BERLIN, ALEXANDERPLATZ

D1196445

Space and Place

Bodily, geographic and architectural sites are embedded with cultural knowledge and social value. This series provides ethnographically rich analyses of the cultural organization and meanings of these sites of space, architecture, landscape and places of the body. Contributions to this series will examine the symbolic meanings of space and place, the cultural and historical processes involved in their construction and contestation, and how they are in dialogue with wider political, religious, social and economic institutions.

BERLIN, ALEXANDERPLATZ

Transforming Place in a Unified Germany

❧ ◆ ❧

Gisa Weszkalnys

berghahn
NEW YORK · OXFORD
www.berghahnbooks.com

First published in 2010 by

Berghahn Books

www.berghahnbooks.com

©2010, 2013 Gisa Weszkalnys
First paperback edition published in 2013

Library of Congress Cataloging-in-Publication Data

Weszkalnys, Gisa.
    Berlin, Alexanderplatz : transforming place in a unified Germany / Gisa
Weszkalnys.
      p. cm. — (Space and place)
    Includes bibliographical references and index.
    ISBN 978-1-84545-723-5 (hardback) -- ISBN 978-1-84545-835-5 (institu-
tional ebook) -- ISBN 978-1-78238-317-8 (paperback) -- ISBN 978-1-78238-318-5
(retail ebook)
    1. Alexanderplatz (Berlin, Germany) 2. Public spaces—Political aspects—
Germany—Berlin. 3. Berlin (Germany)—Buildings, structures, etc. I. Title.
    DD887.W47 2010
    711'.5509431552--dc22

2010007979

British Library Cataloguing in Publication Data

A catalogue record for this book is available from the British Library

Printed in the United States on acid-free paper.

ISBN: 978-1-78238-317-8 paperback
ISBN: 978-1-78238-318-5 retail ebook

To Senta

ᕬ CONTENTS ᕤ

⊰ FIGURES ⊱

⤏ ACKNOWLEDGEMENTS ⤎

This book is the product of three phases of writing, each of which incurred enormous debts of gratitude to people, institutions and places. It would have been unthinkable without the many people in Berlin who welcomed me into their lives and told me about their diverse projects and passions. Prior to, during and beyond my fieldwork I received support from the team of the Rahmenkoordinierung Alexanderplatz and from staff in the Department II of the Berlin Senatsverwaltung für Stadtentwicklung. They opened their doors and files to me and facilitated access to many of the other participants in the Alexanderplatz project. The former members of the Bürgervertretung Alexanderplatz shared with me their ambivalent insights into planning in Berlin; whilst the Platzmanagement Alexanderplatz, the AG Alex (especially the Gangway team), and the young people I met in Alexanderplatz were extremely generous in showing me a different side to the square. Joachim Näther, Dorothea Tscheschner as well as Ingrid Apolinarski at the Institut für Regionalentwicklung und Strukturplanung (IRS) enlightened me on how planning was done in the GDR. The team of Friedrich's Bier & Co were always fun to work with and allowed me glimpses of the 'real' life in Alexanderplatz. In this book, some names have been changed. I am thankful also to the many people who talked to me in and about Alexanderplatz and whose names I never knew. The research was made possible by a generous William Wyse Studentship and an Internal Graduate Studentship from Trinity College, Cambridge, and by contributions towards my fieldwork from the William Wyse Fund and the Richards Fund.

During the first phase of research and writing, Maryon McDonald gave astute comments and much useful advice, which have had a lasting impact on my work. The Cambridge 'writing up' seminars between 2002 and 2004 provided an extremely inspiring forum for discussion. I am especially grateful to Maria Gropas and Rebecca King for reading this work when it was still in its embryonic form and for having been pardoning friends throughout. Marilyn Strathern and Michael Carrithers were critical but kind examiners and sources of support then and ever since. Over the years, numerous people supplied constructive criticism and observations on different versions of the manuscript. I wish to thank, in particular, Simone Abram, Andrew Barry, Eeva Berglund, Georgina Born, Douglas Holmes, Tanya Richardson, Nikolai Ssorin-Chaikov, Andrea Stöckl, Karen Wells and Hadas Yaron. Don Brenneis gave an enormously encouraging review of the manuscript in its last stage. Parts of this book were presented at Cambridge University, the LSE, Goldsmiths, Durham University, Sheffield University, Cardiff University, the meetings of the American Anthropological Association in 2005 and the European Association of Social Anthropologists in 2006, as well as a workshop on anthropologies of planning in Gothenburg in November 2008. I am grateful to all the audiences and participants for their unfailingly stimulating observations.

Finally, the following people deserve special mention, for they provided ample emotional and intellectual sustenance over the years. I am grateful to Matthew Butcher for having accompanied me through much of this project, in which he remains implicated in so many ways. My deep appreciation goes to Gwyn Williams, who not only read a full first draft but also gave unceasing reassurance at a time when it was most needed. Marion Brettar, Stina Torjesen and Alexandra Tzella all contributed with sympathetic words and continuing friendship. Imke Haschenburger, Katrin Omlor and Hannah Schneebeli's passion for Berlin was infectious indeed. Beckie Coleman and Tanya Richardson shared with me, until the very last minutes, the pleasures and doubts of manuscript writing. Andy Barry and Georgie Born gave friendship, generous intellectual guidance and inspiration. Alex Wilkie offered me a temporary home in London, which made it uniquely possible for this book finally to take shape, and has been a fantastic friend in every way. My warmest gratitude goes to my parents, Gaby and Stefan Weszkalnys for their unceasing love and support. And I thank Pedro Gil Ferreira quite simply for having come into my life.

* * *

Parts and earlier versions of some of the chapters appeared elsewhere: Chapter 3 (2007) in *Society and Space* 10(2) and Chapter 6 (2008) in *City and Society* 20(2). I thank the publishers for their permission to republish the material here. I also gratefully acknowledge the permissions granted to reproduce 'Vision Berlin Alexanderplatz' by Yadegar Asisi as well as the drawing of the Planwerk Innenstadt and the figure-ground plans of Berlin by the Senatsverwaltung für Stadtentwicklung, Berlin.

⤳ GLOSSARY ⤳

AG Alex Arbeitsgemeinschaft Alexanderplatz. An association of youth-work projects operating in Alexanderplatz.

Bürgervertretung 'Citizens' Representation'. A group of citizens who campaigned against the plans for the redevelopment of Alexanderplatz in the 1990s.

D-Mark *Deutsche Mark.* The German currency until the introduction of the Euro in 2002.

FRG Federal Republic of Germany

GDR German Democratic Republic

Heimat Native place, 'homeland', place of belonging.

Ostalgie Nostalgia for 'the East', or for the GDR.

Planwerk *Planwerk Innenstadt.* A planning scheme guiding urban development in post-unification Berlin.

Platzmanagement 'Square Management'. A youth-work institution seeking to bring together planners, developers, business people, youth workers and young people around Alexanderplatz.

PDS German socialist party (Partei des Demokratischen Sozialismus)

RKA Rahmenkoordinierung Alexanderplatz ('Alexanderplatz Frame Co-ordination'). The planning office in charge of managing the Alexanderplatz development project and coordinating the incipient building works.

SenStadt Senatsverwaltung für Stadtentwicklung, Planen, Bauen, Wohnen, Umwelt und Verkehr. The Berlin Senat's Administration for Urban Development, Planning, Construction, Housing, Environment, and Transport.

Wende 'turn'. The period between the fall of the Wall and reunification.

All translations, unless otherwise indicated, are mine.

⊰ Chapter I ⊱

Introduction

> Alexanderplatz exists as writing on street (square?) signs and as a combination of letters in the novel by Döblin. Two worlds. Even at the time when the novel was written, Döblin's square did not exist… We have to accept [Döblin's square] as an image, otherwise we are hopelessly lost. But we may not confuse them: this fiction and this empty space. (Kieren 1994: 12–13)

This book is about a place in time and a time in place. It tells a story about Alexanderplatz, a public square of outstanding symbolic significance in contemporary Berlin. Alfred Döblin's celebrated novel *Berlin Alexanderplatz – The Story of Franz Biberkopf*, first published in 1929, has turned Alexanderplatz into a famous trope of fiction. Döblin cast Alexanderplatz as a conduit of the complexities of a city transformed by the Great War, new forms of transportation and means of communication. Its intensity seemed to defy narrative conventions, and Döblin borrowed from cinematic montage to combine incongruent images, documents and disparate voices. In this way, as Walter Benjamin observed in his reading of the novel, Döblin could convey the cacophony that made up the square whilst asserting its authenticity, grounding the text in the life of people he had encountered (Donald 1999: 128). This book may be seen as a kind of ethnographic homage to Döblin. Its aim is to demonstrate Alexanderplatz as a multiplicity generated in the conflicting practices and agendas of people in contemporary Berlin.

The vantage point of this book is a moment in the 1990s when Alexanderplatz was invoked, not for the first time in its existence, as an antithesis to urban ideals. The dismantling of the Berlin Wall in 1989 and Germany's *Wiedervereinigung* ('reunification') in 1990 had set in train a dramatic process of urban renewal and restructuring. It provided an important arena for impassioned public debate over the meaning of existing sites and the city's future shape. Alexanderplatz, too, became an object of planning and debate. Rebuilt in the 1960s German Democratic Republic (GDR) as a central element of 'Berlin – Capital of the GDR', Alexanderplatz was quickly identified as a problem of urban design. A design competition was held in 1993. The winning design by the architects Hans Kollhoff and Helga Timmermann led to a proposal for a new Alexanderplatz, adjusted during several years of deliberation and redrafting. It envisages ten high-rise buildings that will supplant the square's existing layout. They will provide offices, shops and apartments for the New Berlin, to be built in public-private partnership with several real-estate developers. In the future, Alexanderplatz is to be a 'People's Place' and a supposed revaluation of Berlin's eastern centre (Senatsverwaltung 2001). In a brochure on the project, Berlin's then Senator for Urban Development declared, invoking a comparison with Potsdamer Platz, another post-unification flagship project:

> Whilst Potsdamer Platz was a project born of the time immediately after the Wall fell and, in its position on the border between East and West Berlin, is a symbol of outer and formal reunification, Alexanderplatz, as a project in the centre of Berlin, will be a special symbol of the inner reunification so important for the identity of Berliners. (Strieder 2001: 3)

The new plans for Alexanderplatz merge concerns about space, development and the nation into a teleology of city planning that has particular salience in a unified Germany. The controversy around Alexanderplatz, which this book charts, is in many ways about the uniqueness of the planning of Berlin as the old and the new German capital. As a condensation of the political, economic, social and ultimately moral concerns surrounding Berlin's development, Alexanderplatz is an excellent case in point. I try to look through the spectacles of those who – as city planners, critical citizens, property developers or youth workers – have made this place matter. But this book is not just about Berlin. Alexanderplatz raises questions that point beyond its geographical context – questions about, for example, citizenship and belonging, expertise and planning, time and space, the nature of ethnography and the object of anthropology.

Thus, this book attempts to give, through the use of ethnography, a particular account of place. Ethnographic convention has it that the ethnographer should first select a locale, usually equated with a particular people, and subsequently lay out its diverse constituents (politics, economics, ritual, kinship system, etc.). My account inverts this procedure,[1] as I examine how a locale, Alexanderplatz, comes into being in different domains and to different effects. That is to say, what I do is not attempt to describe the diverse 'constituents' of Alexanderplatz, but rather to suggest how Alexanderplatz is multiply constituted.

Figure 1: Vision Berlin Alexanderplatz by Yadegar Asisi

Where?

I want to begin with a story of arrival. More specifically, with multiple instances of arrival, at Alexanderplatz – the place that Berliners fondly, or some might say lazily, refer to as '*der Alex*'. 'Nobody lives in Alexanderplatz', an impatient administrator told me, prior to fieldwork, when I enquired about the effects of the envisaged building works on Alexanderplatz's residents. By implication, everyone who is in Alexanderplatz has to arrive there somehow. The use of stories of arrival has been popular in anthropology to convey evidence of 'having been there', in that unfamiliar place whose hidden meanings the researcher claims to uncover (Hirsch 1995: 1; Okely 1992: 14; Pratt 1986). My aim here is different. It is to lead the reader into an account of what sometimes appeared to be different Alexanderplatzes that people told me about. In the end, however, Alexanderplatz as it emerges in the pages of this book will inevitably be in some sense my own.

The most appropriate way of arriving at Alexanderplatz, some people say, the one that makes you appreciate its physical impact most intensely, is by car. This imagery was invoked by the East German urban design historian Simone Hain in a public discussion concerning Alexanderplatz in the summer of 2002. She described her experience of sitting in a car sweeping along the vast Karl-Marx-Allee approaching Alexanderplatz from the East, whilst the setting sun shed its golden light onto the surrounding buildings. Her words conjured a feeling of elation sensed at the speed of the vehicle, the flurry of passing images, and the realisation that Alexanderplatz constitutes the grand finale of a comprehensively orchestrated environment.

By contrast, after a dangerous bicycle ride along the same Karl-Marx-Allee, a friend suggested that Alexanderplatz appeared like a safe haven. Or again, disembarking from the tram in the early morning, I was often one of those hastily crossing Alexanderplatz to reach the underground or city trains taking people elsewhere, and for whom the square is merely a thoroughfare for commuters. Being spilled out into the square, from the dark underground tunnels, as part of a swarm of co-travellers can be a profoundly disorienting experience as you find yourself in this open space, both celebrated and loathed for its vastness.

In 2001, entering Alexanderplatz from the train station, one would pass through a narrow passage lined with food stalls on one side and, on the other, two long concrete benches camouflaging air-conditioning shafts. There, in front of the department store Kaufhof with its white seventies-style façade, people would often sit at midday, eating Chinese noodles, sausages and chips bought at the stalls, waiting, or simply watching passers-by. A handful of vendors would offer a selection of jewellery, including cheap beaded bracelets, conspicuous finger-rings and more expensive silver necklaces, carefully displayed in portable stalls lined with black velvety material and with their sides folded back. Looking right, one spots the *Brunnen der Völkerfreundschaft* ('Fountain of the Peoples' Friendship') built in the socialist 1970s. Water gushes out of this vibrantly coloured structure. When the weather is fine, people crowd on the edge of its basin, some licking ice cream bought opposite at Janny's Eis. Sitting there, I would sometimes gaze up at the blue-checked Forum Hotel, on which the shadow of the nearby television tower is cast like a gigantic sundial.

Alexanderplatz is a space of watching and gazing, a well-known empty space and simultaneously a feast for the senses, embodied, smelly and noisy. The smell of Bratwurst and the perfume of a woman walking past mingle with exhaust fumes. Along with the smells go the sounds: the droning and screeching of cars, the buzzing of the tram, scraps of conversation, the repetitive calls of a man selling newspapers, another selling lottery tickets. Whilst fumbling for cigarettes in my pocket, the woman next to me offers me her lighter, smiling and asking: 'Isn't it strange how one is observed at Alexanderplatz? This is Alexanderplatz, isn't it?'

Had I come on a cold winter's day, I might not have experienced any of this. Then, the square often appears grey and dreary, with only a few people, bent under umbrellas, hurrying into the warmth and shelter promised by the shops, and scraps of paper and plastic bags being blown across the square. I might have come to inspect the small jewel of modernist architecture standing in the southeastern corner of the square, the carefully restored Alexanderhaus, designed by architect Peter Behrens in the 1920s. I'm appalled to discover that its twin, Berolinahaus, has apparently been left to deteriorate. I remember visiting the Mitte district administration which used to have its home in this building on a day in 1995, taking what must even then have been a rare example of a paternoster lift. With a knowledge laden with historical consciousness, I go closer to inspect the building, the shop signs left over from GDR times, and the thick plaster of posters shred-

Figure 2: Alexanderplatz on a summer's day in 2001

ded and faded, stuck on after Berolinahaus had been closed down and before a wooden fence was erected to protect it from trespassers.

Swivelling the postcard rack at the small newspaper stall in front of Alexanderhaus, I find various pictures of Alexanderplatz: sepia reprints from the early twentieth century, contemporary images resembling the photographs I took and a lushly coloured drawing depicting what the square might look like in ten or twenty years' time. Is Alexanderplatz of the past, present or future? These postcards differ from those that my father picked up for me in a flea market in my hometown in West Germany, which show an even barer 1970s Alexanderplatz. Since unification, flowerbeds and grass and a line of potted trees have been added to embellish the square. However, when asked what has changed about Alexanderplatz, a woman waiting under the famous *Weltzeituhr* ('World Time Clock'), a couple of metres away, tells me that the most significant alteration has been the reintroduction of the tram in 1998. As in the 1950s, it now traverses the square from north to south, slicing the empty plane.

Almost hidden behind trees, I can glimpse a graffiti-sprayed container – a surprising sight which some feel adds refreshing splashes of colour and life. On the basketball field in Alexanderplatz's northeastern corner, young people are swiftly passing a ball to each other. Across the humming street, I recognize *Haus des Lehrers* ('House of the Teacher') with its distinct mosaic, created by Walter Womacka in 1964. It iconically depicts peace and war, work and culture, science and society in socialist harmony. When I sit down on the grass to have a rest, I can feel the vibration from the trains speeding through the tunnels below. It reminds me of all those parts of Alexanderplatz concealed beneath its surface.

This sketch, taken from fieldnotes from 2001 and 2002, raises some of the theoretical concerns of this book. The first is with the inherent temporality of my anthropological object, Alexanderplatz, as indicated here by the fleetingness of my description. Since then, the Kaufhof department store stands expanded and redesigned by Josef Kleihues, the architect who directed West Berlin's 1980s International Building Exhibition (IBA) and who has been prominent in the shaping of Berlin's unified cityscape. Forum Hotel has a new multinational owner and a new name. Berolinahaus has been renovated and filled with shops. The square's surface was ripped open to allow for the installation of lifts and air conditioning shafts that will be part of an improved underground train station. People have come to fill the stairs and benches that embellish the square after a €8.7-million makeover, and the chewing gum stains on its light-grey granite paving have already become the object of new controversies.[2] A shopping mall has been built adjacent to the square, a seeming testimony to its development potential. These are some of the things that, at the time of my fieldwork, were still very much held in suspension. In this book I decided to keep them as possibilities rather than facts, although the writing has inevitably been influenced and be made more difficult by their appearance.

My second concern is to show that out of the myriad ways in which Alexanderplatz can be described, heard, smelled or embodied emerge different Alexanderplatzes. This book sets out Alexanderplatz as a multiplicity. I now speak, borrowing from Mol (2002), of 'Alexanderplatz multiple'.[3] The inspiration, however, came from a number of intellectual endeavours. Since the early days of anthropological post-structuralism, reality has come to be understood as forged from metaphorical complexes which cannot be peeled away to find a truth underneath (e.g., Parkin 1982). It is no longer a novel point to say that a thing is things, or that a place is places (e.g., Kopytoff 1989; Rodman 1992).[4] Multiplicity has appeared as an epistemological and, more recently, as an explicitly ontological issue in anthropology. Within Science and Technology Studies (STS), there were similar attempts to destroy the unity of objects. For example, Actor Network Theory (ANT) illuminated the distributed networks of people and things. However, it seemed to retain an assumption of discrete and identifiable human and non-human actants thus conjoined, and focused on the relationships between them that form the network (e.g., Law and Hassard 1999). Partly dissatisfied with ANT, anthropologists and STS scholars have now begun to speak of 'assemblages' (Collier and Ong 2005; Latour 2005). Drawing on the work of Deleuze and Guattari (1987), assemblage has become an extremely productive term, which expresses a sense of the decentring of the subject (and the object) and of the emergence, contingency and instability, though not incoherence, of forms – not unlike what I see in Alexanderplatz.

Multiplicity is inherent, but grasping this multiplicity and its implications is not easy. I began to understand Alexanderplatz as assembled and multiple when rushing across town to attend a get-together of citizens, here, and a meeting in the planning administration, there; when having to decide whether I would gather more pertinent ethnographic material by attending a public discussion on Berlin urban development or by observing a demonstration of the Republikaner party of the political right happening, at the same time, in Alexanderplatz. In interviews, people would show me documents and drawings, old leaflets and letters they had written – bits and pieces of the Alexanderplatz debate. I participated in countless meetings – of planners, citizens, youth workers, etc. – where people assembled, bringing together insights, grievances and objects that together constitute the place in question.

Importantly, this assembling of Alexanderplatz in various contexts and locales refers not simply to its spatial distribution. As already noted above, Alexanderplatz is also distributed across time; and it is indeed its historicity that has been critical in the contemporary controversy around it. My use of the term *assemblage*, though inspired by people quite literally assembling, thus works more broadly to suggest how a place, such as Alexanderplatz, continually becomes in different ways. When speaking of different discourses, practices or social forms from which Alexanderplatz springs, this is not to suggest that the different Alexanderplatzes they generate are discrete. As a multiplicity, Alexanderplatz contains both fissures and overlaps. The multiple Alexanderplatzes, as I show, whilst recognizable to each other are not commensurable; they are incongruous and, at times, incompatible.[5]

Berlin (in) Alexanderplatz

My depiction of Alexanderplatz as a space of arrival is not accidental. Alexanderplatz is often considered to have marked an entrance to Berlin – in the seventeenth and eighteenth centuries, as the space outside the city gates where roads from north and east converged; or since 1886, as an important train station; or today, as a place where newly arriving punks, young people in search of alternative life styles, come to meet like-minded people. In narratives of arrival, Alexanderplatz sometimes stands as a pars pro toto for Berlin. The manager of a café in Alexanderplatz I interviewed for this research, an East German woman in her mid-thirties, recalled how she arrived at Alexanderplatz in the late 1980s, as a young girl from rural Mecklenburg-West Pomerania determined to make it on her own in the city. Her only thought was: 'No matter what happens, you are in Berlin!' Such comments point to the metonymic quality of Alexanderplatz, as it 'stands in' for Berlin as a whole.

Alexanderplatz as an entrance to, and a pars pro toto for, Berlin also emerges from the artistic imagination. When first screened in 2001, the film *Berlin Is in Germany* enjoyed considerable popularity in both East and West Germany. It is the story of an East German prisoner who is released after eleven years and, with his now devalued possessions, including a GDR passport, driver's licence and money, arrives at Alexanderplatz. Overwhelmed by the changes brought about by the fall of the Wall, an event he had experienced only from his prison cell, the protagonist struggles to set up a new life; but his criminal past keeps coming back, putting obstacles in his way. I went to see the film with my friend Thomas, an urban planning graduate who was involved in various citizen activist groups. After the film, Thomas pointed out to me that *Berlin Is in Germany* is in many senses a re-working of *Berlin Alexanderplatz*, Döblin's celebrated novel. It was Döblin who helped Alexanderplatz attain its special place in the German cultural imagination, a place sustained, for example, by Rainer Werner Fassbinder's television adaptation, originally broadcast in 1980, and by the surging interest in the modernist city in recent literary and urban scholarship.

Döblin's compelling fiction has thus become constitutive of Alexanderplatz as a plural time-space (Reed 2002). On an icy morning in early December 2001, I joined a guided tour bringing together an eclectic group of people, including both Berliners and tourists of different ages. Aided by our tour guide, we set out to retrace the steps of Franz Biberkopf in the narrow streets and courtyards of the famous Scheunenviertel just northwest of Alexanderplatz, the area that served as inspiration for Döblin's novel. The specific literary topography might have set the parameters for our own 'interpretative activity'; however, this did not preclude the incursion of the personal recollections of some participants (cf. Reed 2002).

An elderly woman, for example, was here to revisit the place of her wartime childhood, which she had left for West Berlin in 1952. Whilst we were walking, she pointed out to me the new buildings that had been added during GDR times and street names that had been changed. She loudly objected to the tour guide's description of the area as having been a slum before the war, feeling her own memories insulted. The place she invoked appeared unlike the grim picture of deprivation, alienation and deceit painted by Döblin and his interpreters (Barta 1996; Haag 1992). When another participant told us about the shop that her grandfather had once owned in this area, in Alte Schönhauser Straße, she commented: 'So, we are both doing *Auf-*

arbeitung.' This woman sensed a common project, which she described by invoking the notion of 'working through' the past, commonly used in reference to Germany's dealings with its Nazi past and, now, the socialist period, too.

The last stop on our tour was Alexanderplatz itself. The stalls of the annual Christmas market were set up, inviting passers-by to stop and look at the hotchpotch of goods on sale or to have a glass of mulled wine. Our guide read us a final passage from Döblin's novel, explaining that Alexanderplatz stood for the *Großstadt* ('metropolis') itself. Berlin – 'the city' – was the novel's other protagonist. With its electric lights, noises and traffic, the thriving metropolis almost drives Biberkopf into madness. It echoes an early–twentieth century psychological discourse on the city that cast spatial phobias as a danger intrinsic to the modern urban experience (Donald 1999: 136). To furnish us with an image of the bustling metropolitan square, our guide showed photographs of 1920s Alexanderplatz. The square no longer looked like this today, he explained, because it was almost entirely rebuilt during GDR times. 'Memorize it well!' the guide pleaded, and finally held up an image of the vision for Alexanderplatz developed by Berlin's planning administration in the 1990s.

Those who in the 1990s began to plan what Alexanderplatz might become in the future also appealed to Döblin. The following excerpt adorned the frontispiece of the Alexanderplatz competition brief:

> From the east, Weissensee, Lichtenberg, Friedrichshain, Frankfurter Allee, the yellow street-cars plunge into the square through Landsberger Strasse. Line No. 65 comes from the Central Slaughter-House, the Grosse Ring, Weddingplatz, Luisenplatz; No. 76 from Hundekehle via Hubertusallee. At the corner of Landsberger Strasse they have sold out Friedrich Hahn, formerly a department store, they have emptied it and are gathering it to its forbears. The street-cars and Bus 19 stop on the Turmstrasse. Where Jürgens stationery store was, they have torn down the house and put up a building fence instead. An old man sits there with a medical scale: Try your weight, 5 pfennigs. Dear sisters and brethren, you who swarm across the Alex, give yourselves this treat, look through the loophole next to the medical scale at this dump-heap where Jürgens once flourished and where Hahn's department store still stands, emptied, evacuated, and eviscerated, with nothing but red tatters hanging over the show-windows. A dump-heap lies before us. Dust thou art, to dust returnest. We have built a splendid house, nobody comes in or goes out any longer. Thus Rome, Babylon, Nineveh, Hannibal, Caesar, all went to smash, oh, think of it! In the first place, I must remark they are digging those cities up again, as the illustrations in last Sunday's edition show, and, in the second place,

those cities have fulfilled their purpose, and we can now build new cities.
Do you cry about your old trousers when they are moldy and seedy? No,
you simply buy new ones, thus lives the world. (translation quoted from
Döblin [1929/1990: 219–20])

Impermanence is a central imagery of Döblin's novel. The city is a place
where incessant movement, demolition and rebuilding are the only con-
stants. As the opening of the competition brief and at this particular juncture in Berlin's history, the imagery is invested with new significance. To
many city planners, East Berlin in particular – the former capital of the
GDR – might indeed have appeared as a city that had, once again, 'fulfilled
its purpose'.

A comprehensive process of spatial reordering has accompanied Berlin's
unification and its reconstitution as the capital of the united Germany.
During the forty-year division, the two Germanies had gradually developed what the anthropologist John Borneman (1992) has called a 'dual
organization'. The two Berlins likewise came to be regarded as two distinct and opposed cities, but with each understood only in relation to the
other. In asserting their distinctiveness, urban planning and design were of
utmost significance. Numerous plans and projects were drawn up and
implemented, sometimes as an implicit response to, and often in competition with, what the 'other side' was doing. Now, the two city halves are
being stitched back together, and Berlin 'is busy reinventing itself' (Richie
1998: xxiv). This book shows how urban planning has become a key arena
in which this reinvention is taking shape.

Bringing the city back to an assumed normality has been considered the
unprecedented task faced by its politicians, planners and administrators.
It echoes Borneman's description of German unification more generally:
'Unification of the nation involves suturing these two halves together, making real in the present the fantasy of a past unity, whether by the denial of
difference, the annexation of one half by the other, or an incremental con-
vergence of lifeworlds' (1993: 288). Pipes, cables, roads and underground
train lines have been reconnected; plans and schemes have been thought
up to bring Berlin's future into being. This book attests to the severity of
this process, its conflictual and ultimately partial nature, by pointing to the
obduracy of urban forms (Hommels 2005).[6]

For Alexanderplatz, too, a programme for action has been developed. It
was the third time that Alexanderplatz was to be subjected to a radical restructuring in the twentieth century (Kil and Kündiger 1998). Within a period of seventy years, three distinct programmes have been proposed and
partly implemented. Each appeared to project an ideal of the organization
of the city and urban life. In the 1920s, Berlin's planning director Martin

Wagner envisaged a rationalized scheme that would transform Alexanderplatz into a *Weltstadtplatz*, a square fit for a metropolis with shops and department stores and, importantly, speedily circulating motorized traffic. Wagner's objective was the enhancement of the social make-up of Berlin's underprivileged East. Alexanderplatz was to be refashioned as the modernized counterpart to Berlin's bourgeois West and as a balance to its adjacent areas, the working class districts of Berlin's North and the Scheunenviertel. Alfred Döblin etched the dubious reputation of this marginalized, cosmopolitan area – with its sizeable Jewish and Eastern European populations as well as its petty commerce and crime – into the pages of his novel. For various reasons, redevelopment of housing in the centre remained limited. In Wagner's vision, the rationalized and efficient centre would be complemented by recreational areas and new settlements located on the outskirts – the equally rational and pragmatically organized embodiments of an ideal social community (Bätzner 2000: 151; Frisby 2001: 284).

Little is left of Wagner's only partially implemented scheme, except for two buildings, Alexanderhaus and Berolinahaus, designed by architect Peter Behrens and built between 1929 and 1931. Alexanderplatz's contemporary appearance is largely the result of the refashioning of Berlin's eastern centre in the decades after the Second World War. Dorothea Tscheschner, a planner involved in the team that designed Alexanderplatz in the 1960s and one of my interlocutors, told me how most of the remaining ruins in the heavily bombed square were levelled and eventually replaced in a gigantic rush, nearly in time for the GDR's twentieth anniversary in 1969 (see also Tscheschner 1998: 72). Building in a rush is a function of the temporality of real socialism and its effort to construct the future in the present (Ssorin-Chaikov 2006; see also Brandstädter 2007). And a representative centre for the socialist capital was deemed to play a key part in consolidating the future of the fledgling German Democratic Republic.

When rummaging through the bookshelves of a second-hand bookshop on Karl-Marx-Allee, the former Stalin avenue leading from Alexanderplatz eastwards and lined with 'workers' palaces' that are now listed buildings, I discovered a book whose superbly preserved cladding was a large bird's-eye view of Alexanderplatz. It was copy of Grundmann's *Die Stadt* (1984), a GDR publication on urban theory. The cover seemed to confirm that Alexanderplatz was the embodiment of socialist imaginations of 'the city'. The city's physical appearance was understood as an expression of the form of the future society that was envisaged (Hain 1992: 57). Its production through urban design became a top priority for GDR planners. Alexanderplatz was intended as an exemplar of an emphatically modern socialist city: a centre for societal life, a place for trade and communication and an embodiment of socialist internationalism and technological progress

– symbolized, for instance, by the 'Fountain of the Peoples' Friendship' and the 'World-Time Clock'.

Today, Alexanderplatz's socialist-modernist design does not match planners' visions for a prestigious centre in the heart of a unified German capital. Instead, that Alexanderplatz has become a waste of valuable inner city land and a break with Berlin's historical structures. The former socialist exemplar now appears anachronistic; its temporal certainties have been displaced by a sense ambiguity.

Inventing East and West

I came to Alexanderplatz through a fascination with the 'place-making practices' (Gupta and Ferguson 1997b) that seemed so prominent in post-unification Berlin. I had moved to Berlin in the mid-nineties, having completed school in the Saarland, one of the 'old' West German federal states. For me, as for many of my age mates, the newly unified Berlin exerted an incredible attraction. Berlin spelled adventure and 'cool'; it offered space for exploration and, perhaps, for taking part in a big social and cultural experiment.

Like many others who moved there from the comforts of their parental West German homes, I starkly remember my first freezing cold winter in a ground-floor flat in Friedrichshain, with a coal oven I hardly knew how to work and no telephone. Yet we relished in the ambivalences of the new East (or what was oxymoronically called the 'former GDR'), stuck to the old names of streets and underground stations even after they'd been changed, and noted with surprise when 'East German' terms like *1-Raum Wohnung* ('one-room apartment') slipped into our vocabulary. I began to feel somewhat uneasy about my own Western identity and was pleased (and relieved) when an East German course mate at university, weeks after we first met, voiced her astonishment when she learned I was a *Wessie*; she had assumed I was from East Germany, too. A box of photographs from that time reflects how I moved across the city from Friedrichshain to Schöneberg to Kreuzberg. There are pictures of friends at a gig in Mauerpark, flea market stalls perhaps near Bornholmer Straße, baklava in a Kreuzberg shop window, a man playing accordion at the canal near Bahnhof Zoo, and a party on a roof top looking out over Prenzlauer Berg. The TV tower at Alexanderplatz shimmers in the distance.

After only two years, I turned my back on Berlin, though never completely, to study anthropology in Cambridge, which made me a *Bildungsausländer*, an 'educational foreigner' in the language of German bureaucracy. I returned in 1999 to conduct fieldwork for a study on *Ostprodukte* ('East

German products') and their increasing popularity after unification (Wesz-kalnys 2000). During that summer I supported myself by working in an after-hours shop in Friedrichshain, selling groceries and alcoholic spirits to a population of long-term and increasingly poor East Berlin residents and West and East German students. I also briefly did some secretarial work in the office of architect Daniel Libeskind, now renowned for his design of Berlin's Jewish Museum. Libeskind had participated in the competition for Alexanderplatz held in 1993, and a model of the design he submitted still stood in the office's corridor – a bulky obstacle, constantly in the way and impossible not to notice.

On this return, I was struck by what I saw as the proliferation of spaces of consumption attendant on East Berlin's incorporation into the Federal Republic (FRG). Alexanderplatz, a place I remembered as windswept and colourless, also seemed affected. However, an ethnography of Alexander-platz's changing face as a 'just-so' story of the transition to capitalism seems limiting now (cf. Verdery 1996). Likewise, Alexanderplatz's proposed trans-formation is not simply a reflection of a global trend towards neo-liberal planning. Even if no local voices appear to challenge notions of capitalism and, for that matter, post-socialism, globalization, development or neo-liberalism, this should not keep the anthropologist from critically inter-rogating such persuasive meta-narratives (Englund and Leach 2000). More thorough research on Alexanderplatz revealed additional and far more in-triguing vistas.

On 9 November 1999, back in the UK, I listened to the radio, broadcast-ing live from the festivities in Berlin celebrating the tenth anniversary of the fall of the Wall. Later that day, I phoned my friend Antje, a 29-year old woman from Brandenburg who had moved to Berlin a few years ago and was now completing a course at a technical college, sharing a flat with a former school friend of mine. I had interviewed Antje for my study on *Ost-produkte*, and the question of East and West after unification had been very much part of our conversations ever since. Antje seemed despondent and spoke about her shattered hopes and the lost opportunity to choose a new way after unification. In retrospect, people's desire for unification seemed, to her, to have been 'all about money'. Antje told me that a huge poster had been hung up on Haus des Lehrers at Alexanderplatz, declaring: 'We were the people'. The poster alluded to the demonstration held in Alexanderplatz on 4 November 1989, during the short period running up to the collapse of socialism, in which an astonishing half million GDR citizens asserted their sovereignty with chants of 'We are the people'.

People I met who claimed to have been there remembered the many, partly self-styled, dissident speakers, the posters with imaginative slogans being waved in the air, and the crowd that for the first time actually filled

Alexanderplatz – but in a way unanticipated by its planners. More than a decade later, experiences of the event had merged with the ubiquitous televised images and recordings of the speeches and chants, making it hard to tell who had been an active participant, a bystander stuck at the very back of the crowd, an onlooker at the window of a building at Alexanderplatz, or who had in fact been there at all (cf. Lass 1994). Through this event, Alexanderplatz came to be both a place where the demise of the socialist system was inaugurated and a metaphor crystallising some of the tensions surrounding unification. Alexanderplatz, as we shall see, is now summoned as a place that embodies 'the East' and a specific East Berlin/German identity. Commentary on Alexanderplatz speaks of the ways in which both East and West have come to be redefined, reimagined and, one might even say, newly invented.

Scholarly, including ethnographic, studies have played their part in this process of what I term the invention of 'the East' (and, since this is a relational category, simultaneously of 'the West'). Unification spawned a flurry of studies concerned primarily with the changes in post-socialist, eastern Germany. Previously, there had been little international anthropological interest in Germany, and West Germany still attracts only limited attention.[7] Scholars found in the reunified nation-state an exciting laboratory where issues of social scientific interest could be observed, including changing discourses on gender,[8] memory and remembrance,[9] consumption, citizenship and questions of (national) identity more generally.[10] John Borneman has produced a series of extremely insightful analyses of both the divided and united Germanies and Berlins, focusing on questions of the state, narratives of history and belonging, and discourses on East and West.[11] The accounts produced by these scholars and the questions they pose are pertinent to this book, but I wish to dwell a little longer on the nature of that divided/united reality they describe. I am interested in those quotidian practices and discourses in which East and West German people and places are made.

With the fall of the Wall, East and West came to constitute a peculiar new reality. A reunited national identity was to be shaped, but often it seemed that, instead, there emerged new divisions. People began to talk about each other as *Ossies* and *Wessies* – the notorious terms for East and West Germans, which depending on context and speaker may be derogatory or deeply ironic. East and West were (re)invented not as innocent geographical reference points but as categories of description and self-description, conveying ideas about difference in the united Germany, and as 'referential universes' (Augé 1998: 43). Differences between the GDR and the FRG, East and West, before and after, are sometimes rendered in terms of the contrastive materiality of place. Antje, for instance, often claimed that the West felt brighter and more colourful. On her return from a first trip to West Germany, she noticed how much the GDR's pervasive grey-ness had affected her mood. Another friend suggested: 'The grass was really greener on the other side'.

Although not physically dislocated, East Germans seemed to find themselves in a different place. Some people would say, with some bitterness, that unification had been like going on a holiday – but one from which you would never return. The GDR, as the East German sociologist Wolfgang Engler (1999) observes, had become a 'lost country'. For many East Germans, the past – which ended in 1989 – is another country indeed. 'With the collapse of their state and social system', Borneman suggests, 'East Germans lost their time and space coordinates' (1992: 319), which were subsequently replaced by different ones. The time before the 1989 *Wende* ('turn') is often referred to as *früher* ('in the past') or *damals* ('then'), but also as 'in the GDR' or 'in GDR times'. These narratives speak of a profound temporal and spatial upheaval. As a friend of mine once said, 'nowadays people don't live in the East anymore; we live in the West'.

Berlin's spatial reordering affected not only the locations selected for the new seat of government, but the entire city and especially its Eastern half. Street names were changed and monuments dismantled, buildings renovated or newly constructed, in a fashion similar to other post-socialist cities.[12] Importantly, these spatial changes also entailed a temporal reordering, including the erasure of memories, the inscription of histories and the projection of new futures into the cityscape. Most of the familiar signs of the previous political and social system gradually disappeared and were replaced by what was, for some time, a disorienting topography. Institutions, infrastructures, urban imaginations and practices were altered. Such reconfigurations also impinged on more intimate domains of life.

Berdahl's study of the former borderland highlights both the materiality and metaphorical significance of the border as a space 'in-between', in which she senses the formation of fluid and ambiguous identities amongst villagers (Berdahl's 1999a). Whilst Glaeser (1998, 2000) explores how East and West Berlin policemen began to 'view each other through space', De Soto's (1997, 2000a) focus, in turn, is on contestations of the meaning and uses of specific spaces, the creation and imposition of new histories in a process of what she terms *Gegenwartsbewältigung*, a coming to terms with the present in a unified Germany. There is a resounding of such readings of the spatial constitution of identities in my account, but I seek to complicate the subject, for example, when I explore citizens' protest regarding the new Alexanderplatz.

Attempts to preserve Alexanderplatz's existing architecture were routinely interpreted as a nostalgia for the East and the expression of a particular 'eastern' identity, a view that the citizens themselves were keen to reject. I argue that analyses of Berlin as a post-socialist city can speak, at once, more straightforwardly about a process of 'transition' (as the endpoint of development seemed already prefigured in the existing Federal Republic) and have to be more attuned to overlapping discourses and material practices as well as actors' shifting positionalities. Post-socialist 'legacies' and 'dissidences' coexist alongside West German 'alternatives' – for example, in a self-consciously bottom-up, socially oriented urban politics – which are difficult to disentangle and which makes Berlin's transformation perhaps more complex than that of other cities in the former Eastern Bloc (see Alexander et al. 2007; Bodnár 2001; Brandtstädter 2007; Burawoy and Verdery 1999; Richardson 2008; Verdery 1996).

Susan Buck-Morss has noted a crucial difference between the projects of the (capitalist) nation-state and of state socialism, which she sums up as follows: 'For nation-states [the salient] dimension is space; for class warfare, the dimension is time' (2000: 22, emphasis omitted). Her observation provides diagnostic purchase on the discernible changes in unified Berlin, reminding of the need to keep both time and space in analytical play. But it also needs to be related to the changing fate of these concepts in anthropology and social theory, more broadly, which is worth reviewing briefly.

The 1990s, in particular, saw a burgeoning concern with 'space' in the social sciences, occasionally explained as a response to the apparent dissolution of spatial certainties in the post–Cold War and 'global era' or, alternatively, a rejoinder to those who have declared the inattention to space (in favour of 'time') a grave oversight of scholarly analyses (Boyarin 1994: 8–10; de Certeau 1984; Foucault 1980: 70).[13] Anthropologists' interest in space is not novel, however (Lawrence and Low 1990; Low and Lawrence-Zúñiga 2003). Conversely, there are grounds to suggest that anthropological interest in time is once again growing strong. These writings go beyond culturally different conceptualizations of time, to show how temporality is a symbolic process produced in social, economic, and political material practices and relations of power (e.g., Born 2006; Greenhouse 1996; James and Mills 2005; Munn 1992). Having heard Buck-Morss's assessment of socialism's special preoccupation with control over temporal regimes, it should not surprise that some of the most exciting work on 'time' comes out of the post-socialist context where anthropologists now explore the differential and competing temporalities produced by the Soviet Union and Eastern European states (e.g., Kaneff 2004; Ssorin-Chaikov 2006).

The socialist-capitalist Alexanderplatz would indeed seem to be depicted best through concepts in geography and anthropology, which posit temporality and spatiality as entwined qualities of social relations (Boyarin 1994; Massey 2005: 18). I already invoked Alexanderplatz as a 'chronotope' and 'plural time-space' into which are folded layers and fragments of personal and public histories. Later in this book, I will explore how the future is constructed in the empty spaces that have appeared in post-unification Berlin. Such an understanding undermines notions of space, place and landscape as taken-for-granted backdrops for social action. Whilst physicists have long understood the impossibility of separating space and time, Boyarin (1994: 4–6) suggests that anthropology has been slow to free itself of a Cartesian worldview, as well as the remnants of Newtonian physics or Kantian philosophy: whether conceived as external absolutes inherent in the material realities around us, or as properties of cognition, we have largely continued to treat space and time as universal, discrete categories (see also Casey 1996; Munn 1990).

Recent anthropological approaches to landscape, instead of viewing landscapes as static and immutable, now highlight their processual and dynamic, that is, inherently temporal, nature (Bender 1993; Hirsch and O'Hanlon 1995; Munn 1990, 2003). 'Senses of place' (Feld and Basso 1996) and the ways these are articulated, embodied and lived are becoming the focus of ethnographic enquiry. This project was similarly implied in Margaret Rodman's programmatic paper 'Empowering Place: Multilocality and Multivocality' (1992). There, Rodman urged an attentive look at the problem of place – its complexity and multi-layeredness – to match the then contemporary preoccupation with 'voice' in anthropology. Rather than viewing space or place as a clean slate into which diverse actors inscribe meaning – or a text from which the ethnographer can subsequently read the structure of social relationships and other symbolic orders (Bourdieu 1977; Moore 1986) – space is now firmly understood as a temporal event constituted through social relations (Munn 1990, 2003; see also Corsín Jiménez 2003).[14]

In this book, I do not offer a formal definition of time, space or place. Place has frequently been taken as a kind of socio-materially condensed point carved out of a continuous space – a notion that the scholarship discussed above has thoroughly subverted. 'Place', as I explore it here, resonates with German terms, including *Ort* and *Platz*, which can stand both for place and (public) square. Rather than considering place as the finite opposite of infinite space (Casey 1997: 294, cit. in Richardson 2008: 21), however, I make a case here for considering the (potential) unboundedness of actual places. Instead of offering a definition, then, this book aims to make apparent both semiotic and, importantly, ontological complexity.

My approach is one that sees time/space as 'done' by people, in the above sense, as networked, pieced together and assembled. It posits that spatiality and temporality inhere, in processual and transformative but also historical and static ways. In doing so, I do not wish to supplant the reality that physical or Cartesian space and time have for people, including the planners that appear in this book. Rather, we are now in a position to ask what might be concealed by such reified and objectivist notions as those upheld in urban planning.

Anthropologies of the City

Despite important revisions of what ethnography's subject matter should be, my choice to carry out an ethnography of planning in Germany may still appear atypical. This is partly because of the persistent hierarchy of anthropological field sites in which 'Europe' continues to be at the bottom (Gupta and Ferguson 1997c; Parman 1998a; Rogers 1998). In this view, Germany and its close association with Weberian bureaucracy would be construed as Teutonic antithesis to anthropological romanticism (Appadurai 1988; Chapman 1978; McDonald 1989). These days are not over, although anthropologists are now producing studies of state technocrats, petty capitalists, World Bank employees, science and scientists, and plenty of other subjects and objects whose connections to the 'tribalist' anthropology of yesteryear are sometimes discernible only for anthropologists. Urban anthropology, too, is no longer remarkable. Still the question remains of what could be an anthropology that is not simply in but *of* the city (Low 1999: 2)?

To briefly rehearse the development of urban anthropology: The city has been perceived as fundamentally different from the sites and subjects conventionally investigated by anthropologists, and it was precisely this difference which the early ethnographers in the city problematized (Hannerz 1980; Howe 1990b).[15] Chief concerns were, for example, the distinctiveness of the urban form, how people managed the transition to urban life, and how kinship and community structures persisted in, and adapted to, an urban environment. The 1980s saw a move away from attempts to define the city. What were once considered typically urban phenomena, such as the state and bureaucracy, became readily understood as structuring human life regardless of location. Whilst acknowledging urban specificity on an experiential level, Grillo (1985) argued for a focus on complex societies and nation-state institutions.

The 1990s again brought forth an anthropology focused on what was perceived to be typically urban, pursuing an array of issues considered to be particularly discernible in the city, such as migration, ethnic and racial segregation, social marginalization and poverty (e.g., Baumann 1996; Bourgois 1995; Green 1997; Passaro 1997; Stoller 1996; 2002). Another strand of enquiry examines the specific conditions of city life that produce common experiences and 'shared metropolitan knowledge' amongst urbanites (Rotenberg 1993a: xii). Setha Low (1996; 1997; 1999) has proposed several images or heuristic devices for the study of the city – ranging from the gendered, divided and contested, to the global, fortress and post-modern city. Quite clearly, these concepts are not mutually exclusive. However, they take the city itself for granted, treating it, for example, as a circumscribed geographical space or a self-contained social system (Howe 1990b; Shields 1996). There is a risk of, on the one hand, passing over relational constructions of the idea of the city itself (Creed and Ching 1997; Ferguson 1997; Herzfeld 1991; Williams 1973). On the other, we may fail to fully attend to how the city becomes constructed as an object of scrutiny in the first place.

A different approach, partly pursued in this book, starts from the question of what practices of objectification are at play? It asks how people imbue urban spaces with meaning and examines the city and urban place as topoi, that is to say, not just as condensed social worlds but also as the expression of ideas about the city.[16]

Discourses on urban planning have been crucial to the constitution of the city as a distinct object of knowledge.[17] And contemporary Berlin is characterized not only by the relentlessness with which a series of urban planning schemes have shaped its cityscape historically. More than ever perhaps, Berlin also exhibits a profoundly self-reflexive stance to its very city-ness and the process of its transformation (Färber 2005: 7).

It has become somewhat commonplace to understand urban planning as symptomatic of the specific 'governmentality' that Foucault (1991a) associated with the emergence of the modern nation-state. Governmentality, as Nikolas Rose (1999: 19) suggests, is a concept intended to be both interpretative and analytic, or diagnostic. It refers to a specific phenomenon, namely the governmentalisation of the state, which Foucault and his followers locate in the emergence in eighteenth-century Europe of new institutions and practices assisting in the exercise of a particular kind of power. Inspired by Foucault, anthropologists have set out to describe the multiplicity of institutions, schemes and practices through which the 'state effect' is achieved (Mitchell 1991; see also Hansen and Stepputat 2002b; Navaro-Yashin 2002). Taking this approach, one can easily end up seeing the state everywhere and merely replace one (criticized) image of a Hobbesian Leviathan, a juggernaut state sitting in sovereign dominance above society, with another, seemingly modelled on the invisible dangers we have all heard about so often, such as toxic pollution and radiation, in which the state insidiously seeps into all aspects of life.

However, another important insight is that the extent to which the state is, or ought to be, implicated in the government of individuals, objects or certain realms has been a persistent theme in contemporary rationalities of government (Foucault 1991: 103; Rose 1999: 18). That is to say, governmentality works less through coercion and repression than through the ordering of spaces (both physical and conceptual) and the arrangement of objects and people within them (Mitchell 1988; Rabinow 1989; Rose 1999; Scott 1998).

Anthropologists, such as Baxstrom (2008), Herzfeld (1991), Holston (1989) and Rabinow (1989), each in their own distinct ways, have demonstrated the articulation of urban forms and government through the spatialization of human beings, the instrumentalization of time, and attempts to materialize political, economic and social relationships of power and morality. The emergence of explicit, orchestrated attempts to govern urban space, and the birth of the idea of urban planning itself, have been generally traced back to the mid-nineteenth century. The period of industrialization brought concerns about the sudden escalation of urban growth and spawned the invention of numerous regulative devices. Additionally, fears of diseases and of urban insurrection provoked a search for apparatuses of control and containment (Albers 1997; Düwel and Gutschow 2001; Hall 1996). Paul Rabinow's *French Modern* is an elegant demonstration of how in the early nineteenth century, 'the "city" was emerging as a new object of analysis and intervention' (1989: 31; Foucault 2002), and modern planning emerged at the intersection of new ideas about man, society and space, analytical tools, administrative discourses, problems of government and so on.

Germany has been considered somewhat of a vanguard of the discipline and administrative practice of city planning. Urban planning constituted a key element in the young nation-state's governmentality. Early German efforts at harnessing the industrializing city at the turn of the nineteenth century found praise and emulation worldwide (Ladd 1990: 7ff.). By the turn of the nineteenth century, urban planning had become a quest for ever more holistic and rational programmes taking into consideration a plethora of issues, including not only aesthetics and hygiene but also traffic, transportation and economics (cf. Bodenschatz 1987; Düwel and Gutschow 2001; Ladd 1990).

In this view, the idea of urban planning, from the mid-nineteenth century, has always been bound up with attempts to contain, control and regulate the city (Albers 1997; Hall 1996; Ladd 1990). As producers of knowledge about urban slums and their populations, social scientists, both before and after the two world wars, have been intimately involved in this practice. Martin Wagner's plans for the metropolitization of Alexanderplatz can be seen as the result of an increasingly well established and professionalized notion of planning as a comprehensive and forward-looking endeavour.

Planning has undergone a plethora of changes since. It underwent a second wave of professionalization in the late 1960s and 70s, which went along with a new consideration of the role of residents and citizens in the process of managing and developing cities. Later, still, city planning was re-conceived as, in large part, a self-conscious response to market demands – a tendency also visible in the unified Berlin (e.g., Lenhart 2001; Strom 2001). Importantly, from an ethnographic vantage, we need to attend to the specific values shaping the shift towards neo-liberal urban management and planning into 'actually existing neoliberalism' (Brenner and Theodore 2002). In Berlin this includes the dominant role of the public administration in the shaping of planning decisions, the trajectory of pioneering 'alternative' urban models and the post-unification power struggles regarding urban development (see Latham 2006a, 2006b). Moreover, a reimagination of the social in planning, as this book will show, is integral to the new forms of neoliberal urban government (Caldeira and Holston 2005).

In reference to twentieth century analyses of urban planning, Paul Rabinow remarks: 'There is a fixation on a stale alternative between architecture and urbanism as purely aesthetic creation and hence benign, and as motivated appropriation and hence malignant' (2003: 355). Throughout this book, particularly when examining the planning efforts for Alexanderplatz, I seek to part with such a dichotomized analysis. Recent studies of contemporary planning by anthropologists have partly focused on the images and visions that are being dreamt up for cities all over the world (e.g., Cooper 1999; McDonogh 1999; Sieber 1993). They examine the shifting spatial discourses at a time when post-industrialization and economic decline seem to have produced a need to imbue cities and city-regions with new meanings. The shape of urban form may today be determined less by administrative city planners than by an eclectic group of 'imagineers' (Rutheiser 1996), including developers, journalists and academics. Neo-Marxist urban scholarship (e.g., Harvey 1989; Lefebvre 1991; Soja 1996) suggested that capitalism had resulted in the construction of notions of transparent space (and time); and, in response, tried to bring 'lived' space back into the picture. For example, Lefebvre (1991) distinguished between the 'social production' and 'social construction of space' and stressed the social, economic, ideological and technological factors impacting on the physical form of public spaces as well as the symbolic and phenomenological experience of space through which people give meaning to their material environment (Low 2000: 127-8).

In Berlin, I ran into the well-known difficulties of studying up in bureaucratic and private sector contexts: much is happening behind closed doors, interviews are considered the most appropriate form of interaction with the researcher and many issues are deemed either too trivial or too sensitive to be discussed. Images, visions and plans, by contrast, may be gleaned from glossy brochures and websites and are readily conveyed in an interview. They tempt us into thinking that people who are planners comprehend space in this way only; into measuring built realities against planned ideals; and into forgetting that – as the planners I encountered in Berlin were keen to point out to me – urban planning is a practice characterized by messy contingency. Visions and plans never straightforwardly translate into built realities. So, what ethnography needs to explore are the discourses and material practices that trick us into thinking it is otherwise and that reify the plan as a future already achieved. I think it is worth trying to move beyond simplifying juxtapositions of different types of plan and reality, lived and planned space and, correspondingly, between the planner, as a strangely disembodied imagineer, and the citizen, as the embodied practitioner of the city (cf. de Certeau 1989).

In this book, I show that ethnographic analyses of place contestations can examine not simply the dissimilar perceptions and visions of place that people put forward. Rather, they need to attend as well to the discourses, practices and subject positions (citizen, expert, etc.) from which, in specific moments, place can be legitimately known, described and configured.

Practices of place-making and people's subjectivities are embodied, particular, contextual and always enmeshed. I discuss, for example, the pre-eminence of the public hand in the provision of services and in planning and the simultaneous role of citizens as responsible participants in this process. Since Weber and Simmel, citizens have been key to conceptualizations of the city in Europe (Häußermann and Haila 2005), but they are also vital to now common notions of public accountability. All these are categories that are fundamental to the European experience. I see citizenship as an important anthropological idiom through which people articulate their entitlement to place, often in expressed opposition to official planning precepts. For example, I will propose that the activities of a citizen group protesting the new plans for Alexanderplatz constitute a particular 'citizenly engagement' with place. Citizens were not just experienced residents of urban space but sought to cast their knowledge of the square in the terms offered by a particular urban planning discourse.

This book is thus not intended as a case study of the political and economic processes that underpinned the Alexanderplatz project (see, e.g., Lenhart 2001; Strom 2001). Instead, I aim to give some direction as to how to unpick some of the assumptions that underpin contemporary forms of city planning. I do this, on the one hand, by exploring how place becomes the object of a diverse set of rationalities of government, and how discourses on government are deeply implicated in people's own perception and embodiment of place. On the other hand, I propose to refocus the analysis of planning on the object, the place in question.[18]

Anthropology's Objects

In the last section of this introductory chapter, I want to briefly expand on some of the methodological considerations that I mentioned earlier. That is, how does this book seek to invert what was once a conventional anthropological procedure, namely, identifying and examining a site as to its various constituent components? Notions of the bounded field site have been thoroughly interrogated in anthropology during the last decade (Gupta and Ferguson 1997c; cf. Candea 2007). However, much of the discipline continues to uphold a mystique of intimate knowledge gained by the ethnographer in the field via her experience and insight into the 'field site'. In my research, I constantly grappled with the question of how to situate myself in relation to my field site, Alexanderplatz, and that of whether it was right to conceptualize Alexanderplatz as a field site at all.

In the light of prevailing round-the-clock conceptions of fieldwork, my research often felt unsatisfactory. I blamed it on the sheer size of my field – a city with more than three million inhabitants – and on its fragmentation and anonymity familiar from sociological accounts of the urban phenomenon. 'One nowhere feels as lonely and lost as in the metropolitan crowd', Georg Simmel observed (1903/1980: 26). Perhaps, the sense of incompleteness resulted from the different temporalities and spatialities structuring my research and lived by people in Berlin. They ranged from the administrative planning offices to the realities of Alexanderplatz for those who live, work and spend their free time there. My research included GDR planners, members of a citizen group and several other people who engage with Alexanderplatz through their work, such as youth workers, investors and artists. I attended public lectures, hung out with young people and, in an attempt to learn about the Berliners who live the 'real' Alexanderplatz, worked as a waitress in a pub near the square. Serendipity and lucky, often fleeting, encounters – perhaps inevitable in the city – were essential to my research. But my problems in comprehending Alexanderplatz, as I eventually realized, were perhaps less to do with the nature of this field than with the ways in which it was always already pre-defined and over-determined as an object of knowledge.

During my fieldwork, I lived in a small apartment in one of Berlin's central districts, Prenzlauer Berg, which since the fall of the Wall had experienced an influx of students, especially from West Germany, and became a 'hip' area, sporting numerous bars, cafés and shops. On Saturday mornings, I would take a stroll across the idyllic market in Kollwitz Platz, where, aside from ordinary vegetables and fruits, one could buy French gourmet cheeses, a variety of organic breads, handicrafts, lush bunches of flowers and a take-away cappuccino. That but a decade ago, on the night of unification, some people had pronounced in the same square the 'Republic of Utopia', instead of both the disappearing GDR and the imminent FRG, was not part of my experience (Kil 1992: 508–9).

Prenzlauer Berg acquired its special reputation already during GDR times; renowned for the artists and dissidents who found their 'niche' in the largely neglected nineteenth- and early–twentieth century buildings. After unification, shrewd developers were quick to recognize the profitable potential of Berlin's infamous *Mietskasernen* ('rental barracks'), which the GDR government had intended to flatten and replace with modern residential blocks. Comprehensive redevelopment programmes turned them into pleasant living spaces, with central heating and integrated sanitary facilities, but also into pricey residences (Häußermann and Kapphan 2000: 172–9). These urban reconstructions were accompanied by processes of gentrification, including the displacement of a part of the existing population and the impoverishment of those who stayed, as elsewhere in the central eastern districts.

Shortly after arriving in Berlin, I attended a series of podium discussions assessing the outcome of redevelopment programmes in Prenzlauer Berg (see also Levine 2004). Here, people expressed fears that, especially if the Berlin government further reduced subsidies for housing development, the established population of Prenzlauer Berg would eventually be pushed out. Thus, whilst renovations have been generally welcomed, some see this as gentrification with clearly troubling effects. In the much-loved *Podiums-diskussionen* happening every so often in Berlin, I encountered numerous self-conscious citizens and critical observers, some of whom I also met for interviews and conversations. These public discussions were packed with divisive ideas about the city and its development; or rather, they were moments in which such ideas were formulated, discussed and scrutinized.

Television, newspapers and films provided another form of 'situated knowledge' (Gupta 1995: 385). Berlin's several daily newspapers and independent publications such as *Der Scheinschlag*, reporting on urban development issues, filled me in on the latest news. Photocopied articles and newspaper clippings were frequently handed out at the meetings of the citizen group I got to know and collected over years. Notwithstanding the scepticism regarding their truthfulness, media reports were considered important sources of information that people sometimes enriched with information of a rather different type, gained through hearsay and personal interaction. In addition, Berlin's transformation has spawned a literary industry, both popular and academic, that was hardly possible to survey. Newspapers, documents, books and publications are all ethnographic artefacts to be considered. Many of the concerns raised by people in Berlin, some of whom understood themselves as scholars and experts, are echoed in the academic literature and, as such, provide a commentary that is indicative of the wider evocations of my research subject.

Strathern's question of 'how one knows when one is at home' (1987: 16), posed in a collection on anthropology 'at home', would seem capable of producing quite diverse replies. Strathern refers to the different kinds of knowledges that people can be assumed to have – for instance, of a particular place or culture, and the impossibility of 'measur[ing] degrees of familiarity'. Fieldwork 'at home' involves processes of both familiarisation and defamiliarisation. Coming to Berlin for fieldwork after having lived some years in Britain felt to some degree like a return, albeit one for a different project. For friends and family, I was indeed coming home as I became again more accessible. Berliners, however, challenged my claims to familiarity. A colleague in the pub where I worked, for example, commented that my attempt to write about Berlin was brave. Obviously, I could not know the city very well: I was neither born there nor had I lived there for any significant period of time. My familiarity with Berlin seemed paltry compared to hers, a native Berliner, who would not dream of writing a text about Berlin with all the claims to authoritative knowledge this implied.

In an important sense, I found that I remained somewhat of an 'outsider' throughout my research, and that the account I was compiling – if not doubted outright – was, then, at least compared and contrasted with those of many others. A friend recently asked me whether I considered myself an expert on urban planning or on Berlin. 'No,' was my spontaneous, diffident reply. 'No' because there are many people in Berlin, some of whom I met and some of whose work I read, who are veritable and recognized experts. Expertise is strongly relational, and the kind of expertise I would claim for myself in relation to theirs shifts with context, mood and disposition. Anthropologists have long recognized that knowledge production is a situated practice and inevitably partial (Abu-Lughod 1991; Haraway 1991; Kulick 1995; Joan Scott 1994; Strathern 1991). Being interrogated regarding my own claims to knowledge, and examining the seemingly self-evident notions of experience and identity from which knowledge claims are made (not just East and West German but also planners, citizens, youths), I therefore see as constituting part of the cultural critique that is anthropology.

In delineating my field of research, I inevitably got entangled in the knowledge practices of other people. The world I encountered when investigating Alexanderplatz sometimes mirrored that conjured in the studies of political scientists who have made Alexanderplatz their own object of investigation (Lenhart 2001; Strom 2001). Theirs is a world made up of distinct institutions and political bodies, of ideally separate actors who have interests and hold stakes. As the planning for Alexanderplatz has largely remained in the hands of Berlin's public administration, a brief note on Berlin's governmental 'structure' is useful.

Berlin is both a city and one of Germany's *Länder* ('federal states'), governed by a parliament, the Senat. The city districts each have an elected council with limited authority and responsibility. The Senat consists of Berlin's mayor, the deputy mayor and several senators, elected by the parliament, each overseeing a particular *Ressort*, or dossier, and heading an administrative agency. At the time of the Alexanderplatz design competition, several of Berlin's Senat administrations were concerned with urban planning matters: the Administration for Urban Development, the Administration for Construction and Housing, and the Administration for Transport. By 1999, these had been fused into the Senatsverwaltung für Stadtentwicklung, Planen, Bauen, Wohnen, Umwelt und Verkehr ('Senat's Administration for Urban Development, Planning, Construction, Housing, Environment and Transport'), abbreviated to SenStadt. Significantly, whilst the planning for Alexanderplatz was initially in the hands of the local council of district Mitte, in which the square is situated, in 1994 it was handed over to the Senat's administration. This was justified by labeling Alexanderplatz a place of 'extraordinary significance for city politics'. As a SenStadt administrator asserted in a conversation with me: 'This task [cannot] be looked at from the church tower of Mitte but ought to be looked at from the town hall.' However, the decision has also been seen to reinforce political oppositions and power differentials between levels of the local state (Lenhart 2001).[19] 'Higher' administrative levels were construed as more encompassing and, therefore, representative of a wider public and, presumably, a general 'public interest' (Ferguson and Gupta 2002). What would happen at Alexanderplatz lay, quite literally, outside the purview of the district's planning office, which is all too frequently considered to be attentive to local demands only.

Much of my research was conducted in the Senat's planning administration, particularly in Department II responsible for *Städtebau* ('urban design') where I did an internship, and in the Alexanderplatz Frame Coordination, an office set up to oversee the incipient building works at the square. As both researcher and intern, I was almost instantly welcomed, attended countless meetings and chatted to people over coffee and lunch. People would help me in seeming acts of hospitality or delayed reciprocity, occasionally framed in kinship terms, where they offered support in my educational endeavours just as somebody would one day support their child. Significantly, they also felt obliged to fulfil expectations of transparency and accountability by opening their meetings and files to me.

Now, from this perspective, the controversy around Alexanderplatz had much to do with the apparent multitude of claims to authority over the square's development – seen as divided along party lines, by administrative realms of responsibility and by East/West antagonism. Also, there were the experts and advisors thought to be in a position to both authenticate and challenge official claims; the developers with their specific hopes for profit-making and image-building; and the sometimes diametrically opposed interests of the public. This view of what was going on did not belong to political scientists alone, but was also reflected in the practices and language of both the administrative planners and the members of a citizen group I met during my stay. The notion of 'the debate', so ubiquitous in the Berlin planning context, can similarly be analyzed as both a context in which Berlin's transformation is discussed and as specific social form, consisting of people, institutional procedures, documents, places and so on. It is in debate that controversial sites are assembled and that linkages are both performed and severed.

In a sense, what I ended up doing was a multi-sited ethnography (Marcus 1998) conducted in one place. Marcus's proposal of a multi-locale ethnography is now well-rehearsed; and there are extremely successful examples following, pace Marcus, discourses, conflicts, people and so on. They confirm anthropologists' ability to capture contemporary, 'global' or dispersed phenomena whilst remaining faithful to many of the conventions of ethnographic fieldwork. I could have chosen very different routes to constructing a multi-sited field around Alexanderplatz, for example, by charting the international circulation of planning discourses or by comparing the place-bound citizen activism I encountered with different forms elsewhere. I did not do so. Not because I wish to defend the bounded field site (Candea 2007). Quite the opposite. With Candea, I agree on the virtue of 'thick' ethnography in appreciating complexity. However, I suggest something more radical. The book aims to interrogate assumptions about the ontology of 'place' and the complexity contained 'within its bounds', and in this way to posit some still open questions about anthropology's objects. Yet I hope it leaves sufficient gaps and loose ends to make clear that there is no new holism involved.

The connections between the different sites that my research considered (themselves assemblages of people, discourses, technologies, material practices, objects and so forth) did not always seem natural. For those inhabiting them, they could appear markedly distinct in terms of both their location and the people and concerns associated with them. Just like boundaries, connections – more often than not – had to be actively fabricated or pursued; and some of the people I encountered were busy establishing connections across perceived boundaries: mediating and networking were some of the key activities they engaged in. Nonetheless, my moving between sites stirred confusion.

'You are everywhere, aren't you?' commented an astonished planning administrator when greeting me before a meeting which he had not expected me to attend. His astonishment speaks of the ubiquitous quality of the ethnographic research method. What distinguishes ethnography, for me, is the ethnographer's ability to move, not always unproblematically, *across* different sites, to juxtapose and discern difference, whilst simultaneously achieving a certain degree of intimate knowledge of any one of these. Paradoxically, this also means that the ethnographer rarely belongs. The relative sense of belonging and connectivity we manage to forge as ethnographers with the people 'we work with', I would suggest, relies not simply on a metaphysics of (co)presence. Increasingly, with anthropology's reorientation towards different domains of 'the contemporary', we rely on intellectual affinities, practices of self-reflexivity and a common pursuit of knowledge (Collier and Ong 2005; Marcus 1998: 125) as well as shared languages, worries and delights that frequently precede and outlast the fieldwork encounter. Fieldwork, too, can be an emergent if partial form of life (cf. Fischer 2003).

Importantly, the methodological reinvention resulting in experiments such as multi-sited fieldwork came from a critical sensibility of diverse origins in the 1970s and early 1980s. As Georgina Born and I discuss elsewhere,[20] one can find traces in propositions inspired by neo-Marxist theory and political economy for research on world-systems conjoining micro and macro levels in anthropological accounts. Such concerns were later replaced by, in part more nuanced, analyses of cultural complexity (Hannerz 1992) and a new sense of interconnection. In a world perceived to be changing rapidly with the onslaught of globalization and its effects on notions of locality, anthropologists began to search for new methods.

But it was not simply the concern with 'transnationality' or the globalized world, which has led anthropologists to rethink their methodologies. Simultaneously, Marcus and Fischer (1986) urged anthropologists to consider new formations of power, elite politics and social phenomena of a scale quite different from those to which they (and their methods) were accustomed. An engagement with processes of rationalization in the context of modern institutions, which had rarely, in this way, been the focus of ethnographic enquiry (e.g., Born 1995; Herzfeld 1992) as well as with Western discourses on science and technology, resulted in the more frequent encounter with expert subjects and in a parallel reconsideration of the nature of anthropology's objects.

In a similar vein, this book seeks to pull together different debates around the nature of the ethnographic field, the distribution and distributedness of our anthropological objects, and the engagement with some of those most emphatically 'modern' domains of contemporary life. The discussion of 'assemblages', more generally, is acutely attuned to the self-reflexivity that characterizes both 'our' and 'their' knowledge practices and modes of being, whilst suggesting new anthropological objects (Collier and Ong 2005). More specifically, Holmes and Marcus (2005) have proposed to refunction ethnography as to include what they term the para-ethnographic practices of their interlocutors. Although intriguing and important, a focus on those experience-based knowledge practices that seem to creep back into our modern, expert worlds is not enough. Knowledge based on experience, which is social by definition, only comes to matter when held up against those hegemonic forms of technocratic knowledge it seems to subvert. But I do not think that technocracies in their varied existence have been illuminated sufficiently for anthropologists already to limit themselves to studying what they supposedly know best, that is, their 'social' pretensions.

Our objects are frequently overdetermined by the knowledge practices of others, not too different from our own. We've seen how different knowledge practices constitute specific Alexanderplatzes, with different sizes, locations, significance and enlisting particular actors. Anthropology's objects, including Alexanderplatz, are not just spatially distributed and deeply historicized; they are so in politicized, conflicting and, at times, irreconcilable ways. The question then is whether we are willing to see anthropology as both a descriptive and, *as such*, as a problematising knowledge practice (Born 2009). How to deal with this situation is key to the enquiry that drives this book. An anthropological account of Alexanderplatz needs to convey its multiple constitution, whilst recognizing that people live different Alexanderplatzes simultaneously.

* * *

It remains to sketch out briefly the structure of the book. The next chapter will introduce some of the themes and tropes that provide the backdrop to the story of Alexanderplatz. It discusses future imaginaries, such as the metropolis, the global city and the European city, which have been inspected and contested in contemporary planning debates. The chapter shows that empty spaces have been key in locating these futures yet to come, and that there is a much criticized politico-aesthetic in the making at the expense of other ways of knowing and living Berlin. Moving on, Chapter III examines how talk about Alexanderplatz's material disintegration has provided an idiom for discussing the dislocations accompanying unification and the vanishing of a socialist ideal. But such talk may also be understood as a commentary on the failures of government and 'the social', which people perceive in their environment. These perceptions are partly related to specific attempts to create order, including the new plan for Alexanderplatz.

In Chapter IV, I set out how Alexanderplatz was identified as a problem of urban planning in the 1990s, which led to the development of a new design for the square. I examine the knowledge practices and techniques of intervention of Berlin's city planners, administrators and technocrats, and explore some of the ambiguities involved in the public-private partnership between the City and developers. The chapter also tackles the question of how a consideration of the planning for Alexanderplatz helps us grasp the temporality of failure. Turning to critiques of the project, Chapter V looks closely at the attempts of critical citizens and experts to challenge not only the visions proffered by Berlin administrators, planners and politicians, but also the procedures that have rendered these visions legitimate. I view their critique in a line of German urban politics that emerged from the 1970s onwards, and propose the term 'citizenly engagement' to convey a particular kind of relation to place that, I think, this form of citizens' protest suggests.

I then begin to look at the ways in which current governmentalities of planning and the city seem to be changing, using the lens of a social work project for young people in Alexanderplatz. I highlight the ways in which youth workers imbue Alexanderplatz with a 'social' robustness indicating a shift in conceptualisations of the relation between society and built urban space. This partly prefigures the question posed in conclusion: Whose is Alexanderplatz?

◁ Chapter II ▷

Constructing a Future Berlin

Berlin is not just any city. It has critical significance as Germany's new capital. It was also the city that Hitler sought to transform into Germania and that bears the painful memory of the Jewish genocide. During the Cold War, it was a key symbol of the world's division into two antagonistic camps. Retrospectively, Berlin has come to appear a social laboratory for the making of twin nations. Following the Second World War until the fall of the Wall in 1989, the city had been geopolitically marginal and simultaneously central, from an eastern perspective, as the comparatively prosperous capital of the GDR. With German unification in 1990, this ambivalence – though transformed – appears far from having been resolved. An air of incompleteness and anticipation has consumed the city. To a visitor to the city in the 1990s, the numerous cranes, excavators and the fences redirecting one's movement through Berlin's centre seemed to corroborate its state of becoming and its reputation as the largest construction site in Europe. Few commentators on post-unification Berlin fail to mention the notorious phrase by the cultural critic Karl Scheffler that Berlin is a city fated 'forever to become and never to be' (1910/1989: 219). Scheffler's words, a pessimistic comment on Berlin's rapid transformation in the early twentieth century, have acquired a new life today.

Rather than providing a history of Berlin (which others have done much more proficiently), this chapter begins to set out some of the themes and tropes relevant in understanding the debate around Alexanderplatz as emblematic of the huge *lieu d'avenir* that was Berlin in the wake of unification. I borrow the term from Jaffe and Onneweer (2006), who in turn allude to a well-known phrase coined by the French historian Pierre Nora: the *lieux de memoire*, such as archives, museums, cathedrals and monuments, siting cultural and national memory (Nora and Kritzman 1998). By contrast, a *lieu d'avenir* is a site of arrival, onto which expectations and desires for particular futures are projected. Introducing a special issue of the journal *Berliner Blätter*, focusing on Berlin, the anthropologist Alexa Färber (2005: 7) has noted how contemporary Berlin has been characterized by a self-reflective stance taken towards its transformation. Urban planning and development have been an important arena in which the tensions provoked by the 'critical events' (Das 1995) of 1989 and 1990 could be observed and in which the future of Berlin would be settled (Lenhart 2001: 9). The events provoked a series of urban practices allowing change and transformation to be continually commented upon and argued over. Mending the once-divided city and bringing it back to an assumed 'normality' has been considered an unprecedented task to be faced by Berlin's politicians, planners and administrators. Plans, schemes and *Leitbilder* ('guiding images') have been thought up to bring Berlin's future(s) into being, each suggesting a particular temporal sequence in which the city finds itself suspended.[21] The guiding images proposed for Berlin, some of which this chapter explores, are neither abstract analytic terms nor are they a staple of everyday conversations. They are, however, considered of important consequence for Berlin and Berliners and, therefore, much talked about, inspected and contested, and are at the heart of material practices amenable to ethnographic enquiry.

Suspect Debates

A cursory glance at the literature on post-unification Berlin gives the impression that the 1990s were a series of animated debates. The *Schloss* debate, the Holocaust memorial debate, Planwerk debate, the *Palast* debate – there was hardly a site or issue which has not been discussed and scrutinized. The concept of debate has served as shorthand for the diversity of utterances that have emerged from newspapers, television, publications, public discussions, Internet forums, conversations and so on. Debate implies connections of sorts: it posits a specific kind of relationship, an exchange of a communicative, reciprocal and contentious nature. Debate has been valued in and of itself, as an instantiation of a self-consciously pluralistic ethos and the public sphere – the notion of *Öffentlichkeit* prefigured by Jürgen Habermas (1989), perhaps the most influential German thinker on the issue. The need to bring the public into the purview of politicians, planners and developers was felt particularly strongly in post-unification Berlin. In the city where 'the people' had just asserted their sovereignty, broad opportunities for public discussion seemed required owing to the scale of transformation and to the diversity of conflicting interests – of politicians and developers, administrators and experts, East and West Berliners (Schwedler 2001: 35).

Put differently, debate is both product and object of ethnographic description: a context, enlisting snippets of speech and text, images and practices, and an interesting social phenomenon in its own right. Whether under-

Figure 3: City Model displayed in SenStadt

stood as a context or as a political practice, the debate raises questions about what and who is included and excluded (Dilley 1999; Latour 1996: 137–8).

Attempts to involve 'the public' in the shaping of the future Berlin have taken numerous forms. The Senat's Administration for Urban Development invented an entire novel institution, the *Stadtforum* ('City Forum'), which since 1991 has initiated regular open discussions on urban development issues. Planning competitions, like the one for Alexanderplatz, have offered room for citizens' participation within legally prescribed procedures. There have been exhibitions of models for Berlin's anticipated makeover and of already accomplished achievements; bus tours around the city; and open days, for instance, in governmental buildings (Binder 2001b). In the 1990s, a carefully crafted campaign recast *Baustellen* ('building sites') as *Schaustellen* ('show sites'), offering cultural events and guided tours of unfinished constructions, which became popular amongst tourists and Berliners alike. What could have led to much outcry and protest – 'the noise, the disruption, the dirt!' – was turned into a source of considerable pride and entertainment.

The campaign focused particularly on Potsdamer Platz, perhaps the most famous large-scale project in the unified Berlin. A busy central city square before the Second World War, Potsdamer Platz was bombed and subsequently erased to make space for the border strip between East and West Berlin. Adjacent to it, on the western side, were built some key structures of West Berlin post-war modernism, including Scharoun's Philharmonie and the Staatsbibliothek (the German national library), home to the trenchcoat-wearing angels of Wim Wenders' film *Wings of Desire*, which uniquely captures the sense of longing that engulfed Berlin at that time. Potsdamer Platz found itself situated in the heart of the newly unified Berlin. When I moved to Berlin in 1995, I could go and visit the Red Infobox, a colossal structure erected in Potsdamer Platz and containing multimedia displays and an interactive installation, 'Virtual Berlin 2002' (Huyssen 1997: 69–72). I could peep through fences down into gaping, water-filled holes from which the new buildings came to rise.

The anthropologist Beate Binder (2001b) has suggested that the opportunities given to people in the 1990s for inspecting and experiencing the new buildings constituted particular representational practices. They served, not least, to structure people's perceptions of the transformed urban spaces and to create a certain familiarity so that, once completed, people would return. Similarly, a former project coordinator I met claimed that the Infobox's purpose was both to 'integrate citizens into what is happening in their city' and to lead them where they were 'supposed to move in future.' A few years later, I indeed found myself having an ice cream in the new shopping mall, inspecting the casino, hotel and restaurants, watching a film in the multiplex cinema and participating in a guided tour in the Kollhoff tower designed by the architect who prepared the master plan for the new Alexanderplatz. Potsdamer Platz is an undoubtedly popular, if highly generic space, in which even the unacquainted can move with ease, and another layer in Berlin's fragmented landscape.

However, the representational practices of Berlin's imagineers were not always successful, and the very notion of public participation has come under scrutiny. Consider the following encounter. In the summer of 2001, the Brandenburg Gate – one of the supreme symbols of the new 'Berlin Republic' – was undergoing restoration. To facilitate public participation in the choice of the monument's future appearance, a small pavilion was installed nearby exhibiting four models that featured the different historic looks of the Brandenburg Gate: white, ochre, grey and sandstone. People could cast their 'vote' simply by putting a one *Pfennig* coin into a slot below their favourite model.

One day I went to see this supposedly novel instrument of popular participation. A young man had caught people's attention. He patiently inserted an apparently endless supply of coins into the ochre model, undeterred by the stares and comments of bystanders. As he had finished, I asked him what influence his profuse voting might have. The reply was sarcastic. None whatsoever, he thought. According to the leaflet that explained the purpose of the pavilion, these votes would merely 'flow into' the decision. Ochre, popularly called *Milchkaffee* (after the 'milk coffee' or café latte, the beverage of choice in Berlin's newly fashionable areas) wasn't even his favourite. Yet he found the other visitors' criticism offensive. This ought to be a free choice, he asserted, and nowhere did it say that one wasn't permitted more than one coin.

Impressed by what I took as an act of defiance – a tactic perhaps to use de Certeau's (1984) term – I had to smile to myself when stumbling upon a newspaper article the following day reporting that *Milchkaffee* had achieved an astonishing first place. However, the matter of the Gate's future appearance could apparently not be left to 'the people' alone. A colour expert was cited, warning that the charming and bold ochre was a populist colour and recommending a more elegant tone. And, having proclaimed this form of participation to be a way of strengthening Berliners' identification with their city, the Senator for Urban Development now insisted that the last say was nevertheless reserved for the Senat. The decision eventually taken was felt to reflect the choice of 'the people'. In the final count, 'sandstone' – incidentally also the Senator's favourite – had received the majority of votes.

This ethnographic encounter illustrates not simply the immense significance accorded to questions of urban design in contemporary Berlin and how they stir 'debate'. It shows also that the notion of popular participation, though welcome, has aroused suspicion. Resistance need not be vocal (Gal 1991). However, despite triggering a brief flurry of disquiet, the young man's critique would probably go unrecorded in Berlin's planning debates, whose boundaries seem partly set by 'speech' and more specifically (as I discuss in Chapter V) by rational and expert talk.

Whilst debate has been declared of paramount importance, one of the sternest criticisms points precisely to its absence. This criticism has come from certain parts of Berlin's large and vocal *Fachöffentlichkeit* ('expert public'), which includes planners and architects, historians and sociologists, political scientists and journalists, who consider their own expertise to afford them a certain authority. Although some of these experts came to sit on podiums, they also often claimed to have the perspective of the 'floor', that is, to articulate the view of the citizenry more broadly. Their criticism has been directed as much against specific plans and projects as against the forms and terms of the debate. Expectations of openness and inclusion were flouted as certain categories of people – notably East Germans and those with politically 'leftist' allegiances, women and ethnic minorities, and those critical of official planning precepts – felt themselves to be excluded (Hain 2001: 77; cf. Borneman 1992: 331).

Similarly dissatisfied, Dorothea Tscheschner, an East German planner who had been involved in the designing of Alexanderplatz in the late 1960s, told me about her experience in the Stadtforum in which she had participated for some time. She had noted that, in its minutes, some of her suggestions had been attributed to other, West German speakers. It was as if she, as an East German expert, could say nothing that was considered relevant. Many of those who found their expertise temporarily devalued by those in powerful positions in Berlin's planning administration – such as Bruno Flierl, Simone Hain and Wolfgang Kil to name but a few – have contributed different perspectives on the past, present and future of Berlin in prolific writings and discussions, and their names will reappear in the following pages.

Thus, many of the self-consciously 'democratic subjects' participating in debates felt abused in a process where the presence of the public seems exploited to legitimize the decisions of influential politicians and their allied experts (Lenhart 2001: 99–100; Strom 2001: 152–3). Suspicions of this kind emerge as the flip side of notions of participation and transparency, which are understood to be vital ingredients of good governance today (Sanders and West 2003). Significantly, the diverse modalities of action deployed by Berlin's critical citizens and experts cannot easily be understood as resistance (Abu-Lughod 1990; Rose 1999), or be pressed into the strategy/tactic dualism outlined by de Certeau (1984). Whether sceptical or in agreement with official planning decisions, as self-conscious citizens and critical experts, the participants in planning debates embody particular subjectivities constitutive of the government of their city – a notion partly upheld through the institutionalization of the debate. Undoubtedly, the modalities of action are shifting together with the changing governmentalities of place that I describe in this book.

People responded to the blatant and rapid transformation of their city by writing articles and books, forming citizen groups, distributing leaflets, collecting evidence, holding discussions and much more. They gathered around new objects of contestation (Latour 2005), specific to that post-unification moment. I suggest that Latour's 'object-oriented' *Dingpolitik*, a 'politics of things' which recognizes that 'we might be more connected to each other by our worries, our matters of concern, the issues we are for than by any other set of values, opinions, attitudes or principles' (2005: 14),[22] offers a useful entry into the analysis of Berlin planning debates. A particular kind of *Dingpolitik* has emerged in the 1970s, in debates about urban development in Germany as elsewhere, and was reconfigured in the 1990s. The traditional questions posed by political philosophers regarding, for example, representation and procedure still matter, as we will see (cf. Latour 2005: 16). But it is entwined with a different kind of political object – urban place – which matters perhaps precisely because it is so difficult to 'dislocate'.

The many podium discussions by the *Stadtforum von Unten*, which I attended during my fieldwork, may be fruitfully understood in this way. This 'City Forum From Below' was a group of concerned citizens, including

Thomas, an East German urban planning graduate whom I met because of his previous involvement in a citizen group that had protested the plans for Alexanderplatz in the 1990s. Thomas invited me to come along to their meetings, held in a café in the Prenzlauer Berg district or at the office of one of the group's members, a West German architect, who had devoted much time to civic activism since the 1970s. This office was located in a converted shop in a typical old Berlin *Mietshaus* on the edge of Kreuzberg district. When I was a student in Berlin in the mid-90s, I had lived not far from here. It was a cramped space lined with overflowing shelves and decorated with paraphernalia of citizens' activism. There was a poster calling for a demonstration against Berlin's infamous (but never built) inner-city motorway, the *Westtangente,* in the 1980s. The architect had been a cofounder of the *Bürgerinitiative Westtangente,* a citizen initiative that instigated, as it were, the motorway's non-materialization.

Entering this office felt like stepping into a space where I imagined Berlin's reputedly dynamic, civic activist scene might have originated. What was more, here we were in Kreuzberg, a district famously associated with a mixed population, the squatters' movement and civic protest that emerged in the early 1980s (Lang 1998: 120–48). Over the decades, 'Kreuzberg became well known as Europe's preeminent "Turkish ghetto" and at the same time the most dynamic alternative scene' (Mandel 2008: 146). Squeezed against the Wall and marginalized during Berlin's period of division, following unification, as Mandel notes, Kreuzberg was thrown back into the centre and into new popularity owing to its established multicultural and truly urbane feel.

Truthful to those 1980s precedents, another founding member was Kreuzberg's former planning councillor Werner Orlowsky, now in his seventies and a proud, self-declared *Zeitzeuge* ('witness to time') of a bygone era of fledgling citizens' activism and participation in Berlin. His astounding career – a one-time shopkeeper turned leader of the Kreuzberg's squatters' movement in the early 1980s and, eventually, the district's first Green planning councillor – made Orlowsky easily a celebrity in Berlin's urban development scene, but with none of the allures normally attached to the term. Neither in its make-up nor in the topics it raised was the group focused on West Berlin, however. Other members who occasionally joined the meetings included Thomas Flierl, then councillor for ecological urban development of Mitte who would later become Senator for Science, Research and Culture and Katrin Lompscher, an urban planner who had worked, for example, at the planning research institute in Erkner/Berlin and as a researcher in parliament for the socialist party (PDS, or Partei des Demokratischen Sozialismus) and moved on to become Berlin's Senator for Health and Environment.

The meetings of the 'City Forum from Below' always appeared to exude an air of informality, with irregular attendance, voluntary punctuality and amicable squabbles over Berlin's development policies, urban planning in general, and possible topics and speakers for their podium discussions. The casual, egalitarian and uncensored feel of these meetings – peppered with a fair dose of veteran and contemporary leftist and Green politics – at first confirmed some of my ideas about the self-consciously oppositional nature of citizen groups.

The *Stadtforum von Unten* had been founded in 1995 as a complement to the official Stadtforum. The group's members had taken it upon themselves to champion what they perceived to be the citizens' cause – particularly by promoting greater direct participation in planning matters. They were not alone in this endeavour. The large audiences attracted by the public discussions they organized would seem to bear this out. Here, people came *as* citizens to debate, vigorously and vociferously, the issues at hand – be it urban development policies in general or specific issues, such as the former site of the Berlin castle or the May 1 demonstrations[23]. By the very act of attending and by engaging in such vocal exchanges, they seemed to assert the citizens' place within the debates about *their* city. These discussions assembled people, institutions, initiatives, administrative departments, neighbourhood newspapers, press releases and reports around a common, variegated 'matter of concern' (Latour 2005: 19, 21), which could be the former site of the Berlin castle or regeneration initiatives in Prenzlauer Berg in East Berlin.

One can trace an emergent *Dingpolitik* around urban place and development to the 1970s. In a context where the Keynesian welfare model, a narrow focus on economic growth and a technocratic administration unresponsive to the mounting worries of the population had come to appear increasingly untenable (Brenner and Theodore 2002: 12; Mayer 1999; 2000), people began to protest against the destruction of their urban living spaces. In West Berlin, West Germany and other parts of Europe, sweeping urban renewal programmes were accused of destroying precious social and material structures and to be headed by what were perceived as 'the common enemy: the speculators and irresponsible real estate owners' (Mayer 2000: 134).[24] At the same time, self-consciously progressive experts and administrators began to pose critical questions regarding the beneficiaries of urban renewal. This led to an important juncture in West German legislation, specifically the 1971 and 1976 amendments to the Building Law, which promoted an improvement of living and work conditions through the renovation rather than destruction of old urban quarters.

Importantly, one no longer had to be a property owner to hold a stake. Residents were now included in the group of *Betroffene*, those 'affected' by urban development. The relation between urban space and 'the social' had been redefined. There was a move away from a conception of the city as mere real estate towards an appreciation of residents' needs, concerns and sense of belonging (Düwel and Gutschow 2001: 226). Simultaneously, the proliferating *Bürgerinitiativen*, or citizen initiatives, helped affirm the significance of a modern notion of citizenship comprising what are typically understood as social, political and civil rights and obligations (Isin 2000).

Its emergence in Germany is generally considered a late phenomenon and possibly the result of the late birth of the German nation state (Brubaker 1992; Preuss 2003; Riedel 1972). The fragmented nature of the German Reich apparently made a poor context in which to develop a sense of citizenship merging national belonging with membership in a political community. Before 1871 and perhaps until the Weimar Republic, *Bürger* remained foremost a social rather than a political category. This had now changed. Especially the 1960s saw a shift with the emergence of the APO ('extra-parliamentary opposition') and related protest movements, seeking political and social reform.

Today, it seems largely owing to these that '[a] country that was previously a stranger to parliamentary democracy embraced personal political involvement and the right and duty of citizens to question those in authority' (Thomas 2003: 4). Citizenship is a prolific cultural practice of immense anthropological interest (Ouroussoff and Toren 2005). Ruth Mandel (2008) has recently provided a splendid analysis of the fraught question of citizenship and belonging in Germany; her focus is on *Staatsbürgerschaft*, that is, national citizenship construed as exclusive category of membership around a symbolism of shared blood, descent, language and culture. By contrast, I offer empirical detail through which I wish to interrogate certain quotidian practices of citizenship defined not in relation to national belonging, but in relation to a belonging to place, involving specific notions of entitlement and, as we will see in later chapters, different sets of 'others'.

I wish to show that places such as Alexanderplatz are always intersubjectively assembled with shifting emphases and intentions by the various actors involved. As citizens' participation became a firm part of planning procedure, 'citizen' became a readily available category in whose name people speak, act and exert political influence. It also opened up, as we have seen, questions regarding transparency and accountability on the part of, and co-option by, the state (Abram and Walden 1998; Nelson and Wright 1995). What I explore here are not disembodied discourses but ongoing discussions and contestations carried out between people in contemporary Berlin. The following sections should be understood, therefore, as an ethnographic tapping into debates of which plans, narratives, citizens, scholars and this text itself are all part.

The Capital

The imagery of the divided and reunified capital has been key in shaping perceptions of Berlin inside and outside Germany. That Berlin would be reinstated as German capital upon unification had been resolved by the FRG already in 1949. By the early 1990s, however, this resolution appeared far from unequivocal (Süß and Rytlewski 1999; Winkler 2003).

Opponents cited concerns about the cost, plus Berlin's troublesome history as the capital of four consecutive German states, and the problematic impression that a unified Germany with a centralized seat of power might give to the outside world. Supporters countered these objections by arguing that the failures and misdeeds of past regimes could not be undone by retaining the Bonn status quo. Rather, they argued, Berlin was a symbol of freedom and the determination to overcome the partition between East and West during the Cold War. Replacing Bonn politicians' accustomed provinciality with the cosmopolitanism of Berlin was expected to have potentially progressive effects on government. Moreover, an 'eastward move' could be understood as a sign of the FRG's appreciation of East Germany and the former citizens of the GDR to which Berlin had, after all, served as capital. Finally, the relocation of state administrations, third sector institutions and businesses to Berlin held out the hope of economic and demographic growth. In June 1991, the German Bundestag voted by a slim margin to move the seat of government from Bonn back to Berlin.

'The capital' is a perennial German theme, as the title of one of the countless collections on the topic suggests (Körner and Weigand 1995). There is the question of 'federalism vs. centralism', which has occupied commentators since the nineteenth-century founding of the German Reich. Was Berlin an 'organic' or rather a 'colonial' kind of capital (Hartung 1999)? How could the seat of the Prussian monarchy, distant from the areas where, for some, German culture originated – foster federalism in the Reich (Siemann 1995). Such questions are given new impetus in the context of the new Europe, with its own tensions between the idea of the nation-state and a commitment to federalism (Holmes 2000). Of tremendous concern, both within and outside Germany, has been the question of what image of political, historical and national self-understanding the cityscape of the New Berlin will represent (e.g., Häußermann and Strom 1994; Ladd 1997; Till 2005; Welch Guerra 1999; Wise 1998).

With the birth of the European nation-state, the expression of national sentiment in the capital cityscape has become a defining feature, not least through the seat of state government and administration (Binder 2001a: 27; Vale 1992: 15). Conceptions of the nation as revolving around a shared 'history' became key; and architecture came to be regarded as one of the prime crystallizations of a particular historical epoch (Forty 2000: 196; Rabinow 1989). Perceptions of the unified Berlin have remained entrenched in these interlocking understandings of architecture, history, nation and the capital. Studies of the conversion of existing governmental buildings in Berlin, and the construction of new ones, speak of the multifarious attempts to reperiodize the German state through specific historical narratives, which might form the basis for a unified nation (see Borneman 1993). The most pressing and problematic question, in this respect, has been how to deal with the remnants of the fascist capital – Hitler's never completed endeavour to turn Berlin into Germania – and how Germany would position itself in relation to its Nazi past, especially through the ways that the Holocaust is memorialized in the urban landscape (e.g., Huyssen 1997; Till 2005). Berlin is to be a 'show window' and a representational site for national self-understanding of what has been coined the Berlin Republic (Binder 2001b: 177–8); and its reinstatement as seat of government is perceived as a partial fulfilment of the desire for a return to a supposed national normality (Welch Guerra 1999: 163).

The socialist past has similarly become the topic of conflictual interpretation and debate. In May 2002, the renowned West German urban sociologist Hartmut Häußermann gave a lecture to a small audience of interested citizens, experts and researchers in a Berlin art gallery, which examined 'topographies of power' and which revolved around a dichotomy of authoritarian and democratic systems. An example of the former, he argued, was the characteristic monumentality of Nazi as well as socialist architecture, whilst the latter could be found, for instance, in Berlin's new governmental buildings that sought to keep power invisible. As Häußermann's analysis suggests, democratic openness and an orientation towards the future, continuity and the simultaneous beginning of something new are but a few of the qualities that an adequate physical frame for the new German state is to symbolize.

The restored Reichstag, the seat of the German parliament, is a prominent example. Its spatial arrangement, designed by British architect Norman Foster, is commonly considered to express, in architectural language, an inversion of a familiar discursive hierarchy of government, and to echo official requests for transparency and *Bürgernähe* ('proximity to the citizen') – ideas that are now felt to be essential to the self-representation of the German government (James-Chakraborty 2000; Welch Guerra 1997). Its new glass cupola, which sits atop the chamber where the Parliament's lower house meets, is open to the public. A glass ceiling allows the governed to watch those who are governing 'down below'. Upon its reopening, the Reichstag quickly became a major tourist site, a 'must-see' for those undeterred by the long queue waiting outside, rain or shine.

Häußermann's claims, however, provoked disagreement: an East German architect retorted that the supposedly democratic structures were no less monumental than those of 'authoritarian' regimes. For him, the new governmental buildings were reminiscent of the monumentality of Brasília; and the endless queues of visitors in front of the Reichstag reflected the submissiveness of the citizens of the New Germany. His was a response to Häußermann's suggestion that inculcating humility in its citizens had been a key objective of planning under the GDR regime, which was achieved by creating a monumental spaces, streets and squares for marches and rallies, in short, a stage for the centralized state and a reminder of individual human insignificance. Häußermann's views were challenged by people invoking their own expertise and experience. They pointed to a diversity of architectural forms and urban planning intentions, which Häußermann's analysis had glossed over. They doubted his interpretation of the capacity of architectural form and urban design to shape a particular citizen subject. The meaning of space and architectural form was not necessarily overdetermined by the state.

Creating a new representative centre for the socialist capital had been considered to be a crucial requirement in the consolidation of the fledgling German Democratic Republic. The *Sechzehn Grundsätze des Städtebaus* ('Sixteen Premises of City Building'), passed by the GDR government in 1950, and the so-called *Aufbaugesetz* ('Construction Law') came to serve as the basis for a radical rebuilding of East Berlin, in particular, and of GDR cities more generally (Flierl 1996: 320; Hain 1992; 1996; Topfstedt 1988: 68). Echoing a Soviet urban model of centrality, the city structure was conceived as a hierarchically ordered socio-spatial system managed from, and oriented towards, its centre – a mirror image of the centrally organized socialist state (Flierl 1996: 322–3). The new centre of 'Berlin – Capital of the GDR' was to be simultaneously the centre of the socialist state itself. The area between the Spreeinsel, the eastern endpoint of the Unter den Linden Boulevard, and Alexanderplatz became redefined as the political core of the so-called 'central axis' reaching from the Brandenburg Gate to Strausberger Platz in the east (Hain 1992: 37).

Importantly, however, many of the grandiose plans proposed for the capital centre remained 'unfinished constructions' (Ssorin-Chaikov 2003), unrealized achievements which seemed to assert the idea of the socialist state precisely through what was absent. The diversity of these proposals – ranging from a dominant high-rise building, a *Stadtkrone* ('city crown'), representing state power, to a television tower and the Palast der Republik ('Palace of the Republic') as a 'House for the People' – reflects a perceptible shifts and conflicts as regards conceptions of urban design, state and government in the GDR. As the eminent East German architectural theorist Bruno Flierl suggests, the two structures that were eventually built, the television tower and the so-called Palace of the Republic, 'demonstrate that it was not the state that occupied this space inside the city' (1996: 350) – but the people.

In the 1990s, the Palast der Republik, or rather the space in which it is located, came into the spotlight of a frenzied post-unification search for a locus for local and national self-identification (Binder 2001a; Bodenschatz 1995). The Palast is located on the former site of the Berlin Schloss, the royal palace of the Hohenzollern family. Heavily damaged during the war, the Schloss was demolished in 1950 and replaced by a large open square, Marx-Engels-Platz, and later surrounded by several state buildings. The Palast hosted the GDR parliament's assembly hall as well as restaurants, cafés and other amenities for 'the people'. In the early 1990s, the building was closed and quite literally emptied out due to an asbestos renovation.

The site, which had quickly been renamed Schlossplatz, spawned a convoluted nationwide debate, involving local and federal politicians, urban planners, a citizen group vehemently supporting the rebuilding of the Schloss, and other, mostly East Berlin, groups and individuals favouring the preservation of the Palast (Binder 2000a; 2000b; 2001a). Those supporting the rebuilding of the Schloss and many, mostly West German, planning officials and politicians largely understood the Schloss' demolition as a part of the GDR regime's project to erase the traces of a feudal history and history, more generally, from the cityscape. An architectural competition was held with unclear results; and an expert commission was set up by the Berlin Senat and the German Bundestag to decide about the function of a replacement building.

During my fieldwork in the early 2000s, the debate around the Palast, which had become the 'Schloss debate', was still in full swing. An elderly couple I met at Alexanderplatz in 2002 were not the only ones who surmised that the Palast's asbestos contamination was merely pretext. They noted that many well-known asbestos-contaminated buildings in West Berlin were still in use. Finally, the woman suggested: 'For ten years, they've been fiddling with [the Palast] and have finally managed to tear it out of my heart. Now, I no longer care what's going to happen to it. It was probably a piece of the East they didn't like.' The general tenor in a public discussion organized by the 'City Forum from Below', which sought to destabilize the consensus-building attempts of the official City Forum, was that due to indecision regarding the design, function and financing of any new building, the problem ought to be left to future generations.

For some time, the Palast came to be used for temporary cultural events (Staiger n.d.), but the final demolition started in 2006 and was concluded by Christmas 2008. In 2007, the German Bundestag set aside €440 million

in its budget and a new architectural competition was opened. The recon-
structed Schloss will have three baroque façades and a contemporary one,
facing east. Incidentally, the new Schloss is to host, amongst other things,
the collection of Berlin's museum of ethnology, thus putting the engagement with cultural 'others' right at the heart of the site that has come to be
so closely associated with debates about national sentiments in the reunified Germany.

Similar to Alexanderplatz, the Palast was summoned as a place embodying a specific East German identity. And, although Alexanderplatz is not
situated within what has been declared Berlin's 'historic centre', it acquires
significance partly in relation to attempts to consolidate Berlin as the German capital and to merge East and West in a new urban topography. The
debate about the Palast highlights the 'multivocality' of place (Rodman
1992) in contemporary Berlin, inflected by a discourse on East and West
and a specific politics of history (Binder 2000a; 2001a; De Soto 1997). It
condenses some of the themes I will return to in this book, namely, the frequently contradictory and irreconcilable perceptions of the former socialist sites, and the perceived absence of 'history' from the planned socialist
centre. In an intriguing twist, what has been seen as an iconoclastic gesture
par excellence (Yampolsky 1995) – the demolition of the Schloss by the
GDR regime – has been countered with a double iconoclasm. The construction of a quasi-simulation of the Berlin castle instead of the Palast may
be seen as a kind of iconoclasm in reverse. I wonder whether now, as the
Palast has been demolished, the emptiness that it left will continue to have
salience as a trope for the sense of perfidy, puzzlement and loss attendant
on unification.

Topographies of Immorality

> Since the Berlin Wall came down, the city has undergone a profound
> modernization. Berliners in both East and West had to come to terms
> with a new life situation. Many experienced the radical change as an un-
> reasonable demand. But, today, we know: there was no alternative to the
> modernization of the infrastructure, the comprehensive renewal of apart-
> ments, factory buildings and transport routes. A decade after the fall of
> the Wall, Berlin is on the way to becoming a normal metropolis. (Strieder
> 2000: 5)

The above sentences by Berlin's then Senator for Urban Development introduce a book accompanying an exhibition on Berlin's 'Ten Years of Transformation and Modernization' (Senatsverwaltung 2000). The embodiments

of the normal metropolis that the Senator conjures adorn the pages of the book: newly constructed buildings; high-tech environments equipped with screens, displaying complex graphs and schemata of modern traffic and electricity networks; gasometers and rubbish dumps without which the city could not function. There are also many happy, hard-working people – perhaps representing the 'infrastructure of heads' that the publication considers indispensable to the city's functioning. Eighty billion D-Mark, the reader is told, have been invested into 'life-saving and rejuvenating measures' for the urban organism (Dörries 2000: 79). Text and images present modernization as a process that is self-evident and inevitable. Berlin is portrayed as having embarked on a journey to reconstitute itself as 'normal metropolis'.

Discourses of modernization, such as those invoked in post-unification Berlin, often present the world to be acted upon as an unruly terrain, and promise betterment and improvement through the redemptive powers of development (Crush 1995; Tsing 2000). The Berlin of 1989 and 1990 was widely perceived to hold out promises of economic growth and prosperity. Inspected through the lens of common models of urban development, both East and West Berlin displayed certain anomalies. As a popular GDR joke asked: 'How many districts are there in the GDR?' Answer: 'Only two: Berlin and *SUHL*, the "remaining underdeveloped hinterland" (*Sonstige Unterentwickelte Hinterland*)'. Like West Berlin, which profited from its status as the 'Western bulwark' and received huge aid from the federal government, tax reductions and grants, East Berlin was artificially bolstered by subsidies.

This situation was felt to impart a host of 'legacies' to be dealt with upon unification, as relative development came to be perceived as underdevelopment, especially in the East. Portrayals of East Berlin, like those of East Germany more generally – in newspapers, official pronouncements, or everyday talk – bore the imprint of what Johannes Fabian (1983) has termed the denial of coevalness. Whether in respect of its economy, work attitudes, or an assumed general mentality, 'the East' was construed as having to catch up. It became the contemporaneous but backward 'other' to the more developed Western 'self' – itself seen as a progressive model to be emulated. Simultaneously, the alleged 'backwardness' and 'lack' seemed to offer unparalleled potential for investment.

As two planners of Berlin's Administration for Urban Development note self-critically and in hindsight, Berlin's post-unification development was comprised of high expectations, dreams of chancellor Kohl's infamous 'blooming landscapes', and a (failed) bid for the 2000 Olympics (Süchting and Weiss 2001: 58). Planners foresaw a need for 1.7 million square metres of retail area, 150,000 new homes (assuming a population increase of 300,000) and an additional 11 million square metres of office space. A large part of it was to be constructed around Potsdamer Platz and Alexanderplatz. Up to 7 million square metres of office space were built in Berlin between 1990 and 1998; but there are probably still more than one million square metres of unoccupied office space today.

By the early 2000s, when I conducted the fieldwork, the dreams of economic growth had turned sour, and urban development was deemed an increasingly scandalous affair. Between 1991 and 2001, Berlin lost 150,000 jobs in its traditional industries sector, a number hardly balanced by a parallel growth of the service sector; between 1991 and 2003, unemployment rose from 10 per cent to 19 per cent (Krätke 2004). The supposed real-estate boom, as Krätke notes, which was partly triggered by incentives for investment in real estate in East Germany, quickly developed into a crisis. In addition, in 2001 news broke regarding the so-called Banking Scandal: the spectacularly failed involvement of Berlin's own Bankgesellschaft in real-estate speculation and corruption left the city with about €30–35 billion debt, the larger part of Berlin's overall €50 billion debt burden (Krätke 2004: 523–6).

These kinds of suspicions, as well as numbers and other evidence speaking of the illicit actions and blatantly criminal activities were very much in the news during my fieldwork. Unsurprisingly, the euphemisms of Berlin as metropolis and global city used by its development agency, tourism websites and self-satisfied politicians (see Binder 2001a; Cochrane and Jonas 1999; Lenhart 2001) had provoked a counter-discourse, focusing on the moral values embodied in Berlin's emerging cityscape. One late September afternoon in 2001, my partner and I went to look at the building site of Lehrter Stadtbahnhof. Having read much about it in the newspapers, I was keen to inspect this illustrious 'flagship project' and herald of Berlin's prosperous future. Lehrter Stadtbahnhof, a minor inner-city station, is to be transformed into a major railway hub. By adding a north-south axis to the existing east-west axis, it will be able to receive passengers from all directions – reinforcing an image of Berlin as a nodal point in an enlarged Europe.

In the faint light of this rainy day, we ventured down a footpath, passing through the building site underneath the elevated railway tracks. From behind the metal fences, we could make out the gaping lit entrances to some newly drilled tunnels, leading towards Potsdamer Platz. A man cycling past joined us. He seemed to appreciate meeting other people who, like him, were curious about Berlin's transformation. He was on his way to see, in a Potsdamer Platz cinema, the film *Berlin Babylon,* a recent documentary on urban development in Berlin. Now he explained that he had deliberately chosen the route via Lehrter Stadtbahnhof. For him, the site was part of the development 'madness' the film portrayed and of which the visionary name of the band that produced the film's soundtrack, Einstürzende Neubauten ('Collapsing New Buildings'), spoke. Citing a 'Hopi Indian' adage on human greed and destruction, the man asserted that this vast construction site reflected a madness for which he had only contempt.

I imagine that our fleeting acquaintance partly recognized his vision of Berlin's future in the documentary he went to see. Made by filmmaker Hubertus Siegert between 1996 and 2000, *Berlin Babylon* presents a gloomy reflection on the city's post-unification transformation. According to a leaflet, the film depicts the contradictions of a city being rebuilt between 'the fear of emptiness' and the 'longing for completion'. The lyrics of the Einstürzende Neubauten soundtrack reinforce the morale that the images insinuate, namely, that Berlin's new constructions contain the traces not only of what preceded them, but also of the ruins and wastelands that they themselves will become. Some Berlin friends I talked to about the film thought it lacked a critical voice. By focusing on politicians, developers and architects, as well as on such self-celebratory events as the inauguration of Potsdamer Platz, the film reproduced, unwittingly perhaps, the idea of a success story of those in power. Nonetheless, *Berlin Babylon* remains an ominous document about Berlin's future between ruthless development and commercialization.

Spaces such as Potsdamer Platz and Lehrter Stadtbahnhof are part of what I term the topography of immorality that is seen to characterize the New Berlin. Their perceived immorality stems from the profit-seeking interests that are allegedly invested in them. Notions such as 'gold rush' or *Gründerzeit,* referring to Berlin's original 'founders' time' in the late 1800s, have been used both by city officials and by critics to describe the immediate post-unification period (e.g., Hain 2001; Kil 2000; Lenhart 2001). They imply a sense of buoyant expectation and ambition even ruthlessness on the part of those wishing to take advantage of the situation. A particular kind of power is felt to reside in large-scale development projects and new corporate spaces typical of today's capitalist system. It is a power that complements or, worse, overrides that embodied in the new governmental spaces. In this context, and invoking a long-standing ambiguity towards this architectural form (Neumann 1995), the construction of high-rise buildings, such as those at Postdamer Platz, has been particularly contentious. They are problematized as 'cathedrals' of capitalist power, reflecting the dominance of the economic imperatives over Christian values, and an onslaught on European urban design traditions (Binder 2001a; Flierl 1992; Kil and Kündiger 1998).

What makes Berlin's landscape 'the ultimate landscape of power' is, for some, not related to 'the very fact of its construction' (Marcuse 1998: 333). At work is a certain immoralization of global capital itself, which drives the construction of this new cityscape. The new Alexanderplatz, as we shall see, has become constitutive of this topography of immorality, too. It promises to be another future economic centre in Berlin – complete with numerous iconic towers, each 150 metres high, constructed through a public-private partnership, which has generated qualms regarding the undue influence of private developers.

Berlin's new topography of immorality speaks of a perceived imbalance between public and private in the development partnerships championed in contemporary Berlin, specifically, the failure of government to keep private interests in check.[25] Expert discussions are frequently interspersed with moralistic and psychologistic assumptions about officials' behaviour. There is talk of 'inferiority complexes', 'megalomania', post-unification 'euphoria'; of politicians 'intoxicated' by their power; of 'cartels of power' that have taken over Berlin's urban development sector; and of 'greed' and 'evil'. More specifically, at issue is the alleged misconduct, negligence and irrational conduct of Berlin officials; their unswerving belief in 'self-fulfilling prophecies' apparently led to dire consequences for Berliners (Lenhart 2001: 284).[26] Berlin political scientist Karin Lenhart's concern was with the methods and data in which visions for Berlin's future were grounded, a concern she also voiced in a conversation with me. The notion of 'prophecy', familiar from the religious domain, implies the very opposite of what counts as scientific, factual evidence within a prevalent positivist discourse – hence, the opposite of what governmental officials might be expected to rely on for their policy making.

Similar scepticism is expressed in the following commentary on Saskia Sassen, who can be credited with having invented the notion of the 'global city' (Sassen 1991):

> [Sassen] is quite frequently invited to Berlin to give a speech on global cities, but the city boosters' are not interested in her critical point of analysis [...] – it is just the debate on global cities in Berlin which helps to reclaim a status of Berlin as major metropolis within the urban system. (Krätke 1999: 323)

Critiques of generalizing development models, such as the global city and structural adjustment, focus on issues of difference and complexity, and point to what are considered different paths of development, and to Berlin's insertion into a polycentric structure and the 'specific Berlin mixture' (Krätke and Borst 2000). From this perspective, 'global city' visions have engendered misplaced, even harmful, urban development policies. Incidentally, Sassen (2000) appears to have similar misgivings. As remedy, critics propose a more 'local' and 'authentic' image for Berlin's development.

Invoking a moralizing opposition of inside and outside (cf. Gupta and Ferguson 1997a: 7), Lompscher (2000), who also occasionally participated in the City Forum from Below, suggests that instead of relying on 'external flows' of capital and investment, Berlin ought to maximize 'endogenous potentials' (see also Häußermann and Kapphan 2000: 254–9). This is understood as a more sustainable, recognizing important interconnections between economic, social and environmental realms, and ethical form of development (Adams 1995; Beuermann and Burdick 1998). In short, the question of what an adequate strategy sustaining Berlin's future would be has become highly contested in ways that are rooted in both scientific rationalities and moral imperatives.

The European City

In 1999, Berlin got a new and controversial master plan for the development of its inner city, the *Planwerk Innenstadt*. I vividly remember the sense of revelation when I grasped that the Planwerk was a complex drawing rather than a text, as planners' talk about the detail of information that it entailed had made me believe at first. Planners told me how they had come up with this plan by compiling an overview of all the development projects realized in Berlin's centre since unification over several years and how they hoped that it would afford a better grip on the topsy-turvy building boom that had encroached on the city (see also Süchting and Weiss 2001). The Planwerk became an important scheme for governing Berlin's spatial organization, focusing on an area of about thirty square kilometres – stretching approximately from the station Zoologischer Garten in West Berlin, to Ostbahnhof, an East Berlin train station – and especially on the space reinvented as Berlin's 'historical centre' (Bodenschatz 1995) and once enclosed by the medieval city walls.

This drawing adorned the walls of virtually all the offices in SenStadt's Department II, where I did a brief internship in the spring of 2002, and when asked planners would eloquently explain its content to me. The Planwerk's drawing is a compelling visual device. It persuades partly in the way that it already embodies the post-intervention future it anticipates. It is at once spatial and temporal. Once, when discussing it with me, a SenStadt employee commented that the Planwerk was gradually disappearing. Once constructed, the buildings were depicted in grey rather than orange in the drawing (see Figure 4, depicting orange as a darker shade of grey). In the workshop next door, they were currently developing an update. Through the process of updating, aided by computer technology, the Planwerk entails, in a sense, a measure for its own success. The Planwerk is often considered

Figure 4: *Planwerk Innenstadt*, courtesy of Senatsverwaltung für Stadtentwicklung, Berlin

the brainchild of Berlin's then Building Director, Hans Stimmann; and during my internship in the planning administration, I would hear it described as 'Stimmann's urban philosophy'. Most administrators I spoke to seemed to accept it as an appropriate guideline for Berlin's inner-city development; one of them even called it, albeit with a smile, 'my Bible'.

Like any map or plan, the Planwerk not only constitutes a selective representation of a specific geographical space but also renders this space amenable to intervention (see Harley 1988). This drawing was, in the words of a SenStadt employee, a 'hybrid', combining two seemingly incongruous scales and planning approaches: that of the crude *Flächennutzungsplan* ('land-utilization plan') and the detailed *Bebauungsplan* ('construction plan'). With the former, it shares the ability to devise rough long-term objectives for a large chunk of the inner city; but it does so in an explicitly concrete manner on a scale of 1:5000. The hybrid scale is claimed to underscore the Planwerk's professed anti-technocratic impulse and its vivid, sensual planning approach. In contrast to the numerical values and standards deployed by modernist planners, the numbers stipulated by the Planwerk – such as an eaves height of twenty-two metres – were felt to contain meaning. The city is conceived as a 'text' – a notion that gained prominence in architectural and urban theory of the 1970s and 80s (King 1996: 2).

However, in the practice of the 'city fathers' (Huyssen 1997: 58) the post-positivist understanding of the urban text has apparently been reduced to a very particular reading. As Stimmann writes:

> Reading the urban texture means understanding the city as text. The planner, *Städtebauer* ('city designer') and architect, therefore, needs to continually edit his city, examine it for orthographic mistakes, add new chapters in some places and cut in others, view the text from the perspective of current societal and political *Leitbilder* ('guiding images') without writing it completely anew. The city builder is the editor of the urban texture. (2001: 14)

The Planwerk's professed anti-technocratic stance echoes much of the critique of post-war planning and architecture, which emerged in Germany, and in Europe more generally, during the 1960s and 70s. Then, as today, the language used to describe the effects of modernist schemes evoked the perceived violence and brutality resulting from modernist planners' models of the *autogerechte Stadt* ('car-friendly city'), functional zoning and the blurring of private and public in the 'loosely arranged' *aufgelockerte Stadt*, as well as their alleged trust in technological progress and disrespect for history. Two important German publications, *Die Unwirtlichkeit unserer Städte* (Mitscherlich 1965/1996) and *Die gemordete Stadt* (Siedler

1961/1993), decried respectively the 'inhospitableness' and the 'murder' of the city at the hands of both capitalists and post-war planners.[27] Stimmann's writings today convey a similar sense of destruction: 'Modernity's declaration of war against differentiated urban forms of space, mixed forms of use and property led to illegible city layouts and spatial formations, lacking any architectural or societal relations – in particular the dialectic of house and street, private and public constitutive of the European city' (2001: 23).

In 1970s Berlin a critical stance began to emerge which took issue with the *Kahlschlagsanierung* – the 'deforestation' model of redevelopment, involving the demolition of old housing – and tenants' displacement and resettlement in new large-scale housing estates on the periphery. The modernist planners' desire to rid Berlin of its decrepit *Mietskasernen* ('rental barracks') to bring 'light and air' alongside a new social structure into the city fell into disrepute (Bodenschatz 1987). Crucial in the promulgation of these changed views was the launch of the planning institute, IBA (International Building Exhibition), to oversee redevelopment in early 1980s West Berlin. The architects and planners involved succeeded in introducing a much-acclaimed approach, pivoting on the concepts of *behutsame Stadterneuerung* ('careful urban renewal') and *kritische Rekonstruktion* ('critical reconstruction') (Bauausstellung Berlin1984). They also revived the master plan as a holistic planning instrument (Zohlen 2000: 335).

Critical reconstruction as advocated in 1990s Berlin provided what I call, drawing on Scott (1998: 62), a distinct politico-aesthetics. What seemed progressive in the 1980s now appears shrouded in reactionary traditionalism (Huyssen 1997: 69). It seeks to reinstate a functional mixture (of housing, business, commerce, etc.), the historic street layout and associated frontage lines, admissible building heights (22m to eaves, 30m to ridges), and the 'house-on-one-lot' as the basis for all development (Stimmann 1994: 110; 1995a: 13; 1995b: 409). In short, it proposes a return to features considered typical of Berlin and the 'European city' more generally (Schwedler 2001; Stimmann 2001). By invoking a pre-1914 architectural style and street layout – and a supposedly shared history, ranging from medieval times to the early German Empire – it is claimed that Berlin's distinct identity could be preserved or recreated. In so doing, the Planwerk avers that most important goal of planning in contemporary Berlin: the reintegration of the two city halves.

The Planwerk resonates with contemporary planning sensibilities in other ways. It is also conceived as – to stay with the 'city organism' metaphor – a preventive to the prognosticated dissolution of the city (Mönninger 2001; Neumeyer 2001), by emphasizing densification and the infilling of empty lots in the centre. The imagery invoked here is that of the compact European city. Conceptualizing Berlin as a European city does several things at once.

It construes Berlin as belonging to a specific pedigree of cities thought to have evolved within Europe over centuries. It thus chimes with notions of Berlin situated at the heart of an enlarged European Union. Whilst some argue that the image of the 'European city' was chosen because it is more pleasing than the more accurate 'German city' – which could have triggered charges of objectionable nationalism – the architects Hilmer and Sattler (who realized, for example, a project in Potsdamer Platz) have suggested that 'it is simply, "not the American city"' (cit. in Strom 2001: 142; see also Häußermann and Haila 2005).

In a sense, this is a long-standing German moral and cultural critique of 'America' in a new guise (Frisby 2001: ch. 4; Huyssen 1997: 69). The 'American city' is taken to stand for the future of the city per se, and much of this future is cast in a negative light. The 'European city', as the urban planning historian Harald Bodenschatz (1995: 223) observes, has become a *kultureller Kampfbegriff* ('cultural battle notion') in post-unification Berlin. The contrasts invoked are simplistic essentialisms, which overlook that neither the geographical boundaries nor the meanings of Europe have ever been unambiguous (McDonald 1996; Parman 1998b).

Significantly, Europe takes its meaning in contradistinction not only to America but also to an eastern European 'other' – a distinction reinforced by Cold War oppositions. Europe was construed as the quintessential West – rational, democratic, politically stable and urban – and distinct from an irrational, communist, rural East. Despite the new 'others' that are now being enlisted, since the breakdown of this ostensibly clear-cut division (Shore 1993; Stolcke 1995), proponents of the 'European city' still find the eastern 'other' present in Berlin's cityscape. The results of socialist urban planning are construed as something alien, imposed on the supposedly 'organic' structures of the European city. Aside from the American city, there is another city that the Planwerk is battling with: the socialist city.

Solids and Voids

In important respects, the concept of the 'European city' evoked in contemporary Berlin echoes the critique of modernist planning formulated by James Holston (1989) in his account of Brasília. The resemblance with Holston's argument is striking also because, like Berlin planners, he uses a certain type of drawing – the figure-ground plan – to prove his claims. Holston points to the 'dehistoricization' of the city pursued by modernist planners, and their simultaneous effort to invert common understandings of urban development. Instead of seeing the changing cityscape (like all artefacts) as a reflection of changes in social organization, 'the modernist idea is of … [a] blueprint of radiating change which creates a new society on the basis of the values that motivate its design' (1989: 77). Accordingly, it should be possible 'to propel society into a planned future, causing it to skip predicted but undesired stages in its historical development' (1989: 78).

Both Holston and Berlin planners find the modernist idea reflected particularly in an inverted relationship between public and private space, which they demonstrate through figure-ground plans. Both wish these plans to be understood as revealing public-private relations considered typical of the 'pre-industrial'/'Western' (Holston) or 'European' (Berlin planners) city and the 'modernist' city respectively. As Holston writes: 'In the preindustrial city, streets read as figural voids and buildings as continuous ground …. In the modernist city, streets appear as continuous void and buildings as sculptural figures …' (1989: 125).

Whereas the city derived its public order, in the past, from the arrangement of private property, Holston argues, modernist design seeks to eliminate the determining role of private property both formally and concretely (1989: 136). For Planwerk proponents, the modernist-socialist restructuring of Berlin would seem to have been precisely that: a negation of history coupled with a technocratic effort to plan a new society. The apparent inversion of the relationship between public and private space had been achieved partly through alterations of the urban layout, which, in East Berlin, went hand in hand with the expropriation of land by the GDR state. The Planwerk – specifically the concepts of the 'typical house-on-one-lot' and the land 'parcel' – proposes a reversal: the reinstatement of a specific aesthetics of urban space, turning on the preeminence of private property.

In post-unification Berlin, figure-ground plans were an important 'means of persuasion' (Fischler 1995) deployed in the Planwerk's claim to historic city repair. One would continually encounter them in the urban planning arena; they are displayed in myriad books and exhibitions, and were also considered suitable to represent Berlin in the Architecture Biennale in Venice in 2000. Figure-ground plans are valued for their ostensible simplicity. They are thought to facilitate the comprehension – or reading – of the urban structure and the destructions it is perceived to have suffered. It takes little urban planning knowledge to notice the obvious differences in the relation between black figures and white ground in the Berlins of 1940, 1953, 1989 and 2010. If one views these plans, as Stimmann does, as demonstrating Berlin's urban history as 'a history of destruction by both the war and post-war planning' (2001: 18), the black-infilling of voids in the envisaged 2010 city might easily be perceived as repair or a direct substitution for previous losses.

The figure-ground plans are visual devices that work similarly to the displays, guided tours and other representational practices discussed by

Binder (2001b). They also underwrite and help reinforce a particular kind of 'temporalizing effect' (Boyarin 1994: 20) of the narratives in which the unified Berlin has come to be constructed. It is worth to spell out briefly what I mean, here, by the temporalizing effects.

For this, I would like to juxtapose the imagery of Berlin as a European city, a revived metropolis, or a global city with the image of the post-socialist city. The metropolis or the European city entail a narrative that draws directly on pre-war images of the city; the forty year German division (and Berlin's) consequently come to figure as a mere temporary aberration from a 'natural' historical path. Talk about the 'global city', again, situates Berlin with a global stream of time. As Anna Tsing (2000: 332) has pointed out, globalization is frequently understood as a distinctive historical moment – a rupture, ushering in something unprecedented and new – and thus permits a certain disregard for everything that preceded it. Arguably, the recurrent invocation of the image of the fall of the Berlin Wall as marking the end of the Cold War and the supposed 'end of history' has given Berlin a special symbolic position in globalization discourses. Now contrast this with a characterization of Berlin as 'post-socialist city'. It would highlight persistent divisions within the city and the differential development of its eastern and western part (Häußermann 1996a; 1996b).

In other words, talk about Berlin both as a 'global city' and as a 'post-socialist' city emphasize rupture – but of very different kinds.[28] Of course, the two views intersect and often rely on identical kinds of data from which urban restructuring processes are read, analysed and subsequently packaged as scientific explanations. I suggest, however, the contrast between them rests, to paraphrase Fardon (1995), on the distinct 'temporalizations' entailed. Each of the future imaginaries of Berlin as European, global or post-socialist city makes partial sense of changes within, and of connections between, the historical Berlin(s) and other geographical entities within a wider politico-economic context.

Against the partial conceptions of Berlin's history implied by the European or the global city images, sharp criticism has been launched. For instance, for those taking a self-consciously East German perspective, the Planwerk's objective to contribute to the reintegration of the two city halves appears spurious. The urban design historian Simone Hain suggests that '[t]his plan is based on a concept of history which sees the post-war historical period as abnormal, ahistorical and ultimately destructive. It thus in symbolic fashion, ignores forty years of an urban double existence – which was after all of major historical and international importance' (2001: 78). Hain refers not simply to *where* history is located in Berlin's cityscape and what history is *worthy* of preservation but also to what *counts* as history in the first place.

The Planwerk asserts the primacy of a hegemonic history and, as a particular technology, aids its extension onto new territories (Boyarin 1994: 14, 17).[29] Others have argued that the Planwerk's emphasis on 'history' fits specific city-marketing strategies in the late twentieth century (Binder 2001a; Huyssen 1997). The East German architecture critic, Wolfgang Kil (2000), claims that *Geschichtslosigkeit* ('history-lessness'), promoting permanent change as progress, has been both the precondition and the result of Berlin's new constructions. Here, the Planwerk's claim that modernist planning erased history from large parts of Berlin's urban landscape is turned against itself: the Planwerk, too, it is said, attempts to obliterate a specific history, namely, the socialist period. As Bruno Flierl argues, in reference to the Planwerk, its supporters seem to forget that '[a]lthough the GDR has disappeared as a state, the human beings of the GDR are still there – and, for them, there are still the places and stones, the spaces and buildings, which are meaningful to them' (2001: 75). In a context where the recovery of 'historical traces' in the city's layout has been high on the planners' agenda, such an observation may seem bitterly ironic.

In lieu of aesthetic principles and typologies, which were the subject of uncountable expert debates, the kind of history that Kil (2000) has proposed to recover is constituted through the lived experiences of the city's inhabitants, especially of East Berliners. These counter-claims thus rely on invocations of a notion of 'authentic' experience and memory, which is set against the reductive and imposed textuality used as the basis for city planning (cf. Huyssen 1997). Such commentary points to competing claims about how and by whom Berlin's 'true' history may be determined.

Flierl describes the Planwerk as an attempt to turn a previously *real-sozialistisch* ('real-socialist') into a *real-kapitalistisch* ('real-capitalist') city. The Planwerk's preoccupation with the aesthetics of urban form has been criticized as obfuscating the ideological, political and economic forces at work. Infillings in inner-city areas proposed by the Planwerk, for example, allegedly only serve the high-density development. The supposed diversification of ownership in the inner city remains restricted to the façade, as several lots frequently belong to a single developer.

These criticisms are frequently overdetermined by an East-West discourse. A possible consequence is feared to be the displacement of present populations and social polarization – fears which resonate with global concerns about the emergence of 'divided cities' in the context of neo-liberalism (Fainstein et al. 1992; Häußermann and Kapphan 2000). Instead of welcoming the gradual infilling of Berlin's emptiness as a sign of economic prosperity or a return to 'normality', Hain (2000a; 2000b; 2001) suggests that much of the proposed infilling in Berlin's eastern half will be detrimental to the current residents' quality of life. Ample communal spaces and public parks

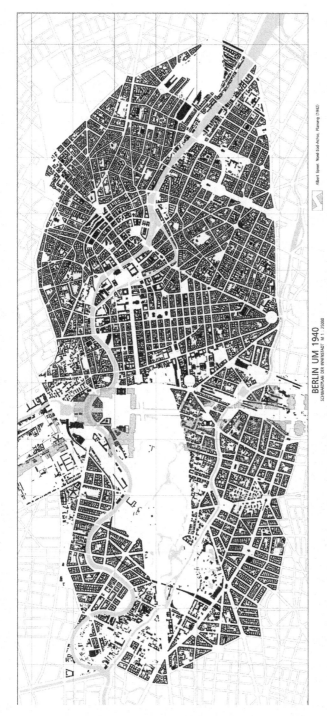

BERLIN UM 1940
SCHWARZPLAN DER INNENSTADT   M 1 : 25000

Albert Speer, Nord-Süd-Achse, Planung (1942)

Figures 5-8: Figure-ground plans of Berlin, courtesy of Senatsverwaltung für Stadtentwicklung, Berlin

BERLIN UM 1953
SCHWARZPLAN DER KERNSTADT M 1 : 25000

Figure 6

BERLIN UM 1989
SCHWARZPLAN DER INNENSTADT M 1 : 25000

Figure 7

BERLIN UM 2010
SCHWARZPLAN DER INNENSTADT M 1 : 25000

Figure 8

created by socialist planning, she argues, will be eliminated in favour of the interests of a select group of politicians, planners and developers.

In the Stadtforum, in SenStadt pronouncements and in expert publications in the 1990s, one could hear repetitive invocations of a new kind of inhabitant, the *Stadtbürger*, the 'urban citizen' or 'urbanite'. An officially launched 'paradigm change' aimed at transforming Berlin from a *Mieterstadt* ('city of tenants') into a *Eigentümerstadt* ('city of owners') further sharpened the conflict as it seemed to imply a threatening conversion to old understandings of urban citizenship as defined through property (see also Hain 2001; Lenhart 2001). The new owners, like the *Stadtbürger*, are imagined as better-off residents, worthy of inhabiting the New Berlin's centre (Hain 2001). From this perspective, the Planwerk's underlying rationale bears an uncanny resemblance to that of modernist planning, in that it seeks to make real, in built form, the blueprint for a future society.

Emptiness

In an important sense, talk about what the future Berlin will become – a capital, a global city or a European city – is talk about how to fill Berlin's emptiness. It seems impossible to talk about Berlin after unification without attending to its empty spaces, from the white spaces in SenStadt's figure-ground plans to the voids in Berlin's cityscape analyzed by the city's scholarly commentators (e.g., Huyssen 1997, Till 2005). Emptiness, as Eric Hirsch notes, constitutes the purest form of potentiality, indicating 'the way we could be' (1995: 4). But as Gary McDonogh (1993) suggests, emptiness is also profoundly ambiguous. Emptiness may denote vacancy, abandon or the failure of state planning; 'it may simply seem wasteful, uneconomic or threatening, but empty space begs explanation' (1993: 7). Talk about emptiness implies conflicting perceptions of the space in question.

In postunification Berlin, empty space seemed both prolific and problematic. There were former industrial sites and buildings that served state functions in the GDR but had yet to find a new purpose. There was the empty stretch left by the Wall, abandoned apartments and plots of disputed ownership. For some time, they provided space for what were largely considered unconventional and often illicit uses: squatting, dance clubs, or the 'Polish market' and a trailer park on the site that later became reconstituted as Potsdamer Platz. The cultural events held in the gradually 'cleared out' shell of the Palast der Republik is but another example.[30] Empty space offered a certain autonomy in its a lack of fit, definition and function. Consider the narrative of Michael, an East German friend in his mid-thirties, who at the time of my fieldwork worked in the district office of Mitte. It came as a reply to my question about his favourite place:

> In the area between the Reichstag and Reinhardtstraße, there is a bridge, Kronprinzenbrücke. Early in the 1990s, when it wasn't yet built, I lived in the area. Whenever I needed fresh air or when I was fed up, when I needed quiet or when I wanted to think about something, I went there. Past the Charité, through Reinhardtstraße, into this former border strip which was then overgrown and wild. There was this half bridge, its pillars, and I loved sitting there.... There was total stillness, but in the middle of the city! One hundred and twenty metres away stood the lit Reichstag; behind you Friedrichstadtpalast; in front of you the Spree; and in between this wasteland, this wild overgrown border strip. A great place. Unfortunately, this lasted only for two or three years. Then they started building the Reichstag – trucks and pneumatic hammers and so on.... So it was really about this connection between quiet, intimacy and seclusion. But you aren't sitting somewhere in the forest where you have to walk ten minutes to the next cycling route. You are 120 metres away from the Reichstag. Incredible! And you know that 400 metres on the left, there's the Brandenburg Gate and in front of you the Spree. And you sit there and you know it's all part of you and with you, this also has history. But this place belongs to you – you are part of it. You can think in quiet, nobody's getting on your nerves. But sometime, you've done enough thinking. Then you get up and that's it.

In a world where urban land is usually possessed and frequently guarded, Berlin's measure of autonomous space seemed remarkable. However, such claims to autonomy clashed with a view of these spaces as zones of illegality and as wasted land, which could be owned, sold and built on. In the 1990s, much effort was put into filling Berlin's ubiquitous emptiness. Artistic, cultural and scholarly attempts to *preserve* emptiness rather than let it be closed partly need to be seen in this context. Huyssen (1997) sees the empty spaces produced by wartime bombing or left by the former border strip as erasures of particular historical moments. The architect Daniel Libeskind famously designed Berlin's new Jewish Museum, which opened in 2001, as a void, a self-conscious emptiness that is to make apparent the absence of the city's Jews who were murdered in the Holocaust.

By the early 2000s, Berlin's new constructions had already begun to generate their own peculiar emptiness – by standing empty, producing *Leerstand* or vacancy. City planners worried about these vacancies, about development projects falling through, and about the absence of profitable investments. However, not to plan or at least account for what was perceived as empty, developable land seemed inconceivable.

Once, as we sat in his office surrounded by plans and other renderings of Berlin present and future, a SenStadt employee told me about a meeting he had attended concerning a high-rise project in Berlin's eastern part. He wondered why they still devoted so much time and effort to making such plans, since everyone knew that investors were lacking. His picture of Berlin's future was murky: with the loss of all its manufacturing industries, Berlin's economic situation was deteriorating, and the city was palpably shrinking. Now the post-unification euphoria, when he, like everyone else, believed that Berlin would boom as in the 1920s, had vanished. 'Nobody believes in growth anymore!' he claimed. Only a moment later, he turned to show me on the map on the wall the areas destined for further development. 'Huge wastelands', he called them, 'deserts' currently used for semi-permanent commerce but, in a city as broke as Berlin, far too precious to be left untouched.

Emptiness, as I noted, is being governed in particular ways. The drawings of the Planwerk Innenstadt filled emptiness with an orange future that is gradually turning into a grey reality. In addition, from the early 2000s, the planning administration devised the so-called *Baulückenmanagement,* a programme for managing 'building gaps'. The programme aimed at reclassifying empty spaces in Berlin's centre, by identifying and subsequently marketing all the 'gaps' in the cityscape. In this way, though not (yet) physically filled, a *Baulücke* is no longer empty; rather, it comes to be conceptualized as an anticipation of future construction.

Whilst doing my internship in SenStadt I could talk to administrators about their efforts to register and inscribe these gaps with a kind of identity, in a fashion quite similar to that deployed by states in governing their populations. At that time, people were busy issuing so-called lot passports including data about their location, size, current use and owner (usually, the Berlin municipality) and about their desired functions. What kind of construction ought it be filled with? The administrator who explained this new invention to me suggested that, just like human beings who are nameless and unable to prove their identity without certain documents, land is nothing without a passport. Managing empty spaces in such a way seemed a first step towards their disappearance.

Emptiness is not a street, not a square and not a park, but an urban pathology. Emptiness can be seen as generated by the disciplinary terms of geography, urban planning and design that constitute it as a conceptual anomaly (Shields 1996: 232–3). Notions of empty space have also played an important legitimizing role in discourses on development and colonization (Blaut 1993: 201; Buck-Morss 2000: 32). Lands to be colonized are considered uninhabited by 'civilized' human life or as without a recognized owner. Sometimes, their inhabitants are conceived as 'people without history' (Wolf 1982). These are spaces to be tamed, developed and exploited, and in which to fashion an ideal society.

The urban development process, particularly in postunification East Berlin, has been likened to a colonization of the East by the West (Borneman 1992: 322; 1997: 96; Hain 2001: 72). Wolfgang Kil speaks of exclusively western political and planning committees that declared the city's entire eastern half 'New Territories', an 'ideational wasteland', and a *tabula rasa* without history (2000a: 59). A similar notion was invoked by the planner Dorothea Tscheschner in an interview with me. Having been part of the planning team that created the new design for Alexanderplatz in the 1960s, Tscheschner now worked as a consultant evaluating buildings for an insurance company, but she also researched and wrote on GDR planning and hoped our interviews could be useful. In one of our conversations over a cup of coffee in her small flat in a GDR residential block located near the former border to Kreuzberg, Tscheschner recalled the way her new Western colleagues would talk about East Berlin shortly after the *Wende*:

> [It was always about] this yawning wasteland of the East, and how you'd be afraid to come here, and [how desolate] the Alexanderplatz underground station looked, and so on. And then I'd ask: 'When were you actually there?' Then, they'd begin to brood [about my question]. It transpired that they were there once, in '91, when the *Treuhand*[31] had shut everything, when East Berlin was a ghost town, because within a year 500,000 jobs

Figure 9: The empty Alexanderplatz

had been dissolved and people were sent home. Of course, everybody was frightened in this dead inner city then. Thus, they came here once, got frightened, and never came back again.

After unification, many of the wide streets and large squares in Berlin's eastern half were reconceptualized as a specific kind of emptiness typical of the socialist system. There, land was conceived as a distinct category of property, a means of production; it was of the state. No other state system, planning administrators asserted in conversations with me, would allow itself to leave the most valuable land in the entire city largely empty. Emptiness was thus seen as a deliberate gesture of the GDR state, demonstrating socialist grandeur. The concomitant erasure of large parts of Berlin's 'historical' centre is felt to underscore the ideological impetus behind this emptiness.

Here, emptiness connotes not only economic mismanagement and development potential but also an absence of 'history'. The former site of the Berlin Schloss with the large parking space in front of the Palast and the subsequent demolition of the building is, as we have seen, a case in point. As an artefact of the reconstruction of the GDR capital, Alexanderplatz is another such instance of socialist emptiness, often cited. To some, as the quote at the beginning of this book evinces, Alexanderplatz seems to exist in nothing more than its name and Döblin's fiction (Kieren 1994). Alexanderplatz's design reflects a planning rationale constructed around progress and a technocratic image of society, but under very specific politico-economic exigencies: 'middling modernism' (Rabinow 1989) in its particular 'real-socialist' inflection. Alexanderplatz was to be a space for work and for leisure, a centre for trade and for societal life (Ribbe 1998: 41). This vast open space surrounded by public buildings and by shops, restaurants and other amenities, had (almost) everything expected from a proper socialist city centre. It augured a teleologically conceived socialist future. After unification, within different frames of evaluation, much of Alexanderplatz was rendered superfluous.

The need for restructuring Alexanderplatz, as an East German SenStadt administrator explained, had been an outcome of Germany's reunification. 'This oasis of socialist planning,' he suggested, 'doesn't match the requirements of contemporary society. Even though some of the existing buildings have been recently renovated, they are not designed for the long-term future.' In light of the various guiding images for Berlin – the metropolis, the global city or the European city – Alexanderplatz had come to appear inadequate.

Now, as I discuss in subsequent chapters, the self-consciously symbolic features in Alexanderplatz seemed vacuous, as the state that had furnished them with meaning had disintegrated. Following unification, the very conception of Alexanderplatz became a contentious issue as different sets of people claimed authorship to its design. Two of these people were Dorothea Tscheschner and Joachim Näther, who had been East Berlin's *Chefarchitekt* ('chief architect') at the time. I interviewed both of them for this research, and despite their many differences and disagreements, some of their views on Alexanderplatz strongly converged. They both suggested that Alexanderplatz's potential had quite simply never been fully exploited during GDR times, and that the makeover that was now envisaged seemed, from their perspective, precipitous and untimely. In their narratives, Alexanderplatz emerged quite literally as one of the 'unfinished constructions' that Nikolai Ssorin-Chaikov (2003) has described in the context of Soviet Siberia, reflecting the always incomplete project of the socialist state. It points to a continuous deferral, a 'could have been'.

The disappearance of empty spaces at the hand of Berlin's current imagineers has provoked its own counter-imaginaries. I heard comments on the obliteration of the large patch of grass in front of the Reichstag, which had once been used for family outings, sunbathing and casual football matches. The vast emptiness of Alexanderplatz has, similarly, come to be understood as a possibility. Social work projects that fill the square's empty corners with streetball fields and propose to turn it into a place for young people; arts performances and events in *Haus des Lehrers* and in the square itself; and residents who conjure up a careful development of the square all propose different kinds of imaginings of that emptiness.

The project manager of the Solidarity Bazaar of the Berlin Journalists, an annual event held in Alexanderplatz which has continued to attract crowds beyond the *Wende*, appreciatively told me about the large spaces for gatherings, demonstrations and concerts that both the former East and West Berlin had offered – spaces where 'the people could articulate itself'. Alexanderplatz, for example, not only hosted the Solidarity Bazaar but had also regularly served as a stage for an orchestrated socialist public, which was subverted as such not least in the mass demonstration on 4 November 1989. After unification, these kinds of public spaces were, in the view of this man, markedly decreasing perhaps because politicians no longer had an interest in engaging in a 'dialogue with the people'. Perhaps, however, 'the people' had unlearnt to articulate itself in the street, which seemed astonishing at this particular moment in time:

> [Berlin] is economically bust, there were huge social cuts, but there is no
> movement as in '89 in the East, that they would take to the streets and
> say: 'We've had enough!' There are the various interest groups [...] and
> each does its own little activity. [...] I don't know whether that is because

it's outdated, because the individualization of society is progressing and groups are therefore getting together less.... But I think in the GDR it did happen in the end, when the problems were red-hot.

The question that was left hanging in the air in this conversation was about the possible disappearance of any potential for protest in a unified Berlin. The narratives related here evoke the significance of empty space – of 'gaps' in the city – and a sense of appreciation quite different from that expressed by planners, who find empty space to be wanting. Some of my interlocutors stressed that Berlin's 'marginal' empty spaces had produced alternative forms of openness and plurality. This brings us full circle to the beginning of the chapter where I sketched out an imaginary of unified Berlin as a space of publicness and debate. In the above tributes to Berlin's emptiness, empty space is public space, a space open to political expression and protest. Similarly, McDonogh suggests: 'When empty space fills, its actors controvert its social construction or planned meaning. Hence it provides a place from which to protest a city and society as a whole' (1993: 15). A vast open plane, once used for demonstrations and protests of diverse kinds, Alexanderplatz often appeared to epitomize 'public space'. This is a particularly salient understanding of empty space, which I will come back to in this book.

What all these different understandings of emptiness share is the way in which they generate the city. Berlin in the wake of unification was a huge *lieu d'avenir*, but the future Berlin, we may say, exists only *in absentia*, in continuous deferral (Buchli 1999; Ssorin-Chaikov 2003). Emptiness is a city with potential for investment and economic prosperity in a globalized world; it is the European city destroyed and rewritten; a socialist capital now reinterpreted as 'history' or lack thereof; it is also a city of publics contesting and deliberating about the future. The future is frequently described as an empty space as yet unknown; here, it is emptiness which describes the future. In talking about emptiness, we have already begun to fill it.

The Disintegration of a Socialist Exemplar

In the summer of 2002, the twenty-first world congress of architecture was held in Berlin. In this context, a public discussion took place in a small art gallery in Berlin's central district, Mitte. The discussion brought together a number of speakers familiar from Berlin's impassioned planning debates including, amongst others, Uwe Rada, known for his critical writing as editor of Berlin's left-leaning newspaper *die tageszeitung,* and urban theorist Dieter Hoffmann-Axthelm, a theologian turned architectural critic and a key figure in Berlin's planning debates. In this discussion, Alexanderplatz was invoked as a vehicle for examining possibilities for integrating 'Eastern' and 'Western European' urban design, but also as a metaphor for what people found problematic about planning processes in postunification Berlin. Another discussant, the East German urban design historian Simone Hain, suggested that in the debate about the future Alexanderplatz social, aesthetic and ethical aspects had often been difficult to disentangle. Some might have hoped that by altering Alexanderplatz's *built* surface, its *user* surface could be altered too.

Hain's reflections alluded to the ways in which urban planning has been concerned not merely with buildings, streets and squares but also with the constitution of urban life and the city dweller. Critical to this idea of urban planning are notions of order and disorder – linking the social and the material – which the present chapter explores. Notions of (urban) order and disorder are historically and culturally contingent, as Timothy Mitchell has emphasized, and their conceptual relation is essentially asymmetrical: '[Disorder] is the void that places order as the centre, existing only to allow "order" its conceptual possibility' (Mitchell 1988: 82). An examination of ideas of disorder can tell us a great deal about the kinds of order that people have imagined or that they take for granted in particular contexts. Such an examination is not merely supplementary. Rather, the complex and shifting discourses on disorder deserve attention in their own right.

Analysts of the formation of urban planning in eighteenth- and nine-teenth-century Europe and its colonies have pointed to the significance of particular kinds of order that urban planning has sought to create (Mitchell 1988; Rabinow 1989). Since the nineteenth century, as the historian Brian Ladd suggests, urban planning in Germany has become the 'pursuit of a combination of spatial order and social reform' (1990: 76). Indeed, the twentieth-century history of Alexanderplatz may be read as a case study of such attempted interventions in 'the social' through planning. From Martin Wagner's 1920s plans for a rationalized city centre to the GDR design to the current plans, each appeared to project an ideal of the organization of the city and urban life (Frisby 2001; Kil and Kündiger 1998).

More recently, critics have pointed to the emergence of an urban policy rhetoric employed by city officials, planners, and developers which is de-vised to constitute inner-city areas as safe and comfortable spaces of con-sumption (Robe 1999). The new design for Alexanderplatz is understood not only as an assault on Berlin's former socialist centre, potentially threat-ening to the East Berlin residents. More generally, it is deemed yet another example of a surreptitious urban politics through which those people not matching the image of the desired 'user' – including homeless people, punks and migrants – will be excluded from public space (Rada 1997; Robe 1999).

These developments have been projected onto a larger scale and are seen to parallel global trends in urban restructuring and regeneration (Rada 1997; Ronneberger et al. 1999). Urban scholars have provided detailed as-sessments of the continual transformation of public and private spaces and the forces at work in urban development processes (Caldeira 2000; Davis 1994; Gibson 2003; Low 2003; Sorkin 1992; Zukin 1991). They point to the ways notions of urban disorder and order are produced through the rhetoric and practice of state planners and private developers. Despite sig-nificant parallels, it remains important to attend to the specificities of plan-ning articulated in diverse social and cultural contexts. Whilst scholarly and public attention, within and outside Germany, has been focused on central sites and the transformation of Berlin into a European capital city, my analysis examines a place that – regardless of its geographically central location and historical significance – has come to appear increasingly mar-ginal. Instead of detailing official discourse, my analysis is concerned with how people's experiences and theories of the cityscape coalesce in an, albeit partial, 'sense of place' (Feld and Basso 1996).

What I offer, here, is not a coherent picture of a 'disorderly' public square but a multi-faceted description of the ways disorder is thought about, expe-rienced, governed and materialized in Alexanderplatz. Key to these inter-related discourses on disorder are two distinct notions of 'society' and 'the social'. One is a familiar idea of 'the social' as a problem space and a domain of government (Foucault 2002: 352; Rabinow 1989; Rose 1999). The other refers to a utopian notion of society as an ideal not yet attained. The latter was particularly characteristic of state socialism (Ssorin-Chaikov 2003; 2006) and as such was embodied in Alexanderplatz.

I will first describe the huge significance that Alexanderplatz held as an exemplary 'socialist square' and how the square's physical disintegration today seemingly mirrors the disintegration of the GDR state. Talk about Alexanderplatz's postunification disorder has provided a way of discussing the dislocations that accompanied unification and the vanishing of a socialist ideal. Secondly, talk about disorder may be considered a commentary on what are regarded the failures of government. Such failures were perceived in Alexanderplatz's disorderly materiality – for example, in graffiti, in rubbish and in particular kinds of people. Disorder was blamed on people who are regarded to have failed or have been failed by society and on those who are feared to pose a threat to public order. Finally, I shall suggest how attempts to create order, such as the new plans for Alexanderplatz, can at times appear to produce the very disorder they are proclaimed to contain.

Diagnosing the 'Weak Heart of the City'

Socialist planning constructed Alexanderplatz as a spatial exemplar. The square was to be a model for GDR cities and perhaps the entire Eastern Bloc and, simultaneously, a show window to the West. It was part of the newly fashioned centre of 'Berlin – capital of the GDR', conceived to consolidate the international recognition of the fledgling socialist Republic. The cityscape was understood as both symbol and expression of the form of society that the socialist state was expected to produce (Hain 1992: 57). The historian Stefan Wolle (1999: 163) has described the GDR as a Potemkin Village and Alexanderplatz was arguably its prime building block: a façade of social and technological progress, the apogee of socialist life (Kuhle 1995).

With its hotel, department store, the Weltzeituhr ('World Time Clock') and the Brunnen der Völkerfreundschaft ('Fountain of the Peoples' Friendship'), and surrounded by the Haus der Statistik ('House of Statistics'), Haus des Reisens ('House of Travel'), and Haus des Lehrers ('House of the Teacher') – buildings representing the components of the socialist state – Alexanderplatz was an embodiment of the socialist future. This was no doubt an aspiration rather than a reality. The indeterminacy of meaning of the socialist architectural reality (Buchli 1999), and the contingencies of planning typical of planning in Soviet Almaty (Alexander 2007), were also reflected in Alexanderplatz. The GDR planners I consulted, who had been involved in designing Berlin's centre, told me that if Alexanderplatz appeared at variance with the envisaged ideal, they would seek to bring the two into alignment. In response to citizens' suggestions and complaints, additional shops and restaurants were added to increase Alexanderplatz's attractiveness. Through these additions, GDR planners effectively adjusted the future to the present. It was a performance of 'teleological time [which] melted the momentous into its eternal end' (Ssorin-Chaikov 2006: 370).

People from all over the country flocked to Alexanderplatz on their trips to Berlin. The parades on 1 May and on 7 October, the national holiday and festivals such as the Solidarity Bazaar of the Berlin journalists made the square a happening place. It was on these occasions that Alexanderplatz emerged as the communicative and societal space its planners had envisaged. The *Weltzeituhr* provided an unmissable meeting point that remains popular today. Crowned by a fragile system of heavenly bodies and displaying the times of ('befriended') places all over the world, the clock seemed to symbolize the ideology of technological progress and socialist internationalism, but also the myth of the temporal and spatial infinity of the socialist world (Lücke 1998). My friend Michael, now an administrator in the local district council, recalled for me his youthful adventures in and around Alexanderplatz. He concluded that in Alexanderplatz, 'there was always this illusion or this hope that something would happen; that you would meet people; that you would experience the unheard-of; that you would meet foreigners from western Europe and possibly talk to them.'

As a place of openness and promise, Alexanderplatz also fostered practices unintended by its planners and hardly officially acknowledged in the GDR. Boris was one of the younger regulars of the pub in the Rathauspassagen near Alexanderplatz where I worked during my fieldwork. Although away during the week to work at a pharmaceutical company in another city, Boris offered to talk to me about Alexanderplatz, his memories and current experiences of it. Having lived near Alexanderplatz all his life, Boris recollected in particular the square's foul-smelling subterranean toilet, so disgusting he never dared enter. It was, in any case, a place with a 'bad reputation', a place about which a mother would say: 'Boy, you aren't gonna go there!' Perhaps the foul smell evoked the illicit activities allegedly going on in these toilets, which made them a no-go area for the little boy. (There were rumours of prostitution and gay cruising.) How he pitied the poor children on school trips to Berlin, queuing to enter the toilet because they didn't know where else to put their bodily excretions. Similarly, whether the Fountain had received its nickname *Nuttenbrosche* ('hooker's brooch') because of its garish colours or because women had offered their services here to Western businessmen was a matter of ongoing dispute. Some of my interlocutors noted that, despite its popularity amongst GDR citizens and foreign visitors, Alexanderplatz never occupied the same status for Berliners themselves. In addition, Alexanderplatz had always been dead at night. GDR work-hours (making for an early-morning start), intense surveillance and ideological constraints may have been responsible for the absence of the visible nightlife one might expect in the centre of a city like Berlin (cf. Schlör 1998).

Alexanderplatz's special allure may have been disputable during GDR times; but after the fall of the Wall, any possibility of a better life and the future that the square had once promised seemed to be fading away. Alexanderplatz had been a place where, as Michael put it, confined East Berliners could 'sniff at the great, wide world'. After 1989, this changed. Then, 'you could go to *Zoo* [station in West Berlin] to sniff at the world; or you didn't have to sniff at the world because you could travel there. You could get to the world and didn't have to care that the world would come to you'.

As the world of socialist certainties fell into disarray, this was apparently reflected in the square's physical disintegration. Alexanderplatz became an apt vehicle for talking about the demise of the GDR state and the future it once embodied. Newspaper articles from the period report on Alexanderplatz as an unruly open-air market dominated by unauthorized vendors selling desirable yet rejectable goods (Humphrey 1999: 34; Veenis 1999), including cheap clothes, Soviet paraphernalia and electronic equipment for hugely inflated prices.[32] The ambiguity that had surrounded Alexanderplatz during GDR times was supplanted by ambiguity of a different kind. 'Dangerous gypsies', 'eastern European conmen', 'violent Yugoslavian youth gangs' and 'illegal moneychangers' allegedly turned the purportedly immaculate socialist showcase into a centre of mischief and crime.[33] Such descriptions of Alexanderplatz resemble, in some respects, those of places in other postsocialist cities (e.g., Bodnár 2001). In Berlin, as in other parts of the postsocialist world, images of 'outsiders' became 'important symbols for discussing particular kinds of dislocation attendant on the exit from socialism' (Verdery 1996: 97), and implying changing conceptions of trade, work and the market (see also Bridger and Pine 1998; Humphrey 1999; Lemon 2000; Spülbeck 1996).

These were not the foreigners that had made Alexanderplatz exciting during GDR times, but foreigners that signified an 'other', repulsive and embarrassing side of Alexanderplatz. Other newspaper articles dwelled on East Berliners' circumstantial inability to fully embrace 'the West'. Readers were offered glimpses of biographies, conveying a sense of lives that had reached a dead end and of people caught in limbo. There is Friedrich who used to be 'someone' – preparing meals for 'the great men of the GDR' – but is now tending a public toilet; Valentin, a former Red Army soldier turned street vendor; and a whole lot of fallen gods, ex–Party animals, so ruffled and tumbledown one might only recognize them at second sight. (The Berliner Zeitungsmann, a West Berlin pensioner who now sold newspapers in Alexanderplatz, took pleasure in pointing out to me that similar characters could still be found in the square.) Being and working at Alexanderplatz, these articles seemed to say, were no longer special. Now, the square was for the poor and destitute, religious fanatics, criminals and those who had not yet made it elsewhere.

The physically deteriorating Alexanderplatz came to serve as a backdrop and metaphor for the disintegration of the GDR state and many of its former citizens. It was, as one journalist contends, a place embodying a specific 'German condition', and a 'point of crystallization of the unresolved problems of unification'.[34] The new state, the FRG, he opines, had not yet succeeded in reintegrating either Alexanderplatz or these people who 'don't want the old times back but don't accept the new ones either'. Alexanderplatz was summoned as a place that had previously embodied an East German identity but was now riddled with troublesome differences. Writing in 1992, the East German architecture critic Wolfgang Kil similarly related the apparent disintegration of Alexanderplatz to East Berliners' altered (self-)perceptions and experiences afforded and imposed by unification. With perceptible sarcasm, he wrote:

> With unification, the former centre of East Berlin has acquired an overpowering competitor. The glitzy West City around Bahnhof Zoo and Tauentzien – with its overflowing shops, stylish cafés and effervescent traffic till late at night – effortlessly eclipses Alexanderplatz – this huge, concrete plane between department store, station and hotel. And promptly, a waft of shabbiness has settled on the former showpiece. The high-rise colossuses are standing around like erratic boulders. Everything suddenly seems to have turned out a few sizes too big and too coarse. All of a sudden, one has the impression, an unpleasant wind was wheezing across the square (2000: 42).

The design competition for Alexanderplatz in 1993 might have appeared like a (partial) solution to the perceived 'unresolved problems' attendant on unification. This solution reflected the pronounced concern with what a shared identity of East and West in the unified Germany might mean (Berdahl 1999a; Borneman 1992; 1997; Glaeser 2000; Mandel 1994). Alexanderplatz was to be reconstituted as a symbol of Berlin's 'inner unification' (Senatsverwaltung 2001: 3). A future built environment was imagined, which would appeal to East and West Berliners alike and express something of their reconstituted sense of 'self'.[35] However, newspaper articles, transcripts of public discussions and the comments of citizen-group members I spoke to suggest that for many Berliners, the proposed solution for Alexanderplatz seemed doubtful. It was expected to bring offices, expensive apartments and exclusive shops that few could afford. The putative symbol of unity would thus draw in 'rich Westerners' but exclude 'poor Easterners'. Some East Berliners felt the proposed reconstruction to be a devaluation, rather than revaluation, of 'their' Alexanderplatz and, perhaps, of themselves.

Inversions of Sociality

By the early 2000s, Alexanderplatz's open-air market had disappeared. The few vendors who were there, selling their goods from portable stalls, had licenses legalizing their trade. Conmen, gambling with passers-by, were but a sporadic, though again increasing, presence. The train station at Alexanderplatz had been restored, and patches of grass and flowerbeds brought colour to the square. These were welcome changes. Yet, as I learned from conversations with residents and other people working in or using the square, it still seemed indisputable that 'something needed to be done' about Alexanderplatz.

One day in December 2001, I went to visit Herr Müller, a local resident and a former member of a citizen group that, as I discuss in Chapter V, had vehemently contested the new plans for Alexanderplatz in the 1990s. As I was waiting outside his home, a 1970s tenement near Alexanderplatz, a man perhaps in his early sixties arrived. He turned out to be Herr Müller. Unlocking the door, the man enquired whether I was waiting for someone. As I learned later, approaching strangers around the house, was habitual for Müller – not only to help them find their way if they looked lost but also to determine their business. This habit felt even more urgent today because of the constant coming and going observable in the area, which was a worry for Müller and for other long-term residents. The newcomers were considered people unwanted or unable to afford a place in West Berlin; they were people whose devaluation by society might contribute to a devaluation of the area and perhaps the position of its residents. Their arrival was claimed to be noticeable simply by looking out the window: the front gardens were littered and nobody seemed to care. As Herr Müller explained, 'a lot of *Fremdheit* ('strangeness') has come [to the neighbourhood] and with this strangeness to the surroundings, too, I'd say. Whether inside the houses or in front of the houses, nobody feels responsible for anything anymore'.

In GDR times, he recalled, the tending of the front garden had been a communal affair in which residents participated with varying enthusiasm. Such activities were conceived of as a significant aspect of citizens' contributions to the shaping of a specific socialist collectivity and society. When housing was privatized, such contributions were no longer encouraged. In fact, Müller claimed, they were actively prevented. Professional gardening companies were paid to do the job. This was regrettable, in his view, because many of the older residents would still find pleasure in such activities. Instead, they now felt estranged from their previously familiar environment.

A similar sense of indifference and neglect appeared to manifest itself in Alexanderplatz. People who remembered it from GDR times would tell me that Alexanderplatz today bore no resemblance to the clean and orderly square they once knew. Instead, as another resident asserted, it had become a spot where dealers and punks gathered; and the Kaufhof department store's attempts to improve things by holding Easter or Christmas markets appeared spurious. Dirt, rubbish and *Schmierereien* (lit. 'smeared stuff'; derogatory term for graffiti) tarnished the walls of the tunnels under Alexanderplatz. Such disrespect for common property and other people's efforts was deemed to have been inconceivable during GDR times.

It seems too simplistic to explain this commentary in terms of a generalized nostalgia for socialist times as it has been reported from Eastern Europe and the former Soviet Union (e.g., Bridger and Pine 1998: 6; Ssorin-Chaikov 2003: 117). Most East Berliners I met would oppose an interpretation of their words and actions as nostalgic. In Germany, 'nostalgia' has become a notorious and politically loaded term. A neologism has been invented, *Ostalgie*, referring to a supposedly romanticizing or distorted view of what life in 'the East' was like, as people try to cope with social and political ruptures and the disappointed expectations of unification. Talk about *Ostalgie* is often felt to belittle the experiences of East Germans by relegating them to the realm of the emotional and irrational as a slightly skewed view of the past filled with memories of a 'good' life that has vanished.[36] Instead, I suggest that what is conveyed here is a specific 'sense of place' (Feld and Basso 1996), one in which indifference and disorder had emerged where people once perceived the possibility of a (never quite achieved) ideal society.

People who don't greet you in the lift, neighbours you can't entrust with the keys to your flat to look after your plants whilst you are on vacation, and those who just don't bother to pick up litter in the front garden – all seemingly embodied the impact of 'the West' and, more generally, the adverse conditions affecting society today. Graffiti, rubbish in the front garden and children's toys left in the corridor were more than a violation of expected norms of behaviour. For Müller and many other long-term residents of the area, they were the traces of irresponsible newcomers, and an attack on previous collective efforts. The flip side and the real threat of strangers moving into the area, in such a context, is 'being made a stranger oneself' (Baxstrom 2008: 147).

What had fallen into neglect were not simply the houses, front gardens and public spaces. It was also a particular kind of sociality. This sociality, I suggest, was one produced by people literally extending themselves outwards into the built environment. From this perspective, actions that destroy communal property may appear to inverse the established sociality. They entail an inverse intentionality. The agents are opposed: they may be long-term residents, on the one hand, and strangers on the other. Social relationships now appeared to be marked by anonymity, indifference and reserve.

These phenomena and the instrumentalization of relationships by money have long been associated with the modern city, and specifically the capitalist one. Social critics, from Simmel (1980) to Sennett (1994), have commented on them with perceptible ambivalence. Socialism held out the hope of abolishing the supposed socio-psychological characteristics of the urban dweller, along with capitalism and the inequality and difference between the country and the city (Grundmann 1984). In contemporary Berlin, however, some people found that confirmation for these interlocking theories of the city and capitalism lay again before them. Theory and experience coalesced in a moral topography of place.

Failures of Government

Alexanderplatz's disorder could also appear to be a matter of rubbish, rats and too many people of the 'wrong' kind. Commentary on this kind of disorder echoed what Stallybrass and White (1986) have termed a metonymic chain linking, for example, the poor to disease and to animals deemed repulsive, such as rats. To say this is not to suggest that perceptions of Alexanderplatz's disorder are crudely or mechanically determined by a dichotomous mental structure or a metonymic chain; but only to insist that order and disorder have been articulated in historically contingent ways, in which the association between substances, creatures and persons constructed as defiled or deviant has long been pivotal.

Talk about Alexanderplatz's disorderliness and ways of dealing with it – through street cleaning, policing or social work – evoked specific ideas about the social as a problem space to be managed through government. In my analysis, therefore, I aim to move beyond a dichotomy of the discursive and the material. Blanket terms such as 'dirty' could refer to both the materiality of Alexanderplatz and particular people, sometimes labelled fringe groups. In this commentary, Mary Douglas' famous observation that dirt is matter out of place seemed apposite (Douglas 1966). The boundaries that were being transgressed were those between salubrity and pollution, and the good and the a-social citizen. Importantly, 'anomalous' matter was felt to threaten not only a conceptual order but also a social one.

Amongst municipal street cleaners, Alexanderplatz had the reputation of being 'the dirtiest place in the whole of Berlin'. The hotel manager lamented that instead of coins, as in the fountains of Rome, in Alexanderplatz's fountain, one could find only rubbish. Blame was variously assigned to the municipal government (for providing inadequate cleaning services), individual shops such as Burger King (whose customers allegedly produced disproportionate amounts of rubbish), or every user of the square. In the summer of 2002, the municipal street-cleaning service installed an oversized, bright orange rubbish bin with the imprint 'For Beginners'. It was a particularly prominent example of the 'official graffiti of the everyday' (Hermer and Hunt 1996), reminding people that even rubbish – unwanted objects with little specific economic or aesthetic value – had an appropriate place.

Rubbish disturbed contemporary environmental sensibilities and seemed to obstruct the playful, recreational activities, the beauty and salubrity that public fountains and gardens are intended to foster (Ladd 1990: 67; Rotenberg 1993b; Worpole 2000). Floating beer cans and broken pieces of glass in the fountain could pose a danger to children, eager to splash around on a hot summer's day but held back by their mother's warnings of the diseases they might catch in the contaminated water. Of similarly great concern were the rats in Alexanderplatz. They became visible particularly at night, straying undisturbed onto the otherwise deserted square. Rats elicited fear and repulsion, especially when venturing beyond the nighttime Alexanderplatz into broad daylight. They became a nuisance feared for their damaging effects on businesses around the square. The manager of a café was outraged that her complaints to the municipal offices only yielded the dismissive reply, 'We can't do anything about it'. The municipality appeared to neglect the care of public space, which she, like many other people, regarded one of its main duties.

Put differently, rubbish and rats could signify a failure of government. This notion has been largely the result of discourses on public health, which powerfully emerged in the nineteenth century. It placed responsibility for the maintenance of public cleanliness and order – through technologies of hygiene such as pavements, street cleaning and enclosed sewers – into the hands of the municipalities and the state (Corbin 1986). If early efforts at containment were to protect especially the bourgeois classes (Stallybrass and White 1986), by 1900, health and hygiene measures were to be applied to the whole of society. Public health had come to be considered part of the

public interest (Ladd 1990). Socio-biological theories of urbanisation posited the city as a threat for the German *Volk*, generating sickness and debil-
ity (Lees 1985: 142). Entwined with a growing sense of hostility towards the
city, public health came to refer to the physical as well as the psycho-moral
constitution of the urban dweller, especially the poor. Injecting elements of
'nature' into the city – in the form of gardens, parks and recreational spaces
– was rendered a luxurious but necessary way of improving their allegedly
coarse and immoral manners. Providing welfare programmes, sewers and
street cleaning became the task of any good city government (Ladd 1990:
67).

In the early 2000s, Alexanderplatz's planners could take for granted
the space of public health and busy themselves with technicalities when
discussing pavement widths or the course of sewage pipes. Sometimes,
however, in the meetings I attended in the planning administration, those
assumed threats to public health *were* problematized. For example, planners remarked that they generally shunned the food stalls in Alexanderplatz
because of their smell and the rats roaming about. The stalls posed technical and aesthetic problems. Neither these 'sheds' together with similarly
impermanent, 'ugly' structures nor the associated elements were deemed
to have a proper place in a central square in the new German capital.

They were not simply matter out of place, however. When viewed from
the perspective of the future Alexanderplatz – as administrative planners
typically did – they could seem unequivocally out of *time*. By contrast,
for other people I talked to in Alexanderplatz, rubbish and rats had come
with unification. Employees at the foods stalls, too, worried about the rats
and bad smells but blamed them on the sorry green shrubs just behind the
stalls. Much abused as a 'piss corner', this place was emblematic of what
a street cleaner felt Alexanderplatz to be in general, namely, 'the largest
public toilet in Berlin'. During GDR times, I was told, all this had, quite
simply, not existed and street cleaners had had much stronger chemicals to
counteract rats and stenches. From this perspective, urine, rats and rubbish
were, quite definitely, matters *in* time.

A Dangerous Place?

One summer evening I sat chatting with some young people who frequented
a facility for youth located in the northeastern corner of Alexanderplatz.
Early on in my fieldwork I had been introduced to the group of youth workers running the facility and began to spend time with youth workers and
young people in the square. They came here almost every day, passing their
time – as we did now – talking and bickering, whilst sitting under the trees

and watching people pass by. Usually, it was the same crowd, but tonight two young men joined us. Their presence seemed to perturb some of the girls. I had not met these young men before and, for them too, I was a new face. On hearing that I was writing about Alexanderplatz, one of the young men, Ahmed, exclaimed that he had been a regular at Alexanderplatz for seven years and could tell me everything I might want to know. He pointed to where a group of Cubans had gathered (most of them had come to the GDR as students and stayed after unification), as they often did during the summer in the early evening. Ahmed noted: 'That's the *Negerecke* ('Negro corner')!' Here, one of the girls interrupted, sharply criticising his choice of words: these people were called Afro-Americans, she knew. Ahmed sneered that she should mind her own business.

Ahmed continued to enumerate Alexanderplatz's various 'corners': the *Fidschi* corner at the public toilets (using a highly derogatory term for Vietnamese migrants); the spot where pickpockets from Romania and ex-Yugoslavia gather; the conmen around the television tower who were also from ex-Yugoslavia; and other corners where people of predominantly Arab origin and without residence permits deal in marijuana and heroin. Two areas, Ahmed claimed, functioned as meeting points for all: the small casino at the bottom of the hotel and what he called the 'unofficial casino' in the park behind the television tower. Ahmed's friend added that Alexanderplatz used to be dominated by Albanians engaging in their 'private trade'. 'Later, the Kurds came,' he explained, 'and we left the area to them.' Then, Ahmed giggled that in front of the department store, one would find the unemployed and welfare recipients – mostly men who have come here to look for women.

'In Alexanderplatz,' he went on to say, 'society's filth assembles.' This was strange, he thought, for just over there was the beautiful district of Prenzlauer Berg; in the other direction, there was Hackescher Markt where, according to Ahmed, people were friendly to each other, too; and another cool district, Friedrichshain, adjoined Alexanderplatz in the east. These were districts characterized by cafés, bars, restaurants and shops catering to a large youthful population of students – and, increasingly, of well-off young professionals – which have become trendy locations and, many feel, 'yuppified' and invaded by tourists. Alexanderplatz, Ahmed concluded, is right in the centre and a place where only 'the socially weak' gather.

Whilst I was scribbling down these explanations, a new landscape – or rather people-scape – of various illicit and marginalized groups spread out before me, in which Ahmed knew how to navigate. In Ahmed's Alexanderplatz, a diversity of ethnic and social groups laid claim to their respective corners of the square. This kind of description – assembled from newspaper headlines, public pronouncements and everyday experiences – could be taken as offensive (perhaps deliberately so), as the girl's response indicates. It both resonated with and jarred vis-à-vis the picture of Alexanderplatz that was painted by worried residents. It also reminded me of what Sirwan, a Kurdish youth I had met at Alexanderplatz, had told me a few days earlier. He spoke of his growing dislike for Alexanderplatz, which was partly related to the dealers whom he despised and wanted no dealings with. Then Sirwan queried: 'You are not going to write about what I just told you?' He was cautious not because he feared getting into trouble with the dealers; rather, he worried that if the presence of such people at Alexanderplatz became widely known, policing might increase, and he and his friends would become subject to even more controls. From prior experience, Sirwan knew well that the police were hardly discriminating in their controlling practices – aside from a discrimination between 'dark looking' people and others. Sirwan was therefore unsurprised that I had little awareness of either the policing practices or the illicit activities he described.

Likewise, when I now said to Ahmed that I couldn't quite see what he was seeing, Ahmed laughed: 'That's understandable. You only see it if you know!' In any case, one wouldn't believe it when Alexanderplatz looked as it did tonight. The evening sun was shedding its last light onto the square. There were people out on an evening stroll, and others resting on the grass. Alexanderplatz looked tranquil.

However, Ahmed and his friend also knew that the police had declared Alexanderplatz a 'dangerous place' in the mid-1990s. 'Since the *Wende*,' Ahmed offered, 'Alexanderplatz has become a dangerous place and more and more criminalized.' The young men, who claimed previous involvement in some 'wheeling and dealing', boasted about how to evade the police's attempts at controlling crime. Perhaps partly to impress, Ahmed and his friend appeared unconcerned about the power of the police or, for that matter, about the ethnographer's potential power to inscribe Alexanderplatz as a criminal space that had so worried Sirwan.

The city has long been associated with crime and danger; but what is perceived as dangerous and what provokes 'city fear' is 'always contingent on the ways in which we *should* fear the city' (Epstein 1998: 213–4, emphasis in the original). Berlin police has applied the label 'dangerous place' to areas – ranging from select streets to entire underground train lines – that have displayed a statistically disproportionate number of crimes. Rendered statistically, occasional events have become a permanent quality of place. In 'dangerous places', everyone is a potential suspect, and the police's rights to control people's identity without immediate cause are significantly enhanced.

Such classifications influenced perceptions both of the place and everyone within it. When Herr Müller recounted his experience of being pickpocketed by a Vietnamese man who had pretended to ask him for change, he did not fail to invoke the crime statistics he thought corroborated his perception of Alexanderplatz as an unsafe place. The classification of Alexanderplatz as a dangerous place appeared to affect the ways in which people embodied the square. Crime and danger were frequently, though not exclusively, expressed in a racialized discourse and associated with certain groups of people to be avoided, and with the night-time Alexanderplatz. At night, danger emanated from emptiness and obscurity – the absence (or hiddenness) of people. In spite, or because, of streetlights and illuminated advertisements, the nocturnal city has come to be imagined as a space where danger lurks (Schlör 1998).

Against all this, the socialist Alexanderplatz, and 'GDR times' more generally, were summoned as an, albeit ambiguous, metaphor of stability and order. Crime and fear of crime was largely considered a phenomenon that had emerged only after unification.[37] During GDR times, Alexanderplatz had been the object of thorough surveillance. Rumour has it that cameras were installed at various buildings around the square, sending images to screens in the Stasi offices. Three different police departments, an East German policeman told me, were deployed to keep Alexanderplatz free of 'undesirable' persons. A punk walking on the *Platte* – as the police called the open area of Alexanderplatz – would have had no chance. Imitating official GDR rhetoric, he noted: 'In socialist society, something like that wasn't allowed to exist. There were only orderly dressed people.' Today, he surmised, Alexanderplatz was gradually turning into another Bahnhof Zoo. Here, the train station in West Berlin was not part of Berlin's glitzy western centre but the locale infamous for drug-related crime and prostitution, such as those depicted in the *Christiane F.* book and film.

Similarly, an East German planning administrator in her thirties claimed never to have felt unsafe walking alone in the city when she was younger. With the ruptures brought by the *Wende*, however, what she called her subjective sense of safety had changed. Neither homelessness and drugs nor the rubbish that people today carelessly strew about, she thought, had existed in the GDR. 'Many problems just weren't there, and others were locked away better,' she noted, 'but one can doubt whether this was a good solution.' The boundary between protective surveillance producing safety and intrusive surveillance producing unfreedom seemed elusive.

A Problem of 'the Social'

Alexanderplatz's disorder and the dangers that appeared to emanate from it were, then, not understood simply as a failure of municipal government. They were, rather, all-too-readily attributed to those people who were seen to have failed society. A street cleaner pointed to the large crowds of people gathering in Alexanderplatz, especially the punks whom he considered 'the greatest dirt producers'. Punks, sometimes called *Bunte* ('colourful'), have self-consciously distinguished themselves from an assumed normalcy through their clothes, hairstyles and boisterous behaviour.[38] When approaching passers-by for money or when shouting at each other or their dogs, they would attract attention.

In Berlin, punks have had their own genealogy from the early punks that centred on style and proclamations of 'no future', to those who contributed to the myth of Kreuzberg as the locus of German counter-culture in the 1980s (Hebdige 1979; Lang 1998: 145–8), to the punks in Alexanderplatz of the 1990s and early 2000s, some of whom were runaways, some of whom came from Poland, and all of whom, in their attempts to create their lives according to their own rules, became potential subjects of Berlin social work services. These people were often singled out and stigmatized because of the 'out-of-placeness' of their appearance and behaviour (Richardson 2003: 85), and were frequently felt to constitute a threat to public order.

Business people in Alexanderplatz frequently appealed to the police and private security services to call punks to order. They feared that these people 'loitering' in Alexanderplatz would scare away potential customers. Some people called for the intervention of the social office and social workers, the experts of the social. Others took matters into their own hands. Residents in a tenement at Alexanderplatz, for example, began to bombard the punks outside the building with water-filled balloons, tomatoes and household refuse. A resident I met suggested that there was enough space elsewhere in the city for these people to go. The punks who people wanted to see 'something done about' were almost invariably portrayed as drunks, scroungers and idlers – able young people who chose not to work but 'to live at our expense' or 'off society'. Giving these people money, another resident claimed, was like feeding pigeons; both were a nuisance, not pretty and virulent. But this, he quickly added, was only a metaphor.

For the conscious citizen Müller, whose participation in the civic action group alerted him to the alleged problem of Alexanderplatz's appearance, punks were predominantly a problem of visual repulsion. These were people he considered even more 'indecent' than other 'folk', 'scoundrels' and 'rogues' gathering in Alexanderplatz. However, invoking the loaded concept of asociality so central to GDR attempts at 'normalizing' its citizens' behaviour (Lindenberger 2008), he continued:

> I don't want to call all of them *asozial* ('asocial'). Certainly, this would be an exaggeration. One could easily be guessing quite wrong.... Not everyone belonging to these circles is inevitably, by nature or by mentality, asocial. They've ended up there for various reasons.

Perceptions of homeless people, punks and so-called street children were neither uniform nor fixed. For some people, they were a pitiful corollary of unification, mounting unemployment, and a widening gap between rich and poor. Such commentary echoed a familiar tension in appraisals of people's apparent failure to conform to society. The notion of asociality is entwined with a discourse on the social as a distinct realm and the idea of the welfare state. Families and individuals are imagined to be tied into a protective social net consisting of tax, insurance, social benefits and solidarity amongst mutually contributing and dependent members (Rose 1999: 123–4). At a time when comprehensive welfare provisioning and, in the GDR, near full employment seemed to make it possible to secure an acceptable standard of living for all, those who are poor may easily be blamed for their own misfortune or considered deviant.

In the German context, 'asociality' has long served to identify, persecute and frequently eliminate supposed social outsiders. Whilst the Third Reich applied the classification of asocial to the unemployed, youthful delinquents, homeless, prostitutes, homosexuals, Sinti and Roma, which were cast as polluting the healthy body of the German *Volk*, the GDR state utilized asociality as a way of demarcating membership and, as the historian Lindenberger (2008) puts it, the boundaries between 'self' and 'other' in the socialist state. GDR law marked out the asocial person – the idler, the prostitute, or the speculator – as a 'parasite' in the workers' state, displaying a type of dangerous and criminal behaviour, and thus the opposite of the socialist citizen proper.

Such legal and moral categories now play into quotidian explanations of apparent failures (or refusals) to conform to society's assumed standards. People appeal to asociality as an individual or group-specific characteristic (Knecht 1999b: 13), indicating a tension echoed in Müller's comment between a structural understanding of poverty, locating its causes in socio-economic structures and an individualistic understanding that posits poverty as a mental attitude or a choice, resulting, for example, from a supposed unwillingness to work (Howe 1990a). Where some people see individual failure, others identify a failure of 'the social', imagined as 'a particular sector in which quite diverse problems and special cases can be grouped together, a sector comprising specific institutions and an entire body of qualified personnel' (Deleuze 1979, cit. in Rose 1999: 101).

In the context of Alexanderplatz, punks occupied a metaphorical position similar to that of the traders, hawkers and beggars in post-Soviet Moscow described by Lemon (2000). 'Social disorders,' she writes, 'are imagined here in terms of human waste – people out of place' (2000: 26). In important respects, punks have emerged as a cipher of social disorder, but as we have seen by no means the only one, against which the persona of 'the citizen' and an imagined ideal of society could take shape. Punks were deemed out of place in a public square – itself often considered the epitome of civic ideals. This is not a matter of mere structural oppositions but an effect of historically contingent and shifting languages and practices of the law and the state. Those considered marginal to society – or asocial – have been delegated to the edges of the city and to secluded and excluded spaces where 'the deviant' can be controlled and 'the pathological' normalized (Foucault 2003; Rose 1999; Schlör 1998; Sibley 1995). In GDR times, as the police officer cited above implied, Alexanderplatz would have been kept free of any elements that seemed to openly question the integrity of this place as embodiment of a future socialist society.

Discourses on asociality are not part of the official language of the FRG's current welfare regime and the majority of its agents are likely to repudiate its assumptions. Importantly, punks have indeed become an object of governmentality, with special services and places for them to meet, eat, wash and get counsel. Chapter VI will have more to say about the qualified personnel assisting them, and the ambivalences regarding the open appearance of supposed social others in the midst of the new German capital, which come to sit uneasily alongside the plans for Alexanderplatz's redesign.

Producing Disorder

In the early 2000s, the new plans for Alexanderplatz had still not materialized. Many people I talked to during my fieldwork found bewildering the square's persistent decline. The busy planning for Alexanderplatz that I observed in the offices of the planning administration and the orderly future that was promised were far removed from people's everyday experience of the square. In the final section of this chapter I want to examine how Alexanderplatz's disorder has been cast as the *product* of attempts to create order. Ironically, the plans to revamp Alexanderplatz appeared to transform one of the 'unfinished constructions' (Ssorin-Chaikov 2003) of the GDR state into the unfinished construction of another, the FRG.

In interviews and conversations there emerged a distinct commentary on the square's continuing decline, which implied that the reasons lay less in its outdated design than in wider economic and political processes, or indeed in the new plans themselves. For example, the peculiar emptiness that had emerged in Alexanderplatz since the early 1990s was related partly to the 'political vacuum' characteristic of the period around unification; partly, it was related to the closure of restaurants, cafés and shops, themselves the result of the lure of Berlin's more consumerist West. A typical notion was that disorder and decline resulted from the impact of forces outside people's control, such as 'the West' or 'capitalism'. By contrast, Boris, the resident of the Rathauspassagen I introduced earlier, located current developments within a stream of time that encompassed both East and West. He told me about a popular bookshop which had been replaced by a bank. For him, this was not symbolic of the frequently lamented takeover of the former socialist East by the capitalist West but, as he said matter-of-factly, simply a sign of 'our times'.

Instead of the expected betterment, the actions of those in power – the politicians, planners and developers – often appeared to generate further destruction. The discontinuation of the water-music in the fountain behind the television tower near Alexanderplatz and the removal of public seating facilities were particularly lamentable changes. Dorothea Tscheschner suggested to me that this seemed like a strategy for making Alexanderplatz so unattractive that a reconstruction began to feel inevitable or even desirable. Perplexing, too, was the apparent devaluation of previously admired buildings, evinced by their destruction. The summer of 2001, for instance, saw the tearing down of the celebrated Palast Hotel near Alexanderplatz, built 'by the Swedes' in the 1970s and where payment was only in foreign currency. Some of the numerous onlookers attracted by the spectacle of its demolition commented on the unreason behind the activities: The hotel was a product of expert engineering and had been recently refurbished for millions of D-Marks. 'Now they demolish it, only to replace it with another hotel!'

The sales assistant in a flower shop at Alexanderplatz expressed disbelief that the new plans for Alexanderplatz would ever become reality; in fact, she doubted the existence of any plan. When set alongside GDR planners' comprehensive schemes, current planners could easily appear not to be planning at all. Instead, she complained, they relied on the vagaries of the market and on private developers implementing their ideas piece meal. Others saw the cause for disorder in the very existence of a plan. As Thomas, a planning graduate and one of the citizen activist who had opposed the so-called Kollhoff plan in the 1990s, explained to me, since the plan had become legally binding, it inhibited even the smallest measure to improve the square's appearance. It set out the specifications for Alexanderplatz's new design including building heights, the amounts of square metres for housing, offices and commercial space, to which developers would have to adhere. But until the developers would fulfil their promises, one could hear planners say, Alexanderplatz had become a *Platz im Wartestand:* a place caught in the moment of waiting for a better future.

Finally, it could seem that the new vision for Alexanderplatz gradually created its own validation. There were, for example, the Rathauspassagen – an exemplary large socialist structure adjacent to Alexanderplatz, combining housing and workspace with space for consumption and leisure (Graffunder 1973). After unification, its exclusive flair had yielded cheap shops selling 'any item for a D-Mark', and a supermarket attracting what were felt to be rather insalubrious kinds of people. In 2001, even these had disappeared due to the incipient renovation that was to bring the Rathaus-passagen up to date. Now, the area looked as if 'the plague had broken out', commented a customer in the *Kneipe* ('pub') in the Rathauspassagen where I worked for some months. The owner of the *Kneipe* observed the area's deterioration with apprehension. When she acquired the space in the early 1990s, she had not expected her new, independent life to become so precarious. Together with what had once been a top location in East Berlin, her business and livelihood crumbled. Her business, like many others, had to shut *because of* the incipient renovation.

Nikolai Ssorin-Chaikov (2003) has provided a compelling analysis of how, at the state's margins in Soviet and post-Soviet Siberia, the idea of the state is reified and deferred in discourses on failure and in discursive gaps. In this always-incomplete state project, 'unfinished constructions' are 'order still unachieved ... as a display of work in progress' (2003: 136). Applied to Alexanderplatz, we might say that 'order' was both once achieved and not achieved yet, its temporal horizons reaching into both the future and the past. Destruction and disorder were evocative of an ideal of the good city or, for that matter, the state. Whilst certain disorders were taken to indicate the disappearance of the GDR state, gutted buildings, streets torn open, and exposed cables and pipes were also the signs of a yet unfinished project of constructing a unified German state of which Alexanderplatz was to be symbolic. For city planners, projecting a future and accustomed to delays, the busy renovation works in the Rathauspassagen and the construction of a new multiplex cinema nearby (replacing a GDR leisure complex) were the first signs of a new future materializing. Their rationale was one of aggregate numbers and of new businesses and jobs created in the long term. By contrast, customers in the *Kneipe* joked that, considering the speed at which buildings were being built and torn down in Berlin today, the new cinema would be pulled down before it even opened. People's speculative comments regarding Alexanderplatz summoned a topos, typical of post-unification Berlin, where construction and destruction, order and disorder are but flip sides of each other. But that plans promising construction and order simultaneously generated destruction and disorder was for many people a rather bitter irony.

I began the chapter by alluding to one of the ubiquitous events where urban development in the unified Berlin was debated. A similar critique as that voiced by Simone Hain was enacted rather differently in the same summer, by Berlin's first theatre group of homeless persons, called Rat-

Figure 10: Performance by the 'Ratten 07'

ten 07. In a humorous public performance in Alexanderplatz, they dressed up as larger-than-life cleaning ladies and, equipped with brooms and foaming detergent, gave Alexanderplatz a vigorous cleaning. Their ostensibly light-hearted performance may be read as a critical parody of the notion of 'cleansing' the urban environment, implying the removal of both dirt and certain categories of people. As the Berlin anthropologist Robe (1999) argues, in contemporary Berlin the *social* problem of poverty has been turned into an *aesthetic* one requiring an ostensibly aesthetic solution. Programmes such as the 'Action Plan Clean Berlin', 'zero tolerance' policies and an increase in private security forces are cited as alarming indicators of an ever more repressive urban regime (Rada 1997; Robe 1999; Ronneberger et al. 1999). What makes these programmes so controversial is, on the one hand, that the kind of metonymic chains (Stallybrass and White 1986) they evoke, and the biologizing and racialized discourses in which they are enmeshed, were deeply implicated in the most distressing practices of human intervention in 'the social', including the atrocities committed under the banner of German National Socialism (Linke 1999; Rose 1999: 115).

On the other hand, there is concern about a blurring of 'public' and 'private' realms. In Chapter II, I noted the moral critique spawned by the apparent excess of private involvement in the urban planning domain. The proliferation of public-private partnerships in planning, for example, unsettles definitions of the state as being uniquely responsible for planning

– a notion particularly common in Germany (Strom 2001: 234). I return to this issue in the following chapter where I explore how the public-private engagement plays out in the encounters between city planners and developers. Similarly, the use of private security services for the surveillance of semi-public spaces seems to undermine the state's monopoly on the legitimate use of violence within its territory (Johnston 1992: 218–9; Weber 1992: 6). At issue, here, are apparently obscure legal bases and lines of accountability. Orchestrated interventions in the social of the kind attempted by the modernist planners of the nineteenth and twentieth centuries can appear dubious today. Rather than interference having ceased, however, the ways in which urban planning now affects the organization of urban life is often perceived to have become more dispersed, more clandestine, and sometimes altogether unaccountable.

Instead of assessing the degree to which the new Alexanderplatz corresponds to this pattern, I have aimed to provide a close-up, and sometimes uncomfortable, examination of the reality that disorder had for people I encountered in and around Alexanderplatz. Disorder was variously experienced as irresponsible strangers and dangerous foreigners, as graffiti and rubbish, as people who self-consciously decide to stand 'outside' society, but also as those people who had simply missed out on the betterment that unification seemed to promise. Such commentary pointed to specific conceptions of society, underwritten by past and present legal and state practices, and to perceived failures of government and 'the social', which were seen reflected in the materiality of the square. It also indicated perhaps less the mourning of a vanished past than the loss of a future. The future that Alexanderplatz once embodied had turned into a future that 'could have been'.

The proposed plans for Alexanderplatz could seem to have contributed to its demise. The plans were criticized for their intended and unintended consequences, including the demolition of GDR architecture, gentrification and the continuing decline of the square. Nonetheless, talk about disorder and that 'something needs to be done' about it served to further consolidate specific ideas of government, planning and the state. The disorderly Alexanderplatz constituted the counterpoint to the carefully developed Alexanderplatz envisaged by Berlin's planners. Plan and failure, order and disorder were entwined: just as the new plans appeared to produce more disorder, the perceived disorder was productive of ideas about order. Disorder made order thinkable as it were.

Chapter IV

Promising Plans

This chapter will look at the planning of Alexanderplatz or, more specifically, at Alexanderplatz as a troubled urban planning project. In the early
1990s, Alexanderplatz was identified as a problem of urban design. A solution was to be found through an urban design competition, launched by
the Senat's Administration for Urban Development (SenStadt) in 1993.
The winning design was to provide the basis for future constructions in the
square. Following the competition, the Berlin Senat proceeded to establish
a public-private partnership and to sign so-called urban development contracts with prospective investors. After a series of public deliberations and
revisions, the winning competition design was passed as a so-called *Bebauungsplan* in 1999, a legally binding plan, for Alexanderplatz. A special
office, the Rahmenkoordinierung Alexanderplatz or Alexanderplatz Frame
Coordination, was set up in 2000 to manage the incipient building works.
Despite all the busy planning and organizing, however, the project experienced serious delays. Explanations varied but many echoed the following
account by an administrator in SenStadt's Urban Design department that
had primary responsibility for the Alexanderplatz project:

> In the beginning, there was the expectation that everything would happen
> relatively quickly. Back then – the competition was in '93, the time of the
> famous gold-rush mood: 'Ah, oh, now to Berlin!' – the investors did press
> tremendously, and we did the planning and the competition within a rela-
> tively short time. Thus, the impression was that things were going ahead
> fast. Despite this, the planning for Alexanderplatz fell behind compared
> to what happened at Potsdamer Platz and in Friedrichstraße. A large
> number of projects were all planned, built and completed at the same
> time. Then it became evident that the amounts [of office, retail space etc.]
> spilling into the market were a little too much. That the market couldn't
> absorb this straightaway was borne out by the first *Leerstände* ('vacant
> buildings'). Those investors who were already quite ahead with their plan-
> ning collectively stepped on the brakes. This is always very astonishing; ...
> they also call it the pig-cycle in the real estate and building sector.

In other words, the Alexanderplatz project was largely constituted within that slightly unpredictable realm of the market, a realm thought to work in ways beyond administrative control. The chapter considers a specific moment in the project's life, where failure began to seem a real possibility. Rather than calling it a failure, however, administrators framed the project in terms of anticipation and postponement. Uninvolved observers would sometimes tell me: 'Nothing is happening at Alexanderplatz!' But from a different perspective, quite a lot was happening. Although it was considered the investors' task to realize the project, Berlin's planners and administrators did not remain idle. They assembled the new Alexanderplatz in numerous reports, drawings, computer images, models, legal documents, publications and meetings. They prided themselves on the comprehensiveness of the planning procedure and saw the delays as being caused by market forces and developers' caprice.

For administrative planners, failure was not located in the new plans for Alexanderplatz. In fact, a lengthy realization phase, it was explained to me, had been anticipated by the project proposal right from the start. Things were going according to plan. Official statements in the early 2000s reinforced the expectation that the new Alexanderplatz would soon be realized. In May 2002, amended urban development contracts were signed, giving altered dates for the completion of the buildings. This chapter explores what was at stake in all the activities, procedures and pronouncements that constructed the new Alexanderplatz at a time when it had not yet materialized.

On (Not) Planning

The Alexanderplatz Frame Coordination (RKA), where I would spend a large part of my fieldwork, was located on the fourteenth floor of Haus des Reisens, the House of Travel, one of the buildings at Alexanderplatz that had received their name to indicate the modernity of the GDR state. (Although no longer official, the names of these buildings have stuck.) RKA staff was extremely welcoming of its ethnographer, and I had been given a desk in a small office room that had been recently vacated due to the reduction of staff numbers. The captivating panorama provided by the view from the office's windows reminded me of Michel de Certeau's description of seeing Manhattan from the World Trade Center (1984: 91). De Certeau took this as an allegory of the planner's God's Eye View. It is a totalizing perspective which derives its power precisely from being aloof to the messiness of city life, and what de Certeau terms the 'walks' and 'operations' of its 'practitioners', the city's inhabitants. From the RKA's window, the movement of an individual gained visibility only by becoming part of a flow of people from the tram stop into the underground station or into Kaufhof, the department store, resembling a trail of ants following their prescribed path.

The magnificent overview was recognized as one of the assets of this office; but another asset was the office's proximity to Alexanderplatz, as a future building site. RKA staff frequently challenged my initial impression of their doings. Once during a lunch break, as they quizzed me on the findings of my research, I commented on the apparent detachedness of their operations from the realities of Alexanderplatz. The response was loud objection: 'But here we are at Alexanderplatz!' Another person added: 'We are eating food bought in Kaufhof!' These were sensible reminders that planners – despite all their ambitions to know Alexanderplatz in very particular ways – were simultaneously, in de Certeau's terms, practitioners of the city. Meetings in the RKA were interspersed with comments on people's experiences and reminiscences about the Alexanderplatz they knew in the past and observations of the present Alexanderplatz, including their likes and dislikes of certain shops or observations on other people's behaviour – for example, how a person's quick pace and lowered head was a definite sign of Alexanderplatz's ugliness. In other words, the Alexanderplatz constituted within the planning office was one that could reach out for a detail of empirical confirmation if required.

RKA life revolved, on the one hand, around the kitchen where staff would take lunch together or a cup of coffee; and on the other, a huge meeting room with an adjacent smaller room, in which visitors could admire a fancy and expensive white model of the new Alexanderplatz, co-sponsored by the developers. It was a miniature Alexanderplatz that assisted patrons and planners in imagining the future (Scott 1998: 57). When SenStadt administrators visited who had their offices in one of the administration's other buildings (for example, one a 1950s and now listed high-rise block in West Berlin, another, a beautifully refurbished former bank, with wide corridors but small and often cramped offices), they would occasionally comment with admiration on the RKA's spaciousness. The significance of these differences lay in the relative importance that the Alexanderplatz project was assumed to have. RKA staff frequently highlighted the magnitude of the project, both geographically and in terms of the large number of actors involved as well as the scale of anticipated 'conflicts'. Further, unlike Potsdamer Platz, Alexanderplatz was an urban centre that would need to be kept running during the construction phase. All this made Alexanderplatz, to them, exceptionally problematic and impossible to manage without a special planning office.

The RKA had its own logo, archive and project handbook containing directives for its workings. Staff were drawn from SenStadt's civil engineering department as well as an independent planning and engineering company. Some of them had previously worked in a similar office managing Potsdamer Platz, for them, a precedent for their experience with large-scale development projects. In their talk about the latter, I sensed considerable pride in what they felt to have been a successful mastering of the challenges Potsdamer Platz had posed. They had invented ingenious solutions for removing tons of sand and for preserving, amongst cranes, excavators and huge water-filled holes, a line of trees marking the pre-war course of Potsdamer Straße. They also claimed their share in devising the Red Infobox, itself portrayed as a reflection of the sense of togetherness and cooperation amongst the Potsdamer Platz investors. Generating 'togetherness' was no trifle on the list of their achievements. Such were the self-professed skills they now hoped to reapply at Alexanderplatz.

The RKA was not an ordinary planning office, therefore, but a peculiar solution to the problems that large-scale development projects are felt to pose. In fact, RKA staff would often insist that they were not really planning at all. They were solving the *Aufgabe* ('problem', 'task') of Alexanderplatz. Their task was not to plan or *gestalten* ('design') but to ensure that the envisaged design would be implemented quickly and smoothly. The office was readily depicted, in metaphors drawn from mechanics or information technology, as a hinge, cogwheel or interface imagined to join the various parties to the Alexanderplatz project. Alexanderplatz, in the words of one of an RKA engineer, resembled a complex Gordian knot whose complexity they aimed to comprehend and unpick in order to retie it in a new form.

A key concern was what was termed the graphic identification of problems and conflicts. In this work of anticipation, plans and drawings were essential tools, rendering conflicts and problems visible. Typical problems were apparent inconsistencies in the drawings provided by different planning entities, such as those discussed in one of the first meetings I attended. In this meeting, participants mulled over the boundaries between two lots or rather two lines in a drawing which, instead of being congruent, crossed. One of these lines represented the edge of a street and the other the boundary of a lot to be sold to a private investor. Now there was an overlap, which created a space that would be public and private at once; an intolerable case of a space that appeared to exist twice. The anticipated problem gained a peculiar reality as people pored over the plan, agitatedly discussing whether this was a case of wrong coordinates and, if so, who was to be held responsible for the blunder. The provisional solution was that, due to the small size of the piece in question, the problem was negligible. For now, it seemed that the land could be treated as 'elastic' (Verdery 1996).

In such moments, I often felt that Alexanderplatz, as I had come to know it, did not feature. People appeared to be talking about an indistinct assemblage of buildings, tunnels, cables, pipes and tracks, which could be located anywhere in the city. When I suggested this to Frau Fürstenau, an RKA engineer, however, she decidedly disagreed: 'It's always this square!' It could not be just anywhere. What was underground, she explained, was intimately related to what was above ground; and the network of underground train tunnels, for example, existed in this form only at Alexanderplatz: 'It's really an entity and I can't mentally divide it.' In other words, this Alexanderplatz was merely a particular representation of the Alexanderplatz 'out there'. All that planners did was to apply a different kind of vision; they claimed to see things that other people did not see. They had a trained eye or simply a different perspective. They could read plans illegible to other people. This was partly, they explained, because they had undergone a particular professional training, and attained through their expert knowledge a particular comprehension of things.

In other words, planners were keen to emphasize that plans were merely representations of a 'real' world which they, too, inhabited. Their particular skill lay in being able to differentiate between the two and remove, if necessary, their private persona from their expert being. Once, when showing me a book assembling the designs proposed in the Alexanderplatz competition, Frau Fürstenau commented that it contained some drawings by her husband. In the past, he had worked for an architecture practice that entered the Alexanderplatz competition but did not win. It seemed to explain her occasional passing comments conveying her dislike for the envisaged high-rise buildings. Now, Frau Fürstenau told me that although she would have favoured a different, more modest design for Alexanderplatz, she did not to feel compromised in her work. Indeed, she felt it was necessary to keep her personal opinion separate from her work. What mattered was to fulfil properly the technical tasks she was given.

A SenStadt administrator expressed similar concerns about mixing his private with his public persona. Whenever he disagreed with official plans, he claimed, he would have his wife write his letters of complaint. Although entitled to write such letters himself as a 'citizen', he preferred keeping work and private opinion separate. Such insistence on keeping personal views out of work contexts was reflected in interview situations, when administrators showed reluctance to discuss their private opinions, or flagged what they saw to diverge from the official stance. With their peculiar bureaucratic ethos, administrators were keen to present themselves, *pace* Weber, as holding an objective, rational and disinterested view (Weber 1991: 215–6; see also du Gay 2000; Mommsen 1989).

These self-conscious technocrats cum bureaucrats wrestled also with that other persona to which they have come to be written in counterpoint: the politician (Weber 1992; du Gay 2000: 46). Rather than planning, RKA

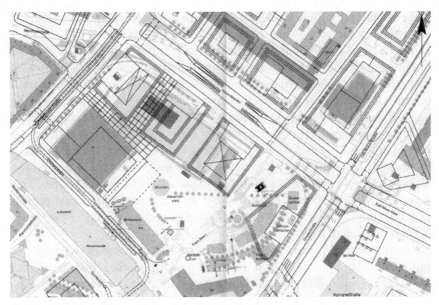

Figure 11: Plan of the Alexanderplatz project

members perceived themselves to be merely executing the 'political will', i.e., the plan for the new Alexanderplatz. However, decisions taken by politicians, in particular by the Senator for Urban Development and district politicians, could suddenly render obsolete all plans made hitherto. Administrators were infuriated by decisions that bypassed all better, expert advice and were instead based on what they called populist considerations. Notwithstanding the perceptible irritation, it was accepted that administrators and politicians had distinct tasks and roles. RKA meetings were therefore not for *Grundsatzdiskussionen* ('discussions of general principles'), a phrase typically used to silence participants who loudly criticized politicians' decisions or sought to suggest different ways of doing things. Meetings were not for challenging planning precepts, political decisions and bureaucratic normativities.

Weber's interest lay in setting out the formation of a specific persona – the bureaucrat – and *Lebensführung* or conduct of life that the bureaucracy both demands and induces (du Gay 2000; Gordon 1987). Similarly, what I have highlighted here are the normativities in which planners and administrators found themselves entangled. In the light of these normativities, RKA staff's insistence that they were not *planning* Alexanderplatz takes on an additional dimension; and the numerous meetings in which I sat over the months researching this book, acquired a special significance.

Assembling Alexanderplatz

The meetings in the RKA provided structure and regularity to my research. There were several meetings per week, sometimes more than one per day. I had permission to attend almost all of them, except for those dealing with issues considered confidential, such as negotiations regarding the developers' contractual obligations. Similarly, in the SenStadt department where I did a short internship, there were regular weekly meetings for different levels of the administrative hierarchy. Inevitably I found my days arranged around meetings.

Meetings – referred to as *Besprechungen,* where things were spoken about, or simply as *Termine,* dates or appointments – were crucial to the RKA's work, and that of Berlin's planning administration more generally. They were occasions where these organizations were realized (Schwartzman 1989). Meetings brought together the various institutions and companies implicated in the Alexanderplatz project, conceived as separate entities with their own organizational rules and technical requirements, hierarchies and avenues of communication, budgets and investment priorities, and different agendas. They included various administrative departments, the planning office of Mitte district, the private investors and their planning bureaus, the infrastructure providers (gas, water, electricity, telecommunications, etc.), Berlin's public transport corporation and the German railways. Finding commonalities and creating linkages between these apparently incompatible or even antagonistic entities was considered the RKA's main task.

Participation in meetings varied depending on who was felt to be implicated in a particular problem, by either causing or being affected by it, or by being capable of contributing certain expertise. Agendas gave direction, and minutes and spurred further action. Participants tended to know each other by the institutions they represented. Such associations were not merely ascriptive. Many of the administrators I encountered had worked in a specific department for several years, and they would zealously argue their case. Traffic planners, for instance, would complain about having been consulted too late, when the frontal lines of buildings were already agreed, leaving insufficient space for pavements, pedestrians and trees. Trees, in turn – considered indispensable to the quality of life of current residents – were something that so-called green planners passionately defended. In discussions like these, the intensely relational self-conception of the expert came to the fore. Experts of one kind were not supposed to interfere in the realms of competence of other experts. If they did, this was easily felt to be an affront. Initially an ignorant outsider, I soon followed a similar way of categorizing participants. Whilst my earlier fieldnotes were often muddled and cluttered with unhelpful comments on a speaker's appearance, later notes confidently identify 'the BVG man' or 'the woman from the traffic department'. Of course, participants would address each other by their surnames, too, and one objective of these meetings, as we will see, was to create some familiarity in the institutional context.

You will have had your own experiences of similar meetings conducted in universities, companies or sports clubs in many parts of the world, whose value today seems so self-evident (Schwartzman 1989; van Vree 1999). Being punctual, speaking in turn and in a calm and collected manner, not interrupting others, sticking to the topic and aiming at a conclusion of sorts are some of the unspoken rules to which participants adhere. Whilst there are few silences, meetings are not about idle chatter. If participants threaten to drift into what is felt to be extraneous talk, the chairperson will politely steer discussion back to the topic. The point is to say something of 'relevance' to the problem at issue.

Such subtle modes of behaviour distinguish the meeting from a speech, a lecture or even a panel discussion. Nowadays, one can find advice on doing meetings in countless handbooks that present themselves as 'toolkits for success'. Handbooks attest to the ongoing significance invested in this peculiar human practice. They elaborate expected forms of reasoning and arguing, invented to ensure what during the last two hundred years or so has come to be thought of as a desirable, non-violent or civilized form of negotiation (van Vree 1999: 3–10, following Elias 1939/1994). Modes of propriety expected in meetings may partly be seen as 'technologies of the self' (Foucault 2000) that run parallel to the emergence and institutionalization of 'the political' and 'bureaucracy'.

For many of the administrators I met, however, holding meetings was not simply an ingrained part of institutional routine. It was an activity with a distinct value. A few weeks into my internship, for example, I tentatively complained to an administrator about my research being limited to, albeit plentiful, meetings. What happened beyond them was not readily revealed. Without permission to observe planners' everyday activities, I feared that my insights into their world would remain superficial. The man looked flabbergasted. Meetings, he insisted, are most important. It was here that problems were brought up and discussed and that – rather than in the individual administrator's office – much of the crucial business of planning was done. What happened outside the purview of meetings, it seemed, was irrelevant. Or rather, only what happened within meetings was deemed significant and real: it had an effect.

Once, as we were about to sit down to a meeting, an engineer from an investors' planning bureau asked me whether I had ever considered how much such a meeting cost. To him, this seemed a worthwhile enquiry. Jestingly, he counted the number of people present who came from what appeared to be every institution imaginable, and calculated what each might be paid for an hour of their time and thus the overall expense of the meeting. His eventual estimate of several thousand euros seemed to him completely unjustified. Economic rationalities, introduced in the world of public administration, made the meetings appear inefficient; to RKA members, by contrast, meetings were an effective way of doing things (cf. du Gay 2000). They appreciated meetings as a means of saving time. RKA staff critically noted that 'paper is patient' and suggested that, by contrast, meetings would yield results fast. Assembling people in a room and creating face-to-face contact was preferred to an indeterminate exchange of letters. Meetings were expected to minimize the 'working for the paper basket'. What was more, everyone would always know what everyone else was doing. There was the expressed hope that meetings would help create cooperation and a sense of togetherness amongst the participants in the Alexanderplatz project.

This points to a second, related concern familiar to students of bureaucracy. Bureaucratic rationality has often been viewed with suspicion, as an allegedly disenchanted and impersonal world (du Gay 2000; Herzfeld 1992; Weber 1991). The bureaucrat herself has been portrayed as but a nameless, replaceable occupant of a position. We have seen how meeting participants were readily identified in terms of a particular position, an institution, department or area of expertise. However, the significant issue here is that 'impersonality' was precisely what RKA meetings were hoped to dispel. It was assumed that as they came face to face in meetings, people would know whom to approach, could attach a face to the voice encountered on the telephone, and might even feel an increased obligation to stick to their promises. Perhaps in support of this endeavour, tables in the RKA meeting room were arranged in a circle with participants facing each other, and we could help ourselves to coffee, mineral water and lemonade – perhaps an attempt to keep us alert but also to assuage the dreariness of rational technical talk.

However, more seemed to be at stake than technocratic self-critique. 'We are only as good as the information we get,' one RKA member told me. The success of Alexanderplatz was dependent on trust amongst the parties involved and on receiving information, which could be gathered, archived and, importantly, acted upon. The assumed priority and vital necessity of information was a concern that RKA staff shared with some of their contemporaries, including scholars and self-conscious networkers (cf. Riles 2000: 92–4). Rather than information having an a priori existence, outside and beyond meetings, meetings were seen to generate information in tandem with generating social relationships. In any case, the RKA was imagined to exist only at the intersection of information flows. Drawings and timetables were important tools, visualizing the information that made the Alexanderplatz project. Significantly, what they visualized also were the relations between the diverse parties to the Alexanderplatz project.

There were multiple translations at work. In order to identify a 'conflict', for instance, the imagined or anticipated fence of a building site, the wall of a building, a cable, or a water pipe had to be translated into lines on a plan. In addition to three-dimensional space, time had to be taken into account and rendered into a two-dimensional drawing. In this way, it became possible to see whether lines would cross and thus result in what was referred to as a 'conflict' – itself a social metaphor. To solve the conflict, the lines needed to be translated back into (belonging to) specific institutions, corporations or developers, which could be invited to a meeting in the RKA. In the meeting, the graphic or metaphorical conflict could easily turn into a real one fought out between the people representing the different parties involved. Put differently, the technical drawings used in the RKA, like maps and plans more generally, could be examined in terms of how they concealed the social context of their making. However, and more significantly, drawings and timetables worked to objectify the social relationships constituting the new Alexanderplatz.

For the anthropologist, commentary on RKA meetings could seem reminiscent of Durkheimian theories of the role of rituals in building a collective sentiment (van Vree 1999: 316). Meetings have come to be seen, cross-culturally, as highly significant constituting and constitutive social form, expressive of social structures, power relations, processes of government and much more (Schwartzman 1989). My interest here is in how they constitute Alexanderplatz as a project. There were, for example, moments of explicit staging of a Durkheimian collective sentiment in the RKA. The following occasion was poignant in this respect. One day in December 2001, I arrived for a meeting and followed those I took to be other participants into the room housing the model of the new Alexanderplatz. There were many unfamiliar faces, mostly men in dark suits, and I quickly sensed that this was not the meeting I had expected. A glass of champagne was pressed into my hands. One of the men was about to finish a speech. 'Although Nikolaus has already passed, St. Alexander came and hid his presents here,' he joked, pulling out a bag from underneath a table. I had accidentally walked in on the developers' St. Nicholas party.[39] Following German family traditions, everybody present received a small jute sack out of which peeped a chocolate Nikolaus wrapped in colourful aluminium foil. We all raised our glasses and toasted the new Alexanderplatz. On such occasions participants might have come to see themselves as partaking of the Alexanderplatz project as a joint endeavour. Meetings as well as the writing documents, the drawing of plans and timetables, the setting of boundaries, the arrangement of tracks and pipes, and the selection of street lamps and paving materials, quite literally assembled Alexanderplatz.

Premises and Promises

When I first began to investigate the Alexanderplatz project, there sometimes seemed to be no alternative to the kind of 'after-the-fact theorizing' that Sharon Macdonald (2001: 17, following Strathern 1992) has warned against in her analysis of the making of a London Science Museum exhibition. I was being presented with a coherent planning project that had been constructed from a set of clearly identifiable elements, and which was now enshrined in a legally binding plan. As Macdonald rightly argues, taking the finished product (the exhibition, the plan, etc.) as the analytical starting point unduly restricts anthropologists' understanding of the complex processes and power relations implicated in its making. Further, such an approach tends to focus on the successes rather than the equally interesting failures, the ideas dropped on the way. We might even overlook how notions of 'failure' and 'success' are constructed in the first place.

Plans and projects are best understood as intersections of exchanges and meetings of different domains (human and non-human, technical and political, etc.), which are *never* complete (Latour 1996). Now, as I have already indicated, the new Alexanderplatz was not yet quite accomplished, but it was eagerly awaited. Its realization, as I will explain, seemed occasionally under threat in the early 2000s, partly related to a growing sense of a precipitate collapse of Berlin's post-unification economic boom. First, however, I will discuss the persuasive rhetoric prevalent in the planning administration. I show how the administrators sought to persuade themselves and me that the plans for Alexanderplatz had everything needed to render it a success. They recounted the procedures that had been followed and the many legal requirements that had been met. They enlightened me on how the new Alexanderplatz fulfilled current planning goals and what rewards it would reap in the future. All this seemingly attested to the soundness and unassailability of the plans.

The administrators' accounts typically revolved around three tropes. First, the optimization of the planning through the instrument of the competition; second, the comprehensiveness of the plan; and third, how the plan corresponded to Berlin's current planning 'philosophy'. I begin with how the competition optimized the planning.

Planning competitions, such as the one for Alexanderplatz in 1993, have enjoyed immense popularity in post-unification Berlin. Between 1992 and

1995, for example, 150 competitions were conducted. Some commentators have diagnosed a 'competition fever' (Lenhart 2001: 198). The competition, as one SenStadt employee explained, was a 'well-established instrument of optimization.' What it was thought to optimize was not only the quality of the designs – by creating 'competition' amongst participating architects – but also the rationality, objectivity and accountability of the selection process. Itself a market-type metaphor (Carrier 1997: 3), it seemed that quality assurance and enhancement were in the nature of the competition itself (see Sennett 2003: 65). The most superb designs, however, are not automatically the most adequate ones.

The procedures surrounding public competitions like that for Alexanderplatz invoke additional authorities, beside the original architect or designer. There were also plenty of opportunities for citizens to give their opinion. Allowing others to inspect, and possibly rebuff, the judgements made, is thought to afford legitimacy to both the competition process and outcome. A clean procedure, I was assured, was better than the obscure decision of a senator based on something developed behind the administrative scenes. It would also ease the project's subsequent acceptance amongst the public. For Alexanderplatz, sixteen architecture offices, of both national and international, East and West German provenance, were invited to enter. There was a carefully appointed jury, including – so I was told – not just 'arty architects' but persons with different kinds of expertise and voting power. As many as fifty people were asked to assume jury positions with such weighty titles as *Fachpreisrichter* and *Sachpreisrichter* ('judges' with architectural and other kinds of expertise respectively), *Sachverständige* ('experts', lit. 'those who understand the thing'), *Vorprüfer* ('pre-examiners') and *Gast* ('guest').

When these men and women gathered to discuss the submissions, they supposedly bore in mind the myriad stipulations that a successful design would have to meet. These ranged from aesthetic qualities to its technical and financial feasibility, considered particularly important for a public project like Alexanderplatz. If there had been queries about the jury's conduct, its members could have pointed to rules, tested and repeatedly amended over more than one hundred years, such as the 'Principles and Requirements for Competitions' set out by the *Deutsche Städtetag* ('German Congress of Cities'). And lest misconduct should become rampant, there was the *Architektenkammer* ('Architects' Chamber') entrusted with enforcing these rules (see Lenhart 2001: 198ff.; Strom 2001: 147ff.).

The perceived value of competitions may be understood in reference to the bureaucratic ethos, so critically reflected upon by Weber; or, alternatively, to more recent, and seemingly ubiquitous, demands for accountability, transparency and reflexivity on the part of policy makers, administrations, businesses and institutions of all kinds (Strathern 2000a). The very form the competition took ensured, in the eyes of many administrators, that it was a success. Competition results were claimed to rest on the scientific insights and rational judgments of numerous people who pledged allegiance to a certain professional ethos. Intensive participation procedures and numerous public discussions that accompanied the competition supposedly underscored the unassailability and viability of the plans. Prospective investors needed not fear further protest or defiance on the part of Berliners.

Simultaneously, the plan for Alexanderplatz, which emerged from the competition and subsequent revisions, took on an appearance of instrumentality, removed from politics and overt ideologies but also from individual authorship (Ferguson 1990; Shore and Wright 1997). In a conversation, an administrator underscored the apparently de-politicized nature of the construction plan. He emphasized the continuity in political will regarding the Alexanderplatz project: the plans had been supported by various governments – the Social Democrats and the Christian Democrats, both separately and in coalition – since their inception.

The competition was, in a sense, its own audit, potentially obviating criticism concerning both the conduct of those involved and its result (Strathern 2000b: 282). It evacuated the process of the conflicting values and relations that people held to Alexanderplatz and the past it was seen to embody, and reduced the issue to one of public amenities, environmental considerations and urban aesthetics. The plan in turn was used to legitimize a future course of action, with seeming timeless validity. When the Berlin parliament passed the construction plan for Alexanderplatz in 1999, the proposed design, in the words of a SenStadt administrator, became Law that would persist into eternity.

I now turn to the second trope that helped people construe he new Alexanderplatz as a feat of post-unification planning, namely, its comprehensiveness. Government, as Rose and Miller remind us, is crucially a problematizing activity, and programmes devised for the amelioration of perceived problems 'presuppose that the real is programmable.... They make the objects of government thinkable in such a way that their ills appear susceptible to diagnosis, prescription and cure by calculating and normalizing intervention' (1992: 183). The plan for Alexanderplatz is similarly not an innocent graphic representation but a specific abstraction that rests on a particular conception of space – space that can be cut up, organized, mapped, known and regulated – constituted within particular regimes of knowing and acting (Fischler 1995; Lefebvre 1991; Mitchell 1988; Scott 1998).

Plans arrange and distribute – human beings and objects, pedestrians and traffic, pavements and streets, commercial and residential space, open and enclosed spaces, public and private spaces, buildings of different heights, shapes, and functions, pipes, cables and tracks – and gather up a welter of disparate knowledges and regulations – pertaining, for instance, to the built and the natural environment or to the social and the economic spheres. The sort of intervention in urban space that I describe here, its coordination and professionalization, are recent phenomena. What was, in the nineteenth century, under the authority of the police and land surveyors, later became the dominion of engineers and architects.

In 'Space, Knowledge, and Power', Foucault comments on the role of architecture in the problematization of space; but architects, he emphasizes, are not comparable to the doctors, priests or judges as the key figures 'through whom power passed' (2003: 356). The true technicians of space, I suggest, are the planners who in public administrations came to be responsible for the execution of certain technologies of power through spatial orderings on a much larger scale. Urban planning as a distinct discipline was not established at German universities until the 1970s (Albers 1997; 1998: 18); although special urban planning and development departments had been invented in German municipal administrations after the Second World War. City planning came to be constitutive of what was considered an 'integrated' planning politics that combined 'the social' and 'the economic' with 'the spatial'.[40]

Whilst the belief in the possibility of organizing and shaping society through a scientifically inspired urban space might have faded away by the late twentieth century (Caldeira and Holston 2005), the instruments – such as the plan – and the operations through which these are established and ascertained seem, in important respects, unchanged. Today's planners base their work partly on assumptions and techniques that made planning conceivable to their nineteenth-century predecessors. For instance, the newly invented science of statistics helped inscribe 'the real' as well as to calculate and compare, amongst other things, the state of society, the economy or public health (Rabinow 1989; Osborne and Rose 1999). It now appeared possible to predict certain developments through numerical calculations. Statistics thus facilitated the increasingly complex task of planning, enlisting a panoply of expertise.

The increasing penetration of the city by social scientists, including Georg Simmel, Max Weber and Werner Sombart, further underpinned the notion that urban developments could be forecast and designed within a given spatial frame (Albers 1997: 38). All this sharpened the sense that urban planning needed to, and indeed could, take into account future changes in the demographic and urban structure. Planning thence comprised not only activities of regulating what was, but also of anticipating and acting upon what would be. Increased emphasis was given to comprehensiveness, that is, the need to take into account all the various realms thought to be constitutive of the city (Ladd 1990: 227).

Those in charge of planning Alexanderplatz in the 1990s, it seems, were gripped by a similar concern with foresight and comprehensiveness. I showed earlier how Berlin's planning administration, under the leadership of Building Director Stimmann, had begun to promote a sensual type of planning, self-consciously breaking with the technocratic aspirations of modernist planning. In Chapter II, I noted the ambivalence of this shift. Here, I want to emphasize that this shift provoked an adaptation rather than an elimination of earlier planning discourses. In the context of Alexanderplatz, a number of reports were produced, including a study of 'Environmentally Relevant Interests' and of 'Human Beings, Uses and Cultural Patrimony', as well as a 'Social Study'. These titles invoke the domains of human life that planners imagined to make up the urban reality on which they were to act; to do so, knowledge about Alexanderplatz's present population, the trading sector, the environment, culture and so on, appeared to be required. Experts in the respective fields were asked to describe and assess the present situation at Alexanderplatz, to anticipate the impact of the envisaged plan, and to suggest measures by means of which this impact could be controlled or minimized. These reports functioned as inventories, diagnoses and prognoses all at the same time. From the reports, Alexanderplatz emerged as an object of knowledge and intervention, embedded within a complex web of effects and the city as a whole – which, in turn, was buttressed by its designation as a place of 'extraordinary significance for city politics' in 1994.

Finally, let me examine how the new Alexanderplatz corresponds to Berlin's current planning precepts. Part of the problematization of Alexanderplatz has been the alleged erasure of history it embodies. History, as we have seen, has been invested with peculiar significance in urban planning debates in contemporary Berlin. The architects entering the competition were asked to provide a programme for a comprehensive reordering, but one that would tie into the past meanings of the square. In the RKA, the historical Alexanderplatz had a quite muted presence, for instance, in the form of reprints of early-twentieth century photographs adorning the walls of the foyer outside the large meeting room. In its most technical form, Alexanderplatz's history appeared in plans that depicted what were – in the planning jargon – the 'plus one', 'zero' and 'minus one' level of the square. There were submerged layers, almost forgotten, such as a church that had been torn down after the Second World War and replaced by Haus des Reisens. Its foundations had been simply covered over during GDR times. A similar impediment to new constructions was a huge bunker that few people knew about and of which there were hardly any plans. One day, the RKA team went on a guided tour around the bunker, inspecting it with a technical eye as a potential obstacle to the new Alexanderplatz and with curious questions on the origins of this rather ambiguous remnant of German history.

More explicitly, history was invoked in conversations with the anthropologist and sometimes for visitors, such as a delegation of about twenty Moscow planning officials and their interpreter who came to inspect the RKA as part of a tour whereby they learned about Berlin's development projects. On arrival, the delegation was ushered into the room with the model of the new Alexanderplatz where the head of the office, Herr von Bismarck, gave a brief talk prepared for the occasion. He opened his exposition with a rhetorical nod to his visitors, remarking, half-jokingly, on Alexanderplatz's 'close connection to Russia'. The square, he explained had received its name upon a visit by Tsar Alexander in 1805. Before, it had simply been the 'ox market' – a trading spot just outside one of the city gates.

The model of the new Alexanderplatz around which we had gathered assisted in weaving a seamless historical narrative. Von Bismarck pointed out the features he was referring to in the Alexanderplatz model, for instance, the elevated train line reflecting the contours of the former moat on which it was built in the 1870s. The railway station confirmed Alexanderplatz's growing importance within the expanding city of the late nineteenth century. With this and the opening of an underground station in 1913, Alexanderplatz became a major public transport node, which it has remained to this day. Hotels, shops and a central market hall further transformed it. In the 1920s, Herr von Bismarck suggested, Alexanderplatz rivalled Potsdamer Platz as regards its effervescence and bustling atmosphere. During the same decade, ideas emerged for a grand architectural overhaul, but only two buildings were realized, said von Bismarck, pointing to the two wooden blocks that represented Alexanderhaus and Berolinahaus.

We then learned that Alexanderplatz had been heavily damaged during the war and became, after 1949, part of the nascent capital of the GDR. Alexanderplatz underwent a fourfold enlargement from 18,000 to about 80,000 square metres, consequently lacking, as von Bismarck observed, any proper (physical) framing, today. Our speedy journey through the centuries concluded with German unification and the concomitant reordering of Berlin's centres. Von Bismarck began to talk about the present-day plans and the role of the RKA. Judging from their subsequent questions, the Russian delegates appeared much more interested in this latter part: finances, contracts and, more generally, the question of how Berlin's government negotiated with private investors – issues that I return to below.

There was little extraordinary about Herr von Bismarck's talk. It was a story that I had been told before; and von Bismarck later confessed to have simply adapted for his own purposes an account from a SenStadt brochure. It was an officially recognized, albeit selective, past that the planning administration has summoned for Alexanderplatz (cf. Herzfeld 1991). History here is imagined to reside in built structures, tied to momentous developments within Berlin. Alexanderplatz's present design is understood as a radical break with the city's structural givens: undercut by tunnels for pedestrians and motorized traffic and surrounded by excessively wide streets (Senatsverwaltung 2001). Within the different frame of evaluation described in Chapter II, which construes particularly Berlin's eastern centre as underused and empty, much of what made Alexanderplatz was rendered superfluous and a waste of valuable inner-city land. To describe Alexanderplatz as a *Platz* ('square') could, from this perspective, appear to be a contradiction in terms (cf. Moughtin 1999; Zucker 1959).

As the product of the high aspirations of GDR planners, Alexanderplatz is now rendered inherently ambiguous. It is perceived to encompass a number of historical layers and ideological systems that do not conjoin as an 'urban' place. The new plans for Alexanderplatz are to alleviate such inconsistencies and ruptures. Simultaneously, they are to make Alexanderplatz fit for the New Berlin. One of the main objectives is the reinsertion of Alexanderplatz into the city, both by reconnecting it with its surroundings and by recovering the street layout and block structure of the pre-war city (Stimmann 1998: 177). The architecture of the envisaged high-rise buildings is said to be an interpretation of the 1920s Behrens buildings that front the square on its southeastern side. The latter's eaves' height is to be emulated by the block-and-tower structure of the prospective high-rises. The new Alexanderplatz will reflect the politico-aesthetic that has begun to characterize unified Berlin: by reconfiguring historical design elements in the light of new economic demands, the construction plan when implemented successfully is expected to help Alexanderplatz regain its stipulated position as a metropolitan square and a centre for shopping, entertainment and business.

Another objective is to achieve greater legibility, which is where urban planning plays into the hands of statecraft, past and present (de Certeau 1984; Scott 1998). Alexanderplatz's current illegibility makes it frightening. Essayist Siegfried Kracauer (1931/1996: 8) described the Alexanderplatz underground station, when first built, as resembling 'modern bathrooms' and as a 'spick-and-span model' of itself. By the 1990s, it had turned into an intricate and ill-lit system of tunnels and platforms, confusing especially to the unacquainted. The confusion extends to the above-ground level. An administrator once told me an anecdote involving a Berlin politician who had been unaware that there even was an underground station in Alexanderplatz, so obscure were the signs indicating its existence. If even the city's governors were unable to find their way, what about the copious numbers of tourists that were to come here in the future?

Finally, the new Alexanderplatz appeared desirable because it corresponds to recent urban planning sensibilities, especially the densification of city centres and its assumed socio-economic and ecological advantages, due to the mixture of residential and commercial functions, the shortening of distances, and thus the reduction of individual motorized traffic. In short, Alexanderplatz is turned into a *lieu d'avenir* (Jaffe and Onneweer 2006), a place filled with a future that accords with the state's promise of securing the well-being and prosperity of the population by enhancing the national economy and by developing its productive and reproductive capacities (Hansen and Stepputat 2002a). Viewed in these terms, the Alexanderplatz project could seem successful indeed.

New Hybrids, Old Ambivalences

The future success of Alexanderplatz was largely underwritten by a public-private partnership between Berlin's government and developers, which also came to appear the project's greatest liability. 'No city originates without investors,' a SenStadt employee noted in an interview with me, 'throughout the entire history of the city ... it was never the City that built itself.' Investors were seen to enable the administration to fulfil its legally prescribed planning obligation; and their intentions to build anything were generally understood to reflect demands in the real estate market. Without these demands, the administrator claimed, Alexanderplatz would have been left untouched. Yet, Alexanderplatz was considered too significant to be left to private investors alone. From their experience at Potsdamer Platz, where discontented developers had attempted to dodge SenStadt's ideas by bringing in their own architects, administrators were well acquainted with the difficulties involved. At Alexanderplatz, developers had therefore been included from the start; they had sat on the competition jury and were consulted in the first decisive planning stages. Beyond this, a public-private partnership seemed to offer a solution.

The urban analyst Susan Fainstein (1994: 225) has noted the 'hybrid status' of public-private partnerships. Although perhaps not novel, it has gained remarkable purchase, especially since the 1980s (Albers 1997; Pierre 1998). Public-private partnerships are considered typical of contemporary forms of governance in which the distinction between what are assumed to have once been two separate spheres – state and market, public and private – has come to appear fuzzy. The sense of 'hybridity', we may say, derives from the perception that public and private are joined in a new kind of relationship that is also understood to be of a different quality. Previously the relationship between these two realms seemed hierarchical, for the public stood (by law) above or before the private. Now, there is a sense of equality and interdependence, described by a SenStadt employee as a 'mutual give and take'.

The partnership thus turns on 'one of the "grand dichotomies" of Western thought' (Weintraub 1997: 1, citing Bobbio 1989), the state and the market, which Habermas (1989) has traced to the late sixteenth century and the particular crisis of representation in which European monarchical courts and other established seats of authority were ensnared at the time. It saw the disintegration of representative publicness – demonstrated in the grand festivities and rituals of the court and the church, and embodied in the feudal powers and the nobility – a publicness that in the light of notions of the public available to us today, seemed characterized by exclusivity. The public subsequently came to connote a realm of authority of the state whose servants were juxtaposed to the figure of the *Privatmann* ('private person'), who is without public office and pursuing his private interests (1989: 11). The market – a realm of private individuals engaging in voluntary relationships – and the state came to be understood as largely opposed (Carrier 1997; Dilley 1992).

To better grasp the ambivalences involved in the public-private partnership Alexanderplatz, I will briefly flag some important assumptions regarding the role of public bodies in planning in Germany. The conviction that ownership of land confers obligations as much as entitlements is shared by all sides of the political spectrum and is codified in the German *Grundgesetz* ('Basic Law'). Adherence to overarching urban development premises is considered one of these obligations. SenStadt administrators would frequently invoke the 'planning sovereignty' of the public hand, reflecting the influence of Roman law and sharply demarcating 'the public' as 'a centralized, unified, and omnipotent apparatus of rule which stands above society and governs it through the enactment and administration of laws' (Weintraub 1997: 11).

Vis-à-vis the investors, RKA administrators cloaked themselves in the garb of their public office, for example, when explaining the numerous regulations to be observed in their building projects. To set up a building site, for example, there were applications to be filed, specifying the space required, the weight and number plates of the trucks and their operating times. Making the investors knowledgeable was considered indispensable for avoiding breaches of the law and possible delays of the building works. Contrasted with the American situation, the emphasis put on this issue may seem remarkable. The political scientist Elizabeth Strom writes of her astonishment at the emphasis put on this issue: 'The state, it is assumed, has a unique responsibility to set parameters for building and planning, and land owners must live with those parameters' (2001: 234).

This arrangement is enmeshed in historically contingent conceptions of the role of the state bureaucracy and of the city as an object to be governed, which crystallized in the early twentieth century alongside changing planning goals and changing perceptions of the city itself. The *Großstadt* had come to be mistrusted. It did not generate the expected ideal of a 'free' play of market forces, but rather was considered 'prone to monopolistic, anarchic or other "unnatural" tendencies' (Ladd 1990: 244). Securing the desired planning goals – adequate living conditions and 'public health' – seemed to require public interference. In parallel, the ever more complex task of city planning evinced a progressive bureaucratization and rationalization. Politicians and councillors began to rely on the assessments of professional staff deemed capable of dealing with the problems of cities, understood to display increasing regularities and similarities (Ladd 1990: 238–9).

Put differently, the deliberations of city officials, then as today, partly reiterate a prevalent theme in European political and economic philosophy regarding the – continually defined and redefined – nature of the relationship between public and private, state and market, and how this relationship should be governed (Carrier and Miller 1999; Dilley 1992; Foucault 1991: 103; Weintraub 1997: 8). From one perspective, the building law – a component of German public law – constitutes a means for the state to regulate those aspects of the private market felt to be potentially threatening to the common good. At the same time, the law may be seen as momentarily marking out certain, albeit negotiable, parameters of competence and thus as productive of the very distinctions between public and private which it claims to regulate.

For the people I met, public and private constituted a persuasive reality inscribed, for example, in all sorts of material objects. Planning administrators and private investors sought to translate the relationship into specific, quantifiable terms, and plans and contracts inscribed, materialized and helped reify these relations. The contracts specified the design premises to which investors were to adhere, the desired completion dates for their projects, and their financial contributions to the infrastructure required. Plans prepared by RKA staff schematically visualized these contributions to the construction of streets, waterworks and sewage, and the design of the square itself – the open space between the developers' prospective buildings – which was to remain public.

Plans and contracts thus embodied a shifting relation between public and private, and indeed a change in the very constitution of these two domains. Municipalities increasingly faced budgetary constraints and were required to apply market mechanisms to their efforts and, indeed, to them-

Figure 12: Signing of contracts between SenStadt and developers

selves. Planners had already begun to find themselves in an increasingly ambiguous role after World War II, being both impartial experts and political advisors (Albers 1980: 157; 1997: 240). With the widespread deregulations of the 1980s and 1990s, 'the city' became an object to be marketed, and planners became managers and facilitators of a process of attracting investment (Albers 1997: 243–4; 1998: 19). My friend Thomas, a recent urban planning graduate and a member of the group City Forum from Below, suggested that planners today no longer see themselves as visionaries; rather, they are mediators between different actors and their interests. This may seem like an extended negotiation between John Locke and Adam Smith, on the one hand, and Thomas Hobbes and Jeremy Bentham, on the other; or, in other words, between the belief in the self-regulating, naturally harmonizing powers of society and the market and the need for a strong, regulating state working to protect the public good against the self-interest of private individuals (Dilley 1992: 6–7; Weintraub 1997: 9).

Public and private, in Berlin's planning context, acquired reality not merely through plans, contracts and laws; they were also perceived in the way people dressed, talked and interacted with each other; and they played themselves out in the ambivalent relationship the city had (and has) with investors. Administrators and city officials might have felt they had 'the law' on their side, but they sometimes appeared to lack the economic and symbolic capital that would make them equal negotiators. Indeed, where economic capital is played down, as in the context of the public-private partnership, symbolic capital would seem to become all the more significant (Bourdieu 1990: 118).

When it came to the negotiation of urban development contracts, SenStadt employees noted with a mixture of disdain and mockery that investors brought an entourage of lawyers and middlemen who would help them to strike the best deals. Similarly, a senior SenStadt official might warn a colleague not to take at face value the promises of investors' representatives. The latter, he explained, were well versed in the art of rhetoric and often intended to coax their conversation partners into believing anything they said. Private investors' rhetorical clout was a force to be reckoned with, as was their economic power. Investors were considered to have mastered cunning strategies to cloak the vagueness of their statements. The 'internal politics' of the investors, obscure to an outsider, and the apparent secrecy shrouding their activities were contentious issues in the RKA. As an exasperated RKA member noted, the representatives of an investor had announced that their building works would commence in March. But as March passed and nothing happened, he realized that they had never mentioned the *year* they were to start.

In the early 2000s, investors' willingness to build was felt to be waning. Outside meetings, in the corridors of the administration, and behind closed doors, there were whispers that the investors at Alexanderplatz were not interested in creating a beautiful, liveable city or in contributing to its prosperity, but solely in 'speculation'. They were suspected to have acquired the land at Alexanderplatz with the objective of making profit rather than actually building anything. This apparent reluctance to build was sometimes explained through uncontrollable swings of the market. Nevertheless, the doings of the agents of the private market could appear 'opaque, mysterious, and beyond [administrators'] control' (Dilley 1992: 5). Opacity was, to some extent, a mutual attribution. I heard representatives of private investors complain, not during meetings but afterwards as we were walking to the underground station, about things happening 'behind closed doors' at the planning administration, about their difficulties in locating the right department that could answer their queries, and about the 'jungle of paragraphs' and the 'jumble' of regulations and restrictions confronting them.

Crucially, investors' seeming defiance and refusal to commit themselves to dates and actions threatened to make the work of the RKA futile: timetables became outdated as soon as they were set, and plans redundant almost the moment they were plotted out. RKA staff anticipated serious implications. If investors failed to comply with a coordinated scheme, Alexanderplatz would remain a building site for several decades, causing inconvenience and upset amongst Berliners. In a sense, RKA staff's task had become to prevent the new Alexanderplatz turning into a problem in its own right.

Investors, it was often said, were all 'doing their own thing'. When RKA staff suggested, for example, that investors might want to employ the same company to measure and predict the damage that their construction works might cause in surrounding buildings and the underground train tunnels, investors were reluctant. They doubted that it would really save them money. They were also (initially) unenthusiastic about having an exhibition, creating a common logo, producing a leaflet or similar such devices that would help present their building projects to Berlin's inhabitants as a joint undertaking. At such occasions, investors' representatives could indeed appear to embody the independent and dispassionate market actor, always in competition with others (Carrier 1997: 9). The ostensibly self-interested nature of investors' actions flew in the face of RKA staff's efforts to generate a sense of togetherness amongst the diverse parties to the Alexanderplatz project or what were termed, in the language of management, synergies. Self-interest and a lack of cooperation were felt to be encumbering. They flouted the purpose of RKA staff's comprehensive and meticulous planning – namely, to ensure the coherence and order of the new Alexanderplatz, and *not* to replace the current 'rag rug' with an equally inconsistent patchwork. In short, they were obstacles to making the new Alexanderplatz a success.

Postponing Failure

In their brief but insightful discussion of sociological approaches to failure, Myazaki and Riles (2005) note that merely to diagnose failure as the inadequacy of knowledge and to fill in the 'gaps' in that knowledge may be insufficient as an anthropological project. Their insight can be applied to anthropological accounts of planning and development failures. Scott (1998) has provided ample example of how state planning has failed its supposed beneficiaries because of the very simplifications that are supposed to make the plans work. Plans, in this view, value *techne* over *mētis*, that is, the detached, standardizing knowledge of the technocrats and state actors over the practical, situated knowledge of people in particular locales. *Techne* fails to capture the richness of *mētis*; in Myazaki and Riles' words, it has gaps. Holston (1989) has dissected the planning of Brasília to show how the city, intended to provide the spatial layout of a future society, denies rather than accommodates, and subsequently reproduces the social reality it seeks to eliminate. Another example is Ferguson's work (1990) on the grand development projects in Lesotho, which failed to achieve their proclaimed ends. The projects' inherent misconception of local realities and the application of standardized development schemes produced instead unintended and sometimes counter-productive consequences.

All these are brilliant studies of planning failure and the little steps leading up to it. However, these analyses suggest a notion of failure as absolute and static, as a definite moment where stated intentions do not match observable outcomes. In an important sense, however, failure is inherent in the idea of the plan. Time and again, planners would explain to me how no plan could ever correspond to the reality that it denotes; there are always surprises and unanticipated alterations to be made. Anthropological accounts have tended to deploy a mode of critique of development planning that centres on the 'gaps' that appear between plan and outcome. What I have done here is to focus on the work that sustains that gap, which allows those involved to retain some sense of the meaningfulness of their actions. I will not describe the ways in which the Alexanderplatz project may be seen to have failed (for example, owing to certain gaps in the knowledge about market developments)[41] but rather want to stay with that moment of failure or, better, the apprehension of failure.

As the comment by the administrator at the start of this chapter indicates, a 'shared perception of failure' (Miyazaki and Riles 2005: 322) regarding Berlin's post-unification development was making itself felt in the early 2000s. Despite this acute sense of a lack of progress and despite the developers' to-ing and fro-ing, the planners at Alexanderplatz insisted that their project would still be a success. The as-yet non-appearance of the new Alexanderplatz was not seen as an obvious indicator of the project's failure. Operating in a state of anticipation, planners asserted that its realization had been merely postponed.[42] Failure (or success?) was temporarily displaced. Like Aramis (Latour 1996), Alexanderplatz had become a 'collective dream' whose completion had come to appear necessary and self-evident.

But Alexanderplatz would not be the first case where the existing cityscape shows astonishing endurance in the face of concerted planning efforts. Hommels (2005) points to some of the notions commonly used to explain why some planning projects get 'unbuilt'. They range from their being over budget, to a lack of agreement amongst participants, to powerful actors wanting to maintain the status quo, to the embeddedness of the socio-technological structure and the materiality of the cityscape, which may make alterations painfully difficult or plainly impossible. Some of these would also hold true for Alexanderplatz, if we consider the political tensions between Mitte district and the city of Berlin; the costliness of the project at a time when Berlin's economic boom seemed to reside; and the difficulty involved in constructing something in a functioning, busy square with an underworld of train tunnels, archaeological remains and a massive, concrete World War II bunker that would have to be forcefully removed.

None of these reasons individually serves as a sufficient explanation, and it seemed that 'locally' only an economic explanation was valid. Planners explained the project's delay by utilizing a distinctly economic knowledge; they espoused an idea of the market as following discernible and regular cycles of boom and bust. This market was capricious but necessary to carry out city planning. No doubt, in pointing to market cycles as the reason for the project's delay, planners also displaced blame. They disembodied it: there was no single person, no entity, no planning doctrine, which could be held responsible.

What I wish to highlight is that the coming together of the dissimilar temporalities of market and state planning had a peculiar effect; it required the treatment of time as elastic. I noted how space was occasionally treated as elastic (Verdery 1996) in the RKA. But so was time. The 'postponement' of the Alexanderplatz project implied such elasticity, as did the prolongation of the period of time given to the developers to commence and complete their constructions, which was set out in the urban development contracts.

Failure, or rather the apprehension of failure, was productive of social action. The Alexanderplatz project was to some extent the product of a process of learning from previous failures in the planning of the unified Berlin. As suggested above, the RKA and its way of managing the project were partly a response to what had gone wrong elsewhere. In its avoidance of failure, it called forth specific forms of social action. The minutes of the RKA meetings, contracts, plans and timetables both anticipated and effected actions intended to bring the new Alexanderplatz into being; as documents they all produced a certain agency (Riles 2006: 21). This was the actual work of the plan,[43] that is, to compel other kinds of actions that the problematization of Alexanderplatz had made indispensable and to allow people to act on a present state of affairs.

At least according to the engineers and administrators involved, their actions had indeed been successful, as they created greater coherence amongst the participants to the Alexanderplatz project. Such commentary always implied a notion of a failure that 'would have been' in the absence of the RKA. What Alexanderplatz allows us to see, therefore, is how the partiality and temporality of failure pan out. We need to ask again whether failure, understood as the nonattainment of objectives, is the adequate term. Failure is not absolute; it is not a matter of intentions and results but of contingency, accommodation and adjustment. Instead of taking the plan 'after the fact' as the baseline for the social analysis, it becomes more interesting to ask, with Hommels, what has allowed an urban structure like Alexanderplatz to obdure?

❧ Chapter V ❧

The Object of Grievance

How was the planning for Alexanderplatz apprehended by Berlin's residents? This chapter examines in much more detail some of the urban cultural practices that have as their object of concern Berlin and its transformation, as I began to discuss in Chapter II. Set up as a public-private partnership and surrounded by a host of events seeking popular participation, the Alexanderplatz project generated concerns about the legitimacy of the planning decisions taken and the role of experts and citizens in the process. Alexanderplatz emerged as an 'object of grievance'. The grievances at issue, as we shall see, were largely those of people self-consciously positioning themselves as *Bürger* ('citizens') or as members of a critical *Fachöffentlichkeit* ('expert public'). They provided grounds for actions that many hoped would avert the new Alexanderplatz and thus the 'wrong' done to Berliners it was thought to embody. By the time of my fieldwork, the Alexanderplatz project implied disappointment for many of these citizens; it was a missed opportunity to set an example for city planning in the unified Berlin. In an important sense, citizens (like planners) thus acted with failure in mind.

As an object of grievance, Alexanderplatz mobilized core ideas of democracy, government and expertise. I suggest that the activities of the civic activists presented here articulate a specific relationship between people and place, within the context of urban planning in the unified Berlin. I call this relationship a citizenly engagement with place. It includes the ways in which participating subjects come to govern their perspectives on place by framing them in rationalizing terms of expert debate. In this sense, the citizenly engagement with place is an embodied process implicated in the self-reflexive stance characterizing Berlin's ongoing transformation. The challenge to planning posed by the citizens I met was less a critique of city planning per se than a moral critique, raising questions about governmental conduct and about who can determine what makes a good place.

A Time of Citizens

After the first phase of the Alexanderplatz competition in the 1990s, and the exhibition of the selected designs, there was much talk of necessarily including Berlin's inhabitants in the deliberations over Alexanderplatz's future. Berlin's then Senator for Urban Development, Volker Hassemer, spoke of the population's need for information, which had to be satisfied to ensure a wide acceptance of the planned reconstruction (Lenhart 2001: 223).

An impressive publicity campaign was conducted under the sponsorship of the investors, aimed at encouraging Berliners to participate in the shaping of Alexanderplatz. There were special newspaper supplements, public discussions, an exhibition on the architect Peter Behrens whose two buildings, Alexanderhaus and Berolinahaus, were the remnants of his larger modernist design for the square developed in the 1920s. The 'Alex-Info-Bus' was set up on Alexanderplatz to serve as both meeting point and information desk where architects, administrators and other experts were available to answer questions by everyone interested in the proposed designs. A leaflet explained that Alexanderplatz was 'the most significant square in the heart of the city' and that, in view of the changes Berlin had undergone and would undergo in the future, Alexanderplatz could not and must no longer remain the same. People were invited to *mitgestalten* ('co-design') and *mitbestimmen* ('have a say') by filling in questionnaires and by describing some of their own ideas. 'Your design suggestions and the results of the survey will be evaluated and will flow into the planning,' the leaflet read, 'for nothing ought to be built over Berliners' heads.'

These events were only the beginning of what SenStadt administrators claimed had been a concerted effort to provide opportunities for popular participation beyond what was legally required. They invoked that assumed collective entity, 'the public', or alternatively 'citizens' and 'Berliners', now thought to be crucial for legitimating political authority in democratic systems and, increasingly, techno-scientific expertise. Like any public, this one was summoned into existence: it existed by virtue of being addressed (Warner 2002; see also Gal and Woolard 2001). But it also required people both to identify as 'the citizen' invited to participate and to act upon this.

If numbers are anything to go by, public participation, or indeed the upheaval caused by the plans for Alexanderplatz, was remarkable. Four to five thousand visitors were counted in the exhibition of the competition designs, podium discussions attracted audiences of up to five hundred, and several hundred opinion-letters reached the administrators at various stages of the planning procedure. I had a chance to view some of these letters – stamped, numbered, neatly filed and stored away in an administrator's filing cabinet. There were letters in all forms and styles: some scribbled, some in clear writing, some typed. Some bullet-pointing important suggestions, others relating more of a personal narrative and memories of Alexanderplatz. Some contained harsh insults; others were phrased in a language stripped of all its emotion-conveying components. Children's drawings that had not been evaluated were filed alongside a series of letters apparently photocopied to be passed around and signed by all the residents of a particular house, asserting their recently gained property rights.

For me, filing through these preserved accounts of reclamations, suggestions, hopes and discontent, they seemed particularly gratifying forms of self-objectification (Brenneis 1994, cit. in Riles 2006: 19), which reflected the animated discussions carried out in people's homes, citizen groups, newspapers, and perhaps in Alexanderplatz itself. Clearly, the members of the citizen group I discuss below were not the only ones aggravated by the plans for Alexanderplatz, though there were also some who expressed approval.

By their very existence, the files holding these letters appeared proof of administrators' adherence to bureaucratic procedure. *Pace* Weber, the production, collection, and preservation of files are crucial to what has come to be understood as the rational management of the modern public bureau (Weber 1991: 197; Riles 1998: 378, 2006). More specifically, these files could be evidence that, in the planning for Alexanderplatz, citizens' views had been taken into account. In a sense, the files were quite literally containment devices. By virtue of accumulating and bringing citizens' letters into proximity (thus establishing a relation between them), they appeared to contain the citizens' voice. What they seemed to contain also was the diversity of letters received. For instance, the official form on which most of the letters were written and the subsequent numbering gave them an appearance of likeness. The process of numbering objectified the individual letters whilst eliminating distinctions and creating resemblance (Parkin 1982: xxxvi–vii). As a function of bureaucratic aesthetics, diversity was contained in favour of comparability.

By the time of my research, the Alexanderplatz debate had been assigned to SenStadt's archives. With the establishment of the legally binding construction plan in 1999, Berlin's administrators saw no further need for public discussion. At the start of my fieldwork, a friendly urban development administrator helpfully provided me with the phone numbers of two members of one of the citizen groups that had earlier actively protested the new plans for Alexanderplatz. During my internship, this administrator, Herr Schneider, became an extremely obliging interlocutor in respect of my questions about the planning administration; now in his 50s, Schneider had not been trained as an urban planner but had been brought to the urban development administration by the confusing vagaries of unification. Commenting on the citizens' protest, Schneider explained that planning administrators had already anticipated a critical public, and that the administration had always been open to negotiation. Only consensus had never been achieved.

Once I arrived in Berlin, I contacted some of the former members of this citizens' initiative, called the Bürgervertretung Alexanderplatz ('Citizens' Representation Alexanderplatz'). We have already met some of them in the previous pages. I shall refer in particular here to Herr Müller and Herr Zimmer, both residents in Alexanderplatz's vicinity; Professor Näther, East Berlin's former Chief Architect; and Thomas, the urban planning graduate who was now looking for work in his field, struggling to make ends meet, but who still found time for his involvement in a diversity of civic activities, such as City Forum from Below discussed in Chapter II. Because the Bürgervertretung had since dissolved, my depiction of what the members had imagined to be at stake in the debate about Alexanderplatz largely rests on their narratives, (co-)constructed in conversations with me, and the documents they had collected over the years.

Thomas' collection was particularly impressive, consisting of several files that he had once begun to systematize both chronologically and according to types of material. Over the months, I spent much time sifting through official reports, newspaper articles, open letters, minutes of parliamentary meetings and Thomas' own notes on Alexanderplatz's history, legal regulations and so forth. Although they seemed no longer of use, Thomas had kept these files for future reference. He hoped that, at some point in his career as an urban planner, the time and effort he had invested in Alexanderplatz – comprised by this heap of paper – would be demonstrably worthwhile. But these files also constituted a reference-point in a more abstract sense. Sometimes when I arrived for appointments with Bürgervertretung's members, a folder thick with paperwork would be sitting atop the table, waiting to be inspected. During our conversation, my interlocutors would occasionally open, or simply point at, it – suggesting that what we were talking about could also be found in there. The folder, it seemed, testified to these citizens' investment in Alexanderplatz, their efforts and resentments, the injuries done to them and their limited achievements. The folder was what was left of their citizenly engagement; it was where their Alexanderplatz – the object of grievance – was now.

Citizens Summoned

Today, in Germany, citizens can seem ubiquitous. This ethnography has already presented them in a number of guises: as the conceptual figure anticipated in planning procedures, and subsequently inscribed in letters and files, but also as the author of letters, the activist, and the eager participant in public discussions. One might also encounter the citizen in the *Bürgerämter*, or citizen offices, that have sprung up in many German cities; or in the peculiar artefacts of present-day German democracy, such as citizens' surveys or citizens' reports. Citizens have remained an important cipher of state legitimacy and are also embodied participants in this process of legitimation.

Before delving into the struggle fought by the Bürgervertretung, I want to briefly give an ethnographic sense of how abstract categories, including 'citizen' and 'expert', take shape. One day in early March 2002, after a meeting in the RKA, administrators told me about an informational meeting which would take place that night. It concerned Rathausstraße, the pedestrian zone leading southwest from Alexanderplatz towards Rotes Rathaus, Berlin's central town hall. It is flanked on one side by the park surrounding the well-known TV tower, on the other by the Rathauspassagen, the large tenement in which the pub where I worked for a few months during the fieldwork was located. Alluding to an earlier and apparently heated meeting with Building Director Stimmann on the matter, RKA staff expected the evening to be controversial.

The venue in the town hall was opened early and quickly filled with people. Many people had to stand through the three-hour discussion. Plans and other images were displayed on two partition walls, and participants could pick up a press statement, which included a computer-designed image of the proposed alterations for Rathausstraße and outlined the anticipated benefits: Rathausstraße would be rid of its small-townish appearance and turned into an attractive, metropolitan centre alongside Alexanderplatz. It would be made accessible by tram and motorized traffic and yet remain a space for leisurely strolls.

The proposed reconstruction was in tune with the intended amelioration of the results of GDR planning in Berlin's eastern centre. As I had learned from Dorothea Tscheschner, the planner who had been involved in the design of the centre during GDR times, the tram had been eliminated in the 1960s, as an accident-prone and outdated means of transportation, finding its 'modern' replacement in buses and private cars. Rathausstraße was considered an exemplary case of socialist urban design, combining housing and workspace with space for consumption and leisure, in the heart of the capital. Today, the tram has been revived in the name of ecology whilst pedestrian zones constitute, in the eyes of many administrative planners, urbanity's very antithesis.

Whilst reading the press statement, I caught snippets of the conversations around me. There was an air of anticipation as attendees speculated about what they might learn tonight. People asked each other where they lived and complained that 'our' money would be spent on measures that were neither desired nor welcomed. A man, who lived opposite in Karl-Liebknecht-Straße where the tram had recently been introduced, talked about how he had the noise levels on his balcony measured, which proved far too high. Tonight, he announced, he would ask 'them' how that could be. An administrator from Mitte's planning office whom I knew from RKA meetings sat down in front of me. We began to chat about Rathausstraße's recent deterioration, as numerous shops, restaurants, offices, the supermarket as well as the pub in which I had worked, had closed down due to the incipient renovation of the building. Now, the Rathauspassagen lay dark and derelict, and the administrator remarked how dismayed she felt walking past them tonight. She reminisced about the beautiful pedestrian zone it had been during GDR times, enlivened by interesting shops and amenities. She had spent much time there as a young girl, meeting friends or visiting the disco in the nearby Alextreff. Looking at the area today, she thought that it blatantly needed improvement. Yet the administrator empathized with the residents; many of them were elderly people who had lived there for several decades and might worry about the anticipated disturbances. A few minutes' later, other administrators, standing closer to the podium, motioned her to join them; and she left me sitting with the 'citizens'.

The evening was long, lively and not always cordial. After some introductory remarks, three representatives of Berlin's public transport corporation (BVG) supplied ample detail on the history of the tram in the area, technical improvements, and the ways in which the tram would help connect the eastern districts to the centre and achieve the desired modal split of 80:20. Subsequently, the discussion was opened. Some people had already made themselves heard, interrupting the speakers, questioning the costs of the project, or simply shouting, 'We don't want these plans!' Historical arguments that Rathausstraße once had the tram running through it did little to persuade, and were greeted with laughter and derogatory comments. Now, people began to raise their hands and stand up to voice their apprehensions, some making use of the microphone provided. They worried about the disappearance of the 'last pedestrian zone in the East', which they considered pleasant for adults and children alike, and how the reconstruction would affect their lives.

The bulk of the discussion turned on the issue of 'noise' and the disruption that the tram and motorized traffic were feared to bring. Noise emerged as a noticeable and, importantly, scientifically *measurable* indicator of people's 'quality of life'. People challenged the forecasts on which the plans were based. 'Who said that buses and underground trains did not suffice?', they demanded to know. And, 'how were the permitted noise limits established?' The man who had had the noise levels on his balcony measured made his claim, but a doubtful expert on the podium suggested that the measurements might have been taken during peak hours. What was required, however, was an average – and that did not exceed the limits at present. Another person responded wryly: 'So if a bomb explodes right next to me and I become deaf, but before the explosion and afterwards it's completely silent, does that mean I'm not really deaf?' A man, who apparently had a professional knowledge about noise, started an argument with the 'noise expert'. Soon, however, other members of the audience urged them to return to relevant issues and to a language comprehensible to all.

Attendees appealed not only to the language of 'science', but also to 'the state'. A woman expressed her preoccupation with the health hazard constituted by the so-called *Elektro-Smog* emanating from trams. She gave an impressive list of political figures to whom she had written – including Wolfgang Thierse, then president of the German Bundestag; then chancellor Gerhard Schröder; Joachim Zeller, the then mayor of Mitte district; and Eberhard Diepgen, who had until recently been Berlin's mayor – and who all sided with her and against the tram. The 'caring' state, though locally absent, seemed not to have disappeared completely. It was imagined to reside elsewhere – for instance, in more prominent figures supposedly embodying stately power.

In other words, opposition to the plans was itself framed in the dominant terms scientific and governmental discourse. At times, the discussion appeared polarized by the conflicting agendas and allegiances of the district and SenStadt respectively. Dorothee Dubrau, Mitte's councillor for urban development was present. In previous conversations I had with administrators, some described Dubrau as populist, others considered her courageous. As one of them commented approvingly: Dubrau would always fight for her people, even 'against Stimmann and the political will'. On this occasion, Dubrau appeared to personify Mitte district's special commitment to its residents. She had produced images of Rathausstraße's planned reconstruction, which noticeably differed from those shown by SenStadt. They buttressed suspicions that the real plans for Rathausstraße had been kept secret. Instead of getting the transparency they might have expected, some participants surmised that, even tonight, information was withheld. 'On the contrary, it is dis-information!' claimed the representative of a citizen initiative active in another Berlin neighbourhood. In her eyes, SenStadt was not taking people's fears seriously and showed neither commonsense nor *Bürgersinn*, that is a consideration for what citizens might wish. She asserted: 'As citizens of Berlin we won't let ourselves be divided.'

As the discussion drew to a close, a BVG representative stressed that the regulation applied here, applied in the entire Federal Republic. Planners could not be expected to stop planning to please certain residents. As a final comment, the head of SenStadt's urban design department encouraged participants to remain *sachlich* ('objective', 'matter-of-factly') and to consider the project's advantages for Berlin as a whole; but of course, SenStadt would try to take all their doubts and worries into account.

Citizens Made

The evening had brought no conclusions; the eventual decision was to preserve Rathausstraße as a pedestrian zone, with the tram but without motorized traffic. According to an RKA member, the decision owed to a comment from the developers made during the event, that a proper street was not needed. For a SenStadt administrator, however, the decision had been populist: to secure future votes, politicians preferred to concur with residents' wishes rather than expert advice. Neither of them suggested that the citizens' views had had any weight in and of themselves.

As Paley observes, participatory events have a 'double significance' (2001: 62). They serve as sites for divulging information, gauging citizens' opinions, and sometimes for changing their attitudes. However, people come not only to hear. They also delineate the problems they themselves see, hoping that those in charge will take them on board. That is, they ostensibly provide an opportunity for demanding accountability. It is in such moments of explicitly democratic encounter that the meaning of citizenship and participation is enacted and negotiated. They are 'localized practices' through which the state appears to gain tangible presence (Gupta 1995), and through which the abstract categories of 'citizenry' and 'residents' take shape. The citizen in these events is imagined as a kind of calculating subject – a person who is, aside from a bearer of rights, also 'a subject of interest, a subject of individual preferences and choices' (Gordon 1991: 21, emphasis omitted; Strathern 2002: 257). In significant ways, these events help in generating 'opinions' and 'interests' (Hindess 1986); by naming them as such, a diverse set of assumptions, values and beliefs is rendered commensurable and thus comparable (Strathern 2002: 257). More importantly still, they are moments where citizens present themselves as both *experienced* and *knowledgeable*. There, *mētis* – the knowledge derived from practical experience – and *techne* – expert knowledge (Scott 1998: ch.9) – if they can ever be told apart, got enmeshed.

Citizens' actions are made possible by, rather than opposed to, contemporary senses of government. In Chapter II, I noted that since the 1970s, citizens' participation has become a firm part of planning procedure in Germany. The Federal Building Law of 1960 already pointed towards a reconceptualization of the relationship between the state and two kinds of citizens: those who own property and those who don't. Tenants were now included in the group of the *Betroffene* ('affected') whose *Belange* ('matters') ought to be considered in the implementation of urban renewal programmes. Since the 1970s, as a SenStadt employee succinctly put it, it had been clear that 'we are here for the citizens and not vice versa'.

Openness to civic action characterizes German political structures today (Berglund 1998: 21). Both planners' understanding of space and society and of themselves as well as prevalent forms of accountability had been recast in the process. 'Society' has come to be imagined as comprised of diverse and conflicting interests, and it seems no longer possible to determine the public good – that peculiar, indivisible collective benefit that planners invoke as both the rational and goal of their actions – without directly taking into account people's own views. Simultaneously, 'citizen' has become readily available as a category of self-identification in whose name people speak, act and exert political influence. Legal reforms thus contributed to the production of a new kind of citizenly persona, with specific attributes and characteristics – a citizen not born, but 'made' (Burchell 1995; Cruikshank 1999).

Focusing on this particular legal juncture in 1970s West Germany, I take the law to be critical in the production of a particular citizenly subjectivity (Borneman 1993; Collier et al. 1995; Holston 2008). Being a citizen comes with expectations of rights and of appropriate conduct, which enable as much as they constrain. This is not to say that all those participating in planning procedures would necessarily understand themselves in the contextual terms sketched here. If pressed, they might have drawn a variety of comparisons. Herr Müller and Herr Zimmer, for example, felt that their involvement in a *Hausgemeinschaftsleitung* ('house-community leadership') in GDR times had been a form of being *engagiert* ('actively involved') comparable to the Bürgervertretung, as were the responsibilities they used to assume in the everyday care for the surroundings of the houses in which they lived. Their comments partly contradict notions of acquiescence, compliance and repression through the GDR regime, and to quite different conditions of possibility (Foucault 1972) for what was arguably a form of citizenly engagement.[44] It is such conditions of possibility for citizen groups, and for citizens' participation more generally, in contemporary Berlin, which are of interest here.

The proliferation of participation, its positive connotations and persuasiveness (Nelson and Wright 1995a: 2) has had broader ramifications, which have been examined extensively in the anthropology of development (Abram 1998; Grillo 1997; Midgley 1986; Nelson and Wright 1995b). Some of the concerns raised in this literature dovetail with those of people I met in Berlin. Here, I wish to address specifically two issues. First, there is the question of whether the state – or, in Germany, the local government usually responsible for planning matters – lives up to its rhetoric of participation, including attendant expectations of transparency and accountability. Some fear that participation procedures may be merely a way of garnering additional viewpoints and of pre-empting potential conflicts or, quite simply, a form of co-option. Others point to the tensions arising from seemingly incommensurable epistemologies. To mitigate these apparent disparities, new models of participation are continually invented. 'Cooperative', 'collaborative', 'communicative' or *bürgernah* ('citizen-near') are but a few of the adjectives available to describe desirable forms of planning today (cf. Abram 2000; Selle n.d.).

In the light of new ideals, what was once considered progressive can come to appear utterly inadequate. For instance, Werner Orlowsky of the 'City Forum from Below' told me about a revealing public discussion on the model implemented in Porto Alegre, the Brazilian city that has become, for many, a symbol for state-of-the-art participatory politics.[45] 'I had always thought that Berlin was at the forefront as regards citizens' participation', Werner said, 'but really it is lagging behind!' In his view, Berlin's participation policies were threatening to become just empty rhetoric. There was less money to finance adequate facilities. What was more, those in charge were no longer driven by the 'lust for participation', which he had felt in his days as Kreuzberg's planning councillor in the 1980s.

The second issue concerns the kind of interests citizens pursue. For some scholars of urban movements, fragmented civic action and 'particularistic' interests – often summed up as 'Not In My Back Yard' (NIMBY) politics – have displaced the goal of 'social justice' that united the citizen initiatives of the 1970s (cf. Mayer 1999; 2000). However, as Berglund notes, in some cases 'the acronym NIABY, Not In Anybody's Back Yard could be more apposite' (1998: 7). In Berlin, the distinction between common and particularistic interests is typically invoked by administrators and sometimes by citizens themselves. What is described as NIMBY in an English-speaking context was called, in Berlin, 'Saint Florian's principle' – in reference to a popular invocation of the patron against fire threats: 'Saint Florian, save my house, light another one!' Implicit here are normative ideas about a public sphere where, to use Habermas' well-worn terms, 'private people come together as a public' (Habermas 1962/1989: 27; see also Calhoun 1992). Particularistic, selfish interests are considered misplaced in the deliberations and actions of such supposedly rational civic agents. But who can determine what is rational and what is particularistic are, in the last instance, the administrators qualified to do so on the basis of their particular 'ethos of office'.

The ideas and concerns sketched out here are constitutive of a discursive framework within which people appraise their own and others' actions.

Public discussions and participatory events afford opportunities for both formulating and challenging what later appears as the 'opinions' and 'interests' of the participants. They are key moments for self-positioning; people are required to speak as someone, which has implications for the kinds of claims they can make. Residents may challenge expert opinions on the basis of their experience of the place in question; or frame their views in the scientific terms, the premier language in which rational argument today is made. Conversely, a participant introduced as the representative of a political party or the district council may note that she is also a citizen of Mitte. Paradoxically, attempts to blur boundaries would seem to underscore the salience of the categories invoked. Public discussions are crucial arenas in which government officials, administrators, private investors, experts and citizens come to form their images of each other and of themselves. It is here that these categories acquire empirical existence and that people enact, shape and confirm their specific subjectivities.

Governing Perceptions

The Bürgervertretung Alexanderplatz had been brought to life after an informational meeting hosted by Mitte district office in the early nineties. When first founded, it had about thirty members who sought both to work with and to challenge the exercise of government through means they considered both practicable and appropriate. They held meetings, wrote letters, stuck up posters in the neighbourhood, contacted other citizen groups, attended public discussions, and managed to organize some of their own, such as the one held in a circus tent in Alexanderplatz, which attracted several hundred people.

The Bürgervertretung's membership was diverse and unified only by opposition to what they referred to as the Kollhoff plan. As Zimmer said, '80 per cent of us were laypersons, ranging from the granny and the housewife to other people doing all sorts of things – but not architecture. We only had one thought: It cannot be like this! It mustn't look like this!' Unfamiliar with the planning terminology and procedures, they relied on the patient explanations given by Thomas, Professor Näther and another architect member.

Any characterization of the group is therefore ambiguous. Its members included citizens and experts, and some considered themselves experts first. When I began my first interview with Professor Näther by enquiring about his citizen group activities, he was offended. I appeared oblivious to his former achievements as an architect and as coauthor of Alexanderplatz, which were, as he noted, what had gained him renown after all. Although he was now retired, his commitment to the citizen group was an outcome of his expertise. Näther and his wife still lived in an apartment in one of the blocks built near Alexanderplatz during GDR times. They expressed appreciation of the famous 'sun and air' coming into their home; they also pointed out the many amenities that used to exist in the area but most of which, to their dismay, had been *wegrationalisiert* ('rationalized away') after unification.

However, what had been at stake for Professor Näther were perhaps less the effects of Alexanderplatz's proposed reconstruction on him as a resident, than the destruction of GDR architecture and of one of his works in particular. His special subject-position as an 'author' of Alexanderplatz had been demonstrated to him, unmistakably, in an open parliamentary session where he was shouted down, I was told, particularly by representatives of the Christian Democratic Party. Apparently, the former Chief Architect was held personally accountable for all the planning injuries the GDR had inflicted on Berlin, and deemed unfit to make any suggestions for future planning. This instance of what Thomas called a 'red socks campaign' against those with previous involvement in the GDR nomenklatura points to how wider questions surrounding the ascription of personal responsibility for the socialist regime also played out in the area of urban planning (cf. Borneman 1993; 1996).

Through its expert members, I was told, the group gained a different 'way of seeing'. I got a sense of how this might have happened when meeting up one evening with Thomas, Herr Müller and Herr Zimmer to talk about the group's activities. The café in the Scheunenviertel, where the Bürgervertretung used to hold some of its meetings and where we had arranged to meet, had closed down, so we relocated to one of the trendy bars that had sprung up in the area since unification. Since the group had dissolved, Müller, Zimmer and Thomas saw each other seldom. Now, sitting over a glass of wine, they reminisced about their activities and the reasons for their involvements. At times, Müller and Zimmer were struggling to remember the technical jargon that had come to be so familiar to them only a few years ago. Thomas quickly emerged as the leader of our conversation; his explanations of the planning procedures and Alexanderplatz's history soon began to dominate. Herr Zimmer and Herr Müller continued to contribute, but Thomas' expertise seemed unchallenged.

The different 'way of seeing' was reflected in the figure of the group itself. They organized themselves into subgroups, gathering and evaluating information under specific rubrics that resembled key categories of urban planning, such as 'the economy', 'urban design', 'the social' and 'traffic'. Subsequent discussions of these subgroups' findings were hoped to aid what was called the *Meinungsbildung* ('formation of an opinion'). In their interactions with each other and with the administration, architects and developers, these self-conscious citizens constructed a common subject position (as citizens) and a set of interests that they could put forward in negotiations with planners and developers.

My interlocutors were keen to point out that the Bürgervertretung had never opposed Alexanderplatz's development as such, but rather its development on a grand scale, which Alexanderplatz, as a place of 'citywide significance', was claimed to require. They conceived their task not to reject techno-scientific expertise, 'but rather to take on a political function which expertise has failed to, or cannot, fulfil' (Barry 2001: 206). This made their critique not anti-inventive, but focused on what was deemed unreasonable and inappropriate about the plans. They questioned the economic rationality and technical feasibility; pointed to potentially exacerbated ecological and traffic-related problems; and highlighted the architectural significance of certain buildings worthy of preservation. They sought to prevent what they feared to be the plan's detrimental effects, specifically the erection of dense high-rise constructions that would obliterate the existing square and result in both a monotonous environment lacking what they termed social dimensions and in gentrification processes. They did not believe that developers would stick to the proposed unifying design but would merely be interested in 'building monuments to themselves'.

Their struggle brought into play some of the broader contentious issues that had polarized the German public in the wake of unification. When Müller talked to me about his fear of being 'driven out' of Alexanderplatz, he likened it to his family's expulsion from Poland after the Second World War and to a more general East German post-unification experience of people losing their homes, thereby invoking the debate around the precept of 'restitution before compensation', which guided the complex question of property ownership and privatization (Dieser 1996), and which is associated with a strong sense of injustice (Dahn 1994).

The Bürgervertretung partly couched its concerns in terms familiar to students of urban development and related protest elsewhere. City self-marketing and the attraction of outside developers are often felt to prevail at the expense of the less powerful residents (Foster 1999). Residents risk being subsumed into the generic category of 'users' (Rutheiser 1999), and their seemingly 'alternate visions' (McDonogh 1999: 367) remain unacknowledged (see also Abu-Lughod 1994; Herzfeld 1991; Low 2000). Scholarly critiques of popular participation in development contexts frequently rest on similar oppositions between locals and outsiders entertaining different frames of reference and knowledges, which the complex relations in the field of Berlin planning debates would clearly seem to challenge.

What I want to highlight is the considerable overlap between the kinds and conceptions of knowledge and the problematics identified by citizens, politicians, planners and other experts (Berglund 1998). The Bürgervertretung's members found their views partly reflected in official reports, specifically a so-called 'Social Study' which had been commissioned by the planning administration and for which they, too, had been interviewed as experts of a kind. Another study was entitled 'People, Uses and Cultural Patrimony', conducted by a group of researchers headed by Harald Bodenschatz, at Berlin's Technical University where Thomas was a student. This report portrayed Alexanderplatz as a precious example of GDR modernist planning and concludes that its redesign is not simply an indicator of attitudes towards this cultural patrimony but indeed of the 'growing together' of East and West in a unified Germany.

These studies recommended a *behutsam* ('careful') approach to existing structures and measures to protect and involve the local population. This was an approach, championed in 1980s Berlin in opposition to large-scale urban renewal programmes implemented in the Kreuzberg district. Instead of what they described as an oppressive and inhumane design, an 'implant' into the city, they demanded an 'organic' linking of Alexanderplatz and its surroundings. Implicit in these bio(techno)logical metaphors was a contrast between artificiality and authenticity, and between what some saw as the overbearing megalomania of the Kollhoff plan and the harmonious modesty of another Alexanderplatz.

The Alexanderplatz conjured up in the Bürgervertretung's open letters, in podium discussions, and in conversations with me was at odds with other representations of the square as a grand demonstration of really existing socialism. In the citizens' view, Alexanderplatz was a 'square for human beings' and 'a place of communication and interaction'. For Thomas, this other Alexanderplatz was partly embodied in the notion of Alexanderplatz as a 'Gateway to the East', indicating an alternative imagining of how East and West could grow together in this place. The notion stems from Wolfgang Kil's writings on postunification Berlin:

> As an idea for the city, a *Gate to the East* does not aim at the familiar guiding images of an unrestrained economic growth. Rather, this idea directs our gaze towards a future whose outline is just about discernible. It attempts to prepare for a world determined by an increasingly direct confrontation between rich and poor. Conflicts of a completely different kind are prefigured, also and especially in Berlin. And if traditional demonstrations of the self-satisfaction of wealth have triumphed again in Potsdamer Platz, then the city has to try and show in another prominent place that it is ready for the potential conflicts of future developments. How about Alexanderplatz? (Kil 2000: 44)

The kind of conflicts Kil had in mind were largely to do with increasing migration, specifically from Eastern Europe into Berlin. The worst that could happen, Kil contended, was that Alexanderplatz would be turned into a top address of real estate development closed to new migrants and gradually pushing the present population to the city's periphery. It was in these debates, and in the Bürgervertretung's activities, that Alexanderplatz came to be summoned as a place constitutive of a particular East Berlin identity.

Importantly, however, rather than constructing a specifically East German subject position for themselves, the citizen group members lay claim to a 'comprehensive' and 'representative' view. That is, on the one hand, they self-consciously rejected the image of the East Berlin citizen opposed to the redevelopment of Berlin's eastern centre frequently invoked in planning debates and echoed in conversations I had with SenStadt administrators. This was the image of an activist who was East German first and citizen second, who had lived in the area for years, if not decades, and who was now anxious not to lose his privileged living space. Sometimes, such a person was believed to be a backward-looking socialist or an elderly member of the PDS, the socialist party, rejecting everything 'Western' and wishing 'to preserve Alexanderplatz as a GDR museum'.

The following excerpt from the text evaluating citizens' letters regarding the proposed design expresses such an elision between 'subjective', 'emotional' sentiment, an Eastern identity and an alleged anti-development stance:

> [The letters] mirror, aside from a general rejection of radical changes, worries about a loss of identity.... Alexanderplatz is regarded by 'East Berliners' as the centre of East Berlin. The redesign of East Berlin's centre in the '60s and '70s is understood as part of both an individual and a collective history of the citizens of the former GDR. [However] [a]ny assessment of the historical appropriateness ... of the [proposed] design must consider that developments in urban design within city centres rarely preserve given structures. Development is always a process of creating and changing. The rebuilding of Alexanderplatz in the '60s and '70s also consciously destroyed and changed numerous old structures ... [The proposed design] attaches itself to the layers of the older urban design history.... Decisions concerning how to deal with existing buildings are never right or wrong; rather, they are orientated towards different design objectives.[46]

In this view, East Berliners considered particular places and buildings to be vehicles for transporting glimpses of an otherwise unattainable past – a past that is retrospectively romanticized. Their protest in the face of proposed 'development' comes to be seen as a way of coping with the collapse of a future that is irrevocably past.

I suggest that an ascribed or self-conscious East German identity worked effectively to close down the political contestation entailed by citizens' actions. Yet the citizens I got to know seemed all too aware of the peculiar,

stereotype which conflates an East Germanness with a particular consciousness and *Ostalgie*, that notorious nostalgia for the East. They did not
recognize themselves in this image. Another document, the group's membership list, which Zimmer showed me in one of our conversations, served
to underscore this point. It demonstrated that not all the members were
from East Berlin. The summoning of additional perspectives was imagined
to result in a more comprehensive outlook and alter perceptions of the
group by outsiders.[47]

Instead of understanding the citizen group as consisting of people with
an unambiguous shared identity and putting forth an 'alternative' vision, I
argue that what comes to appear as the unified point of view is better seen
as part of the process of constructing a common subject position as citizens, through people's interaction with each other and with more powerful
groups (Gregory 1998). This subject position is constituted around shared
grievances, and in the terms of a Latourian *Dingpolitik*, thereby became
both constituted by, and constitutive of, their common matter of concern,
Alexanderplatz. Public discussions, the citizen group's regular meetings
and other participatory events may be seen to have helped in formulating,
on the one hand, the group as a kind of collective actor capable of having an
opinion and, on the other, Alexanderplatz as an object that one could have
an opinion about. Thus, aside from rejecting the image of the East German
protester, the citizen group members engaged, on the other hand, in a work
of objectification that would seem to play down their own experience-based
knowledge of Alexanderplatz in favour of techno-scientific fact.

In formulating themselves as an initiative, I suggest that the Bürgervertretung sought to adopt a specific *expert* perspective on Alexanderplatz.
This was the planners' comprehensive vision, their notorious God's eye
view, considered characteristic of the profession since its inception (Albers
1997; Ladd 1990; Rabinow 1989). It was achieved through the diverse studies and reports – on the environment, traffic, the social and the general
feasibility of the Kollhoff plan – which together with the maps and drawings served to both problematize the space of Alexanderplatz and govern it,
by accumulating knowledge that would allow planners to act on the square.
The Bürgervertretung was construed as similarly comprehensive. They
were not, as one of the members noted, a '*Kiez* initiative' (that is, an initiative defined by and confined to the specific neighbourhood, the *Kiez*) but
aimed to deal with the 'superordinate' ('*das Übergeordnete*').

Whether citizens' comments are sanctioned as relevant is to some extent determined within a whole set of notions, classifications, and criteria
sanctioned by planners and administrators (see also Abram 1998, 2001).
Although professedly open to citizens' suggestions, administrators still apply their very own evaluation criteria. Once, in a conversation, a SenStadt
planner expressed his desire to return to a perspective that was spontane-

ous and innocent like that of an ordinary citizen. As a planner, he would have to wrap his judgement in planning prose. Yet, the same administrator asserted that for citizens' comments to qualify, a simple 'This is rubbish!' would not suffice. It would register as disapproval; but the procedures were about 'quality not quantity'. In exchanges with administrative planners, architects and other official experts, people thus struggle over just how to frame the object in question.

Abu-Lughod's warning not to 'romanticize resistance' (1990) by understanding it always as a failure of systems of power seems pertinent here. An analysis of the Alexanderplatz citizen group does indeed tell us more about 'forms of power and how people are caught up in them' (Abu-Lughod 1990: 42). Notions of resistance, wedded to an idea of power as domination, would indeed be inadequate to comprehend the manner in which people sought to contest and modify the relations of power in which they saw themselves implicated (cf. Rose 1999: 279). Time and again I was struck by the citizen initiative's insistence on rational, scientific and objective argument. They sought to present themselves not only as experienced, i.e., as residents with an experience of living in this place, but also as knowledgeable. Similar to the German environmentalists studied by Berglund, people might have been all too aware that 'emotional cries of moral outrage are not responded to in the same way as charges of procedural incompetence in the law or technical-scientific reports' (1998: 156–7).

Citizens seek to assert themselves in a world that largely considers 'the rational' and 'the emotional' to be what exhausts the constitution of the human subject (Overing 1985). In a context where claims can easily be dismissed on the grounds of being subjective, emotional, nostalgic or as reflecting the St. Florian's principle, and where dispassionate, expert and objective argument is explicitly valued, it should come as no surprise that people seek to inhabit the latter categories. With astonishing verve, these citizens – some of whom were experts – sought to adopt a language and rational critical stance reminiscent of a Habermasian world. In a sense, these citizens claimed qualities for their perspective that administrators and government planners like to claim for themselves. They were not simply buying into an official planning discourse, however. Rather, adopting such language was an expedient tactic: they governed their perspective in order to take part in the debate.

Legitimate Concerns

One day, as I was strolling across Alexanderplatz, I met Herr Müller, one of the citizen group members, and we briefly stopped and talked. Müller was in a hurry; he was on his way to the bank – one of the few reasons for him to visit Alexanderplatz today. Alexanderplatz was not a destination for the Sunday walks with his wife on which the couple keenly observed how Berlin was changing. The square was no longer 'a place to go to', as Müller had put it in a previous conversation, but merely one 'to walk across'.

This personal disinvestment, it seemed, had paralleled his withdrawal from the Alexanderplatz citizen group after the Kollhoff plan had been legally sanctioned. Over the years of planning and decision-making regarding Alexanderplatz, the citizen group registered some achievements, including the preservation of residential blocks earmarked for destruction, an increase in space for housing, and a decrease in the number of high-rise buildings. Nevertheless, they felt that the developers' interests had in the end outweighed those of the population. Thomas had lamented in a conversation with me that their group had never managed to propose a powerful image for Alexanderplatz that could compete with the Kollhoff plan; their critique had always remained constricted by the plan.

I now asked Herr Müller whether he had heard about the recent signing of the contracts between the Berlin planning administration and the prospective investors, which had been widely reported in the newspapers. 'Everything was just a mantle of democracy,' Müller surmised. The citizens could not have prevented this outcome, he thought: 'We don't have to reproach ourselves for anything'. Those in charge – the administrators and politicians – might, however, for they appeared to have brushed aside the glaring problems with the Kollhoff plan that the group had sought to bring to their attention.

Participatory events gave an air of legitimacy to the decisions made, and some citizens felt themselves merely appropriated in this way. They did not doubt the formal legality of the practices involved, but were concerned about what was deemed to be irresponsible and, to some extent, immoral conduct on the part of those who claimed to act and speak in the name of the citizenry (Pardo 2000). As possibilities for a substantive appraisal of the plans seemed increasingly constrained, a large part of the citizen group's critique revolved around issues of government itself, lamenting the neglect of 'traditional democratic desiderata' (Appadurai 2002: 45). Framed in a language of transparency and democracy, it invoked the notion of a *Demokratiedefizit* ('democratic deficit') in relation to planning procedure. The concept involves a perception of the parliamentary system as insufficiently representative of ordinary people's views. They are being left out, it is thought, in favour of select, powerful interests.

Whilst the public was, in the view of citizen activists, very real, the attention to the public's will was not. Importantly, they imagined their agenda to reach beyond the interests of individual members, and their group to be the nucleus of a larger entity. For example, they claimed that 'most' or 'hundreds' of residents had backed their pleas for a 'reasonable' planning concept. Whatever concessions their efforts might have brought from planners were not effected by the group alone: 'There were societal forces at work, too,' Herr Müller commented. Invoking large quantifiers, percentages and numbers could seem crucial to the group's self-understanding as somehow standing in for a broader 'public'. These idioms indicated the magnitude of the support received and echoed, in a sense, the promise of the opinion poll (Osborne and Rose 1999; Rose 1999). By conceiving of democratic decision-making as the expression of public sentiment, and of themselves as representing a 'majority' (of the public), these citizens could claim that the planning administration's decision, by neglecting the majority's will, was illegitimate.[48]

A public imagined larger than the sum of citizens who made themselves heard was similarly a part of the administrators' reckoning. However, this public was effectively considered to be in silent agreement with the proposed plan. For the administrators I talked to, citizens' grievances were largely unfounded. They were partly thought to reflect the difficulties that many East Germans had experienced after unification as well as all their grand expectations of democracy. Invoking his experience of citizens' protest from his days in the 1980s Kreuzberg administration, a SenStadt administrator I interviewed emphasized that he had always been open to citizens' concerns; but negotiations foundered on people's apparent misunderstanding of parliamentary democracy:

> I always thought it was a shame that some citizen initiatives said: 'It's all nonsense what you are doing!' ... This doesn't work. Then we would need a change in the system. I'm not opposed to that ... [But] what we do in the administration is weighing up – as it says in the statute book: *miteinander, gegeneinander, untereinander* ('with one another, against one another, amongst one another'). Wonderful! – and subsequently draw the appropriate conclusion, which can also be communicated. Already this, I think, is quite an achievement.

The citizens I met did not feel that they had misunderstood the enlightened democratic principles East Germans were encouraged to embrace after unification (Borneman 1994: 112, following Weck 1992). Rather, they felt they had moved quite effortlessly from one 'system' to another. However, the new system could seem unlike the 'just' society that the ideology of the market and (real) democracy was proclaimed to bring about.

Legitimacy, I suggest, was not simply a question of numbers but, more importantly, a moral question. Administrators were at pains to explain that their task was not to question the political system but to weigh and balance opinions, and to translate them into the categories of the common good. Whilst appreciating this supposedly neutral stance, the citizen initiative's members perceived the process of weighing up as skewed and repeatedly referred to it as 'weighing away'. As Herr Zimmer, put it in a conversation with me, to be a citizen meant, 'I can say a lot. I can say everything but ... in the end, everything is being weighed..., the economic aspects, the population's objections, environmental concerns and whatever plays a role. And the economy goes like this,' he said lowering one hand, 'and the rest like that,' lifting the other. His gesture conjured the imagery of Justice, weighing different concerns blindfolded and regardless of a person's social standing. Only in this case, Justice had apparently peeped out from behind her blindfold and failed to be impartial.

When administrators gathered and weighed up citizens' views, they saw themselves as arbiters of the public good. The public good, just like the seemingly self-evident urban design objectives and, most of all, the Kollhoff plan served as framing devices (cf. Strathern 2002). For citizen group members, however, the close involvement of private developers in the competition and planning procedures seemed one of the chief reasons why citizens' opinions were given so little weight. Their critique invoked an ideal of the state – one protective of its citizens, prioritising their welfare and defending the common good. Now, the state had apparently forgone its responsibilities, and the power wielded by the investors was both elusive and unaccountable. The apparent bias in the law resulted in a sense of injustice (Baxstrom 2008: 90). Instead of controlling the investors' profit-making interests, SenStadt had incorporated these into the frame for Alexanderplatz's development.

From this perspective, the Kollhoff plan amounted to no more than a specification of the number of towers and square metres necessary for the best possible yield. Perhaps, what was at issue was less a different understanding of democracy than a different understanding of the object in question, Alexanderplatz.

A Citizenly Engagement with Place

The participative events organized by SenStadt to develop the 'construction plan' for Alexanderplatz required citizens to reflect outwards – or aesthetically – on the proposed design. (When they gave the impression they were not doing this, people were asked to scrutinize their motivations and the nature of their interests.) I suggest that, rather than reflecting outwards, what many of the citizens did was to reflect inwards, or on themselves and their relation to Alexanderplatz. The citizens doubted that the investors' relationship to this place entailed the same sense of responsibility that they themselves felt. It could seem that, for the investors, Alexanderplatz was merely a piece of land, which could be built on and from which profits could be reaped. The citizens' relationship to Alexanderplatz was conceived rather differently, but as one bestowing entitlements no less. Theirs was a demonstration of a distinctly 'citizenly' engagement with place.

I find useful Andrew Barry's genealogical double take on the figure of the demonstrator: on the one hand, emergent in the mid-nineteenth century, we find the political demonstrator as a member of a mass of political subjects; on the other hand, there is also the medieval demonstrator in the anatomy lecture theatre as a witness of scientific truths (Barry 2001: 177). The critical citizens I consider were both keen to reveal a political injustice and to demonstrate the failure of the knowledge produced by the planners regarding the best design for Alexanderplatz. Indeed, in the light of Alexanderplatz's blatant disintegration, the citizens' investment in this debate was as much about their political rights as about finding a design that would sustain the kind of urban sociality they saw dissolving around them.

Two notions have been salient in descriptions of people's relationship to place in contemporary Berlin and in Germany, more generally. These are *Heimat* and identity. *Heimat*, as Borneman notes, is an untranslatable: '[*Heimat*] denot[es] habitat, locality, birthplace, homeland, and native place.... [T]o lose one's Heimat is to lose not only one's home but also some of the central referents of German personhood that define familiarity and the conditions in which one feels secure' (1997: 93–4). In post-unification Berlin, as Borneman observes, *Heimat* has become profoundly ambiguous. This ambiguity was mirrored in the comment of an engineer in the RKA, Frau Fürstenau, who was in her late thirties. Reflecting on the debate around Alexanderplatz in the 1990s, she told me that East Germans' sense of *Heimat* has been ruptured with unification and that, as a result, many people began to view places like Alexanderplatz as embodiments of a particular *Lebensgefühl* ('feeling of life'). Although she sympathized with those people who wished to preserve Alexanderplatz – a place of which she had fond childhood memories – she considered it troublesome if they attached their identity to the material world rather than, as she put it, finding it within themselves.

Such a sense of attachment to place appeared to emerge from the citizens' letters addressed to the administration during the planning process for Alexanderplatz. Official evaluations of these letters identified the authors' supposed worry about identity. 'Identity' has become a staple in the vocabulary of architects, developers and local governments, and an important aspect of urban regeneration schemes (James 2003). Terms such as identity must be considered at best ethnographic concepts, and at worst simplistic renditions of a complex sense of place. In the 1990s, planners, administrators, politicians and other experts were preoccupied with (re)establishing what they considered Berlin's identity, especially as regards the design of what has been designated Berlin's historical centre (Bodenschatz 1995). It is apparently thought that identity, too, can be planned. Only that planners, as noted in Chapter II, now found themselves confronted with people's own self-conscious sense of identity, intimately related to an authentic and experiential knowledge of the city, which appeared at odds with the schemes devised by official planning bodies.

I argue that what has been dismissed in Berlin's restructuring of the eastern centre were not just claims to identity but also claims to what may be termed 'societal property'. In our first telephone conversation, Müller had introduced himself as an *Ureinwohner* ('native') of Alexanderplatz – a term he occasionally repeated. At first, 'the native' seemed a pun on the ethnographer's endeavour to study Berlin. But I think it was also a claim of autochthony and a demonstration of a specific kind of relationship to Alexanderplatz. Müller and his family had lived at Alexanderplatz since 1969. Securing their apartment had been a difficult undertaking. For years, he commuted between his workplace in Berlin and a small town in Brandenburg where his young wife and children lived. They were thrilled when they finally received the message that they had been allocated a newly built apartment in Berlin. 'The sun was shining' for them. In the 1990s, the Müllers had gained lifelong tenancy, but still worried about the threat of renewed displacement. His attempts to keep a close eye on the immediate environment, described in Chapter III, and his engagement in the citizen group might well be understood as a desire to direct or affirm a particular kind of future living.[49]

Müller insisted that his citizenly activities had nothing to do with reclaiming privileges he might have lost with the disappearance of the GDR. His involvement, he suggested, had been an expression of his sense of being both a 'proper' member of society, a citizen, both in an expressedly political sense and as a resident, and as such, responsible for this place: 'This is my living environment. This is Berlin for me!' His relationship to Alexanderplatz had developed through observing and experiencing how the new socialist capital took shape. The 1960s in Berlin were the period of *Aufbau* – a period of intense construction and reconstruction, so central to the self-legitimation of the young socialist state 'resurrected from ruins and turned towards the future', as the GDR national anthem proclaimed. There was the television tower, gradually growing into sky, a process that Müller had captured in plenty of photographs:

> I saw the TV tower growing ... how it got taller and taller, and how the cupola was put on it. Naturally we went to watch that. It's clear that you identify with something like that ... and with a lot of what was built around Alexanderplatz. Why should I move away? A lot of it is a piece of [my] life ('*Leben*') or experience ('*Miterleben*') ... about which one was happy and of which one was also a little proud.

Examining the controversies surrounding the post-unification property restitution in East Germany, the East German writer Daniela Dahn (1994) emphasizes the importance of *Besitz* ('possessions') in the GDR, in the absence of legally recognized private *Eigentum* ('property'). East Germans, she suggests, had developed a sense of possession concerning, for instance, the houses in which they lived. Her observations are evocative of Humphrey's (2002) notion of 'personal property' in the context of socialist Mongolia. However, following reunification, these possessions received no legal recognition. Many East Germans found themselves, though not disowned, dispossessed and sometimes displaced.

Alexanderplatz was not a 'possession' or 'personal property' in this sense; yet, it might have been conceived of as property of a similarly elusive kind. The legal scholar Carol Rose (1994) suggests the term 'illusory property' to talk about a sense of property people may have, which is neither public nor private. Illusory property, she argues, 'involves the imaginative construction of property even where the law recognizes none' (1994: 274). Calling this property 'illusory' is problematic, however, suggesting that it is somehow 'unreal' compared to legal types. In reference to Alexanderplatz, I suggest that the notion 'societal property' is more apt.

Alexanderplatz was a prime (although late) example of the *Aufbau* pursued by the socialist state. *Aufbau* was a project claimed to involve – in action and spirit – all citizens. People were engaged in a project of building not just the capital city but socialist society itself – a project of 'exteriorising' themselves as proper socialist citizens. In this sense, the capital Berlin became the 'societal property' of each and every citizen. That is to say, whether in the *Aufbau* of 'Berlin – capital of the GDR' or in more mundane tasks such as the tending of the communal front gardens, the socialist state encouraged individual demonstrations of people partaking in socialist 'property'. With unification, there seems to be little scope for demonstrations of this kind. In the light of what I noted in Chapter III regarding perceived changes in Alexanderplatzes materiality, the citizen group members' work may have partly been an attempt to sustain or replace the sociality they saw disintegrating around them.

Both of the connotations of demonstration outlined by Barry – experimental displays ascertaining techno-scientific truths and manifestations of a democratic will – have political and ethical dimensions. This is pertinent to my analysis of Alexanderplatz as a particular instance of place contestation in the unified Berlin. Previously, I suggested that citizens' protest in urban planning matters must be seen as an effect of current concerns with transparency and participation in (disembodied) government. The discussion of the practices and processes through which citizenly action is made possible was expanded in this chapter. It cannot readily be squeezed into normative frameworks of rational debate but is infused with people's values, memories and senses of belonging to the place in question. Rather, it is a particular citizenly engagement with place. People sought to demonstrate a relation of *Heimat*, autochthony or societal property, of experience, responsibility or simply of citizenship, from which entitlements and obligations towards Alexanderplatz were felt to ensue.

There were multiple facets to people's engagement with Alexanderplatz, which – as with the claims to 'possessions' voiced by East Germans in property-restitution disputes – appear to have gone largely unrecognized in official debates. Whilst notions such as *Heimat*, autochthony and social property all have ethnographic salience, the citizenly engagement is not reducible to them. Claims to an experienced relation to the place in question figure importantly. Yet citizenly engagement with place is characterized precisely by an aim to be self-consciously rational (even if that may never be the kind of 'pure' rationality invoked by philosophers and political scientists) and by attaining an objective, consistent and knowledgeable relation to the place in question. In participation procedures, as in everyday actions, citizens demonstrated their peculiar experienced, responsible and knowledgeable relationship to the place as well as, to use Barry's words, the unacceptability of the planning administrators' and developers' actions (2001: 177).

To paraphrase Carol Rose (1994: 270), participation in the debate may be considered a persuasive activity, of citizens persuading others of their specific relationship to the place in question. These citizens endeavoured to persuade others of their ability to speak knowledgably and legitimately about Alexanderplatz and thus to assert their entitlement to determine what this place should become in the future. This was a question of belonging in a double sense: of how people belong to Alexanderplatz and how Alexanderplatz belongs to them.

Chapter VI

A Robust Square

In this chapter, Alexanderplatz unfolds through a project initiated by a group of social workers that worked with young people in the square. The project sought to constitute Alexanderplatz as a *Platz für junge Menschen*. This was a play on words: Alexanderplatz was to be both a public *Platz*, or 'square', and somewhere where there was a *Platz*, or 'place', for young people. I suggest that 'Alexanderplatz: a place for young people' was a demonstration, in the sense of 'making visible a phenomenon to be witnessed by others' (Barry 2001: 178), similar to the efforts of the Bürgervertretung. In this case, it was to make a strong claim regarding the dire need to find a legitimate place for young people populating the city's public spaces from which they are increasingly expelled. As a public square, Alexanderplatz of course constitutes an archetypal site of political protest and demonstrations of this kind. There is, however, another, more recent sense of demonstration, discussed by Barry (2001: 178), which is the technical demonstration, or *demo* of 'what can be done', which would seem to offer a fitting entry here. I would add that there can be a distinct temporality to the phenomena that political demonstrations invoke. Seen in this way, 'Alexanderplatz: a place for young people' was to make explicit the potentiality contained in the square (Hirsch 1995), by invoking both counterfactual and plausible futures.

The chapter also offers a fresh look at the articulation of 'the social' in city planning. It contrasts the perspectives of the youth workers with that of the city planners who were busy implementing the new vision for Alexanderplatz. I suggest that planners' and youth workers' respective visions entail different notions of 'the social' and how it could and should be made to reflect in the materiality of the city. Planners envisioned a 'robust', plain public square that would serve as a neutral background to a variety of uses. In contrast, the youth workers' vision for Alexanderplatz was a proposal for a kind of 'social' robustness where the specific needs and desires of the square's different user groups would be built, quite literally, into the urban design.

In this ethnography, the social figures in a number of ways: for example, as relations between people and as people's activities, which together create the inherently social space of Alexanderplatz. The social is also seen as the heterogeneous diversity of society, which is imagined to be constituted by many different groups of people that encounter each other in a public square. Finally, the social is conceived as a quality of planning, which is summoned, for example, through forms of popular participation. The chapter thus does not define the social as much as it seeks to set out a range of different configurations of the social in relation to the discourses of planning and of youth work. I examine how these various configurations of the social both provoke and overdetermine people's actions (Rose 1999). My argument critically engages recent scholarly claims that the idea of 'the social' is in demise and that its hold on the political imagination is weakening (Rose 1999: 136; see also Ingold 1996). In this light, the activities of the Berlin youth workers might be seen as a scramble for recognition in a world where their specific expertise appears increasingly redundant. However, I want to challenge this assumption. I suggest that a concern with the social has never disappeared from the discourse on city planning. What we see arising, therefore, is a *new* 'social question',[50] that is, a specific reworking of the problematic of the social in planning.

A concern with the social was at the heart of Alexanderplatz's redesign during the twentieth century. In the 1920s, Berlin's planning director Martin Wagner sought to bring social enhancement to the underprivileged East, eternalized in Alfred Döblin's novel *Berlin Alexanderplatz*, through a rationalized scheme for a world city square. Socialist planning similarly constructed Alexanderplatz as a model, but this time for GDR cities and as expressive of a future socialist society (Hain 1992: 57; Kuhle 1995). This society enacted itself in the parades and festivals that ran past, through, or ended in Alexanderplatz, until that last large demonstration of political dissatisfaction on 4 November 1989, which lead to the breakdown of the socialist regime. The Kollhoff plan developed in the 1990s has similarly been seen to contain a new socio-spatial order to be imposed on Berlin's eastern centre (Kil and Kündiger 1998).

There are, however, alternative imaginings of a peculiarly 'social' Berlin, which are relevant, here, such as Berlin's declaration as a Child and Youth Friendly City,[51] particularly responsive to that constituency's needs and requirements. This was one of the images that provided a context for the youth workers' actions. My focus is on youth workers' interaction with the domain of planning. I will show how in their project 'young people' emerged as a token for the kind of social diversity which, in turn, has come to stand for a particular kind of public sphere.

I first learned about the youth workers' initiative in the RKA planning office. In 2001, when the building works for the new Alexanderplatz had not yet started, SenStadt began to prepare an additional design competition for the open space that would comprise the square in the future. In this context, RKA staff had arranged a meeting with a youth worker who held a position with the title *Platzmanager* ('Square Manager') to discuss the prospects for young people's facilities at the square. I had noticed these facilities before – a beach-volleyball field and a container of the kind used in building sites embellished with bright graffiti – but without grasping the implications of their presence. The *Platzmanagement* ('Square Management') had been established partly as an institution that could negotiate with planners and investors the integration of young people's needs into Alexanderplatz. The head of the RKA encouraged me to pursue this contact. He felt that the youth workers' concern with the 'real life' at Alexanderplatz, particularly that of marginalized groups, had more appeal for an anthropologist than dreary administrative work.

To be sure, I would occasionally feel a similarity between the language and concerns of youth workers and those I had myself as an ethnographer. I soon sensed that what the youth workers expected from me was rather a different expert perspective. As Heiko, the Square Manager, put it: 'We are always interested in exchanging views with other disciplines.' Heiko introduced me to the larger association of outreach youth work projects, the Arbeitsgemeinschaft Alexanderplatz (AG Alex), working in the Alexanderplatz area. Over the following months, I began to participate in some of their activities, attend the monthly meetings and spent many afternoons with the youth workers and young people in the square.

In its attempt to confirm young people's legitimate presence in public space, 'Alexanderplatz: a place for young people' partly instantiates a global effort to involve young people in the planning not only of playgrounds and youth clubs but also of spaces that are not exclusively for them but which they nevertheless use (e.g., Driskell 2002; Simpson 1997). Such efforts may be interpreted as attempts to govern young people's use of public space (Stratford 2002). More generally, they reflect the heightened significance of notions of participation in urban politics and planning, which have accompanied the new formation of neo-liberal government (Abram 2000; Appadurai 2002; Nelson and Wright 1995b). Commenting on recent developments in Brazil, Caldeira and Holston suggest that there has been an observable move from technocratic modernist planning to neo-liberal urban government. In the latter, they argue, 'the social is [no longer] imagined as something for the plan to produce, but is rather something that already exists in an organized fashion.

This organization will be the basis for the creation of urban space...' (2005: 406). I argue that at stake (particularly in the case of Alexanderplatz) is not simply a broadening of neo-liberal governmentality under a participatory guise, but a shift in the nature of ideas about 'the social' in relation to political and technical processes, more generally (Barry 2001; Nowotny et

Figure 13: Container in Alexanderplatz

al. 2001). This shift has filtered into urban policy and planning practice. The youth workers proposed what I call, borrowing a term used in the recent literature on scientific knowledge production (Barry et al. 2008; Nowotny et al. 2001; Strathern 2005), a 'social robustness' for Alexanderplatz. There, planning seeks authority beyond its own domain, in reference to 'society'. The social is not to be shaped by, but to be integrated in, the urban design. What I point to, here, is a particular kind of aesthetics of urban form that is supposed to bring together different knowledge practices as well as design objectives.

This chapter elaborates on a fortunate parallel between the metaphor of 'robustness' used in science studies and the ethnographic terms of Berlin's planners. This allows me to go beyond current appreciations of participative politics in the context of urban planning. I show that such politics involve a rethinking of the relation not simply between state and citizen but also between society, technical expertise and space.

The Place of Young People

[Our aim] is to shape Alexanderplatz as a square that is for children and young people, too.... Of course, Alexanderplatz is a square for people who shop there, who have businesses there, for the Deutsche Bahn, for architects, and for *Imbiss* stalls and festivals.... But it is also a square for

children who live there, and for youths. And it is also a public space for youths who want to create their centre of life in such squares – whether that's temporary, during puberty, whether that's a philosophy of life, or whether it's part of your life culture. [It should no longer be] a taboo or bad for young people … to say: 'This is also our square!'
(Michael, AG-Alex participant)

About a month after our first encounter in the RKA, on a chilly afternoon in November 2001, the *Platzmanager*, Heiko, took me on a tour around Alexanderplatz. Whilst waiting at our agreed meeting point, the World-Time Clock, I glanced at the post–September 11 pleas for peace – 'Peace is the path, not the goal…' – which people had stuck up on the clock's pillar. Some of these posters had been scribbled over, their edges were torn and rain had washed out their bright colours. There was also a call for a *Mahnwache*, a type of picket peculiar to Germany and intended to remind and admonish, to be held regularly in Alexanderplatz over the following months. To me, the posters and the activities to which they invited now seem to hint at the key quality of Alexanderplatz that the youth workers, too, treasured: its publicness.

On our tour, Heiko highlighted features unnoticed by many other people I talked to during my research. Heiko, a West Berliner in his thirties, had formerly worked as a youth worker in both West and East Berlin, including on projects that familiarized him with the specific problems faced by East German youth after unification. Heiko was a generous repository of knowledge about youth work and Alexanderplatz, but his point of reference was not just the young people, planners or developers. His approach could appear 'para-ethnographic' (Holmes and Marcus 2005), seeking to glimpse the apparently complex reality of Alexanderplatz with a critical eye. To get a sense of people's diverse uses of Alexanderplatz, he would regularly spend time in the square, observing and talking to people. It was an attempt to capture and conjoin in the process of managing Alexanderplatz those diverse interests vested in it, public and private, local business people, consumers, developers and young people.

Now, when drawing attention to the different surfaces of the square, Heiko spoke not of the unseemly patchwork that so upset the planners, but of skateboarders' and BMX cyclists' preference for the smooth paving along the tram tracks and in front of the hotel. Heiko distinguished between spaces where youths were permitted and those where they were not – the public, the private and the semi-public spaces safeguarded by discriminatory practices. He showed me the beach-volleyball field and the brightly sprayed 'youth service area' which he presented as pieces of ingenuity, constructed under private sponsorship and, significantly, with considerable input from young people. Heiko recounted how they had developed the ideas, helped build the facilities during a week of hard work and bad weather, and later assumed responsibility for them. (The adjacent streetball field was set up earlier, sponsored by the multi-national firm Nike.)

When I commented on the diversity of people in Alexanderplatz, Heiko was delighted. For him, the presence of East and West Germans going about their daily shopping, of so-called punks and homeless people, of people with different cultures and worldviews, made for a positively urbane place. This space would vanish, however, once the building works in Alexanderplatz commenced. Heiko pointed out the lines of the planned buildings; they would 'swallow' the Container, the lawns where people sat during the summer, and the bench outside the department store. Instead of cordoning off areas for young people, he envisaged Alexanderplatz as a place appealing to all: young and old, rich and poor, punks, skaters and ordinary youths.

The initiative 'Alexanderplatz: a place for young people' was conceived in the late 1990s in the context of increasingly stringent urban policies, and Alexanderplatz's designations as a 'dangerous place'. To recap, at that time, Alexanderplatz had been declared a 'dangerous place' – a label applied by the Berlin police force to areas that appear to display a statistically disproportionate number of crimes. Rendered statistically, occasional events become a permanent quality of place and everyone, including young people, becomes potentially suspect. In 'dangerous places', police powers to carry out random identity checks are significantly enhanced.

Youth workers considered such controls unjustified and disconcerting acts of criminalization. They frustrate what is now a defining tenet of youth work. In this view, illicit behaviours are not indicators of a criminal character but part of the transition from childhood to adulthood: adolescence. Historically speaking, as adolescent 'delinquents' became thinkable and susceptible to the reforming powers of specialized welfare services, a social imaginary of 'youth as problem' was naturalized (Benninghaus 1999; Gillis 1981; Ruddick 1996). It was by being rebellious that 'youth' put itself onto the scholarly agenda after the Second World War, and particularly in the 1960s, as a distinct category of people to be reckoned with, spelling trouble, rebelliousness and violence (Benninghaus 1999; Gillis 1981). Repeatedly mobilized in twentieth-century thinking about young people (Valentine et al. 1998; Wulff 1995), in the wake of German unification the notion of 'youth as problem' seemed to be confirmed by right-wing extremism and racist attacks on the part of youth (Stock 1994; Thiele and Taylor 1998).

The youth workers I met struggled with the notion of youth as a problem. Whilst it provided one *raison d'être* for their work, querying this notion was another. Most of the AG Alex's members practised outreach social work, termed *Straßensozialarbeit* or *Streetwork*, in Germany. The rationale of streetwork, I was told, was to reach those who appear in need of support where they are, 'the street', and to enter a 'partnership' with them, rather than forcing them into an institutionalized setting. In the view of so-called streetworkers, 'the street' (parks, shopping malls, Alexanderplatz) has remained significant in young people's lives (cf. Hecht 1998; Matthews et al. 2000). Street-based social work has yielded to the fact that those nominally marginalized – not only young people, but also the homeless and drug addicts – have continued to occupy urban space in a fashion that may contradict dominant spatial meanings and, by implication, definitions of social categories themselves (Ruddick 1996).

Streetwork has been an attempt to govern those who evade being governed. Crucially, however, its 'clientele' can always walk away. When streetworkers approached young people in the street, they perceived themselves as 'guests' entering a space that was considered, if only temporarily, to be young people's own. This was conceived as inherently social space. Young people created it around themselves; it emerged by virtue of their being there (Corsín Jiménez 2003; Munn 1996).

The district council of Mitte, where Alexanderplatz is located, responded favourably to the youth workers' criticism of the alarming controls of young people in the square. In 1998, a resolution was passed affirming that Alexanderplatz should remain a place meaningful for young people. Surveys confirmed this perception, suggesting that there were – in addition to the 230 children and youths living in Alexanderplatz's vicinity – about 500 young people from all over Berlin who used Alexanderplatz as a meeting point. The AG Alex was asked to devise measures that would sustain Alexanderplatz's attractiveness for young people. Subsequently, the Platzmanagement was set up to provide an interface between young people, youth workers, potential sponsors, the administration and private developers. For the AG Alex the competition for Alexanderplatz's open space provided another chance to press forth their initiative 'Alexanderplatz – a place for young people'.

In passing hours and days with youth workers and young people in Alexanderplatz, I noted a common narrative of explaining the square's popularity. It evoked notions of centrality and accessibility. Crisscrossed by numerous bus, tram and train lines, Alexanderplatz could be reached from almost anywhere in Berlin. 'Everyone is here', a young man offered, 'it's in the centre and, therefore, gravity is stronger.' On many days, youths would sit outside the Container chatting, playing football, or watching the bustle around Alexanderplatz's 'Fountain of the People's Friendship', a reminder of GDR times. Inside, young people played billiards and listened to music blasting out of a battery-powered radio. When nothing was happening, you could always 'go for a walk', as the young men I encountered often did. In the shops, you could check out CDs, mobile phones or clothes, or watch –

as it happened during my fieldwork – the World Cup on large television screens. In the winter, you could skate in an ice rink in front of the department store, where many of the young people now frequenting the Container had met for the first time. To get warm and to grab a cheap bite, you could go to Burger King. Michael, an administrator in Mitte's youth office who, when he was young, had hung out in Alexanderplatz, put it succinctly: 'There is always movement, something's always happening.... You can meet there and hang out, sit on the stairs, look about, eat ice cream, sunbathe, watch the skateboarders and the punks and their dogs in the fountain. So there is, as in all public squares, a little bit of entertainment value.'

Youth workers emphasized that young people's uses of Alexanderplatz differed in ways related to their life situation and the expectations they brought to bear on this place. For punks, Alexanderplatz was both a social space and a workplace; for others, it was a space of leisure. Deserted on weekends, it offered space for BMX cyclists and skaters to try out their tricks. The teenage girls, Heiko suggested, found in Alexanderplatz an escape from their parents' world and the East Berlin suburbs where many of them lived. By contrast, for the young Kurdish men, Alexanderplatz was an entry into an unfamiliar world. Being in Alexanderplatz promised many things: chatter with friends; encounters with the opposite sex; playing volleyball; spotting 'famous' TV stars; bickering; dispelling loneliness; sometimes excitement; and sometimes boredom.

Both, young people's and youth workers' interpretations of young people's doings in Alexanderplatz took shape against the backdrop of a discourse on youth as a problem, which they were keen to reject. The youth worker Sylvia asserted that especially for the Kurdish youths, Alexanderplatz constituted a piece of *Heimat*, connoting a sense of home and belonging (Borneman 1997). Silvia, who would regularly check on the Container, accompany and counsel the youth that made use of it, told me that many of them had arrived in Germany as unaccompanied minors; for them, 'home' was currently a bare bedsit. These young men were not members of the foreign 'gangs' that caused alarm in the early 1990s by allegedly making Alexanderplatz their territory. Indeed, *Heimat* implied quite the opposite of such threatening appropriations.

The most compelling images used by youth workers to assert Alexanderplatz's significance for young people invoked ideas of community and public life. The young people here were not causing trouble, but rather were perfectly capable of tolerance and respect. The translation of young people's doings in Alexanderplatz as an expression of their wish 'to partake of public life' imputed purpose and direction to their actions. These young people did not do what is often considered typical of young people, 'hanging out' or simply 'doing nothing' (James 1986; Wood 1985). They were also not 'wasting time' – offending temporal sensibilities that arrived with capitalist notions of productivity (Thompson 1967). Instead, they performed an activity deemed as having potentially positive effects on their self-development.

In short, not unlike the ethnographer, youth workers claimed their understanding of Alexanderplatz to be derived partly from empirical observations. This was not a disinterested project. The images they invoked as Alexanderplatz's 'background potentiality' (Hirsch 1995), including social diversity, tolerance and public life, had a positive persuasiveness. The youth workers' ambition was to render this potentiality explicit and to sustain it in the face of the new plans that appeared to threaten their efforts. This ambition was perceived as inherently politicized, as it made the existence of youths and their specific life condition into a debatable object rather than simply a social fact (Barry 2001: 7). As such, it constituted an eternal point of contention within the AG Alex.

The following argument in an AG Alex meeting brought this issue into the open. It erupted over the question of whether a one-off workshop for streetwork projects aimed at working with 'youths in exceptional life situations' would be useful. One participant expected the workshop to bring an additional burden of paperwork. Noticeably exasperated, she commented: 'We're working *with* youths, not *about* youths!' The focus should be on doing groundwork, which was to say, on young people themselves. Especially the AG Alex, with its aim of influencing urban development process, she deemed a waste of precious time and energy. Once the building works at Alexanderplatz began, the punks would be forced out, and streetworkers would follow them wherever they moved, making Alexanderplatz irrelevant to their work. Some participants felt that by attempting to influence the planning for Alexanderplatz they overstepped a boundary and risked losing sight of their original realm of expertise: youth.

Networking Alexanderplatz

Heiko's office was a mid-sized, rather cramped room in a modernist block on Karl-Liebknecht-Straße just off Alexanderplatz. In his office, Heiko conducted not only his day-to-day work but also stored posters, spray cans and other materials used for publicity campaigns, and it was here that many of the preparations for the events organized by the AG Alex took place. There were shelves displaying books about Alexanderplatz and leaflets on streetwork and youth participation programs, a large table, office desks and a minimum of equipment, including a photocopier, two computers and a telephone. Communication technologies were vital to what Heiko considered one of his main tasks: networking.[52]

The idea of turning Alexanderplatz into a place for young people had soon proved to be a complex undertaking. Many of the other youth workers I talked to considered Heiko's new role to be challenging. Instead of taking sides, he had to mediate. As Ulrike, one of the AG Alex participants, once remarked, this was reflected not least in the way Heiko dressed. When taking on the job, Heiko shed his accustomed 'social worker outfit' and he was now more often seen wearing a suit. Dressing differently was an important part of embodying a position between what he felt were two distinct worlds: the world of youth work and young people for which he stood in, and the world of private business and administration where he sought support for the AG Alex's ideas. Wearing a combination of casual trousers, shirt and jacket, he thought, mirrored best his attempt 'to fit into both worlds and actually to be in neither of these worlds properly, but somewhere in between.' Clad in his hybrid outfit, Heiko came to embody the network which the telephone and Internet helped him establish by connecting the Platzmanagement's office to a world of public and private bodies and institutions.

The network was a term of self-description with considerable appeal. It described what was conceived of as an entity of a distinct kind, a new form of organization and, importantly, an activity (cf. Riles 2000). Heiko's work appeared to consist of incessant phone calls, appointments with private investors, business people at Alexanderplatz and administrators of various kinds whom he sought to persuade of the AG Alex's ideas. There was a public to be summoned for their cause. There was press to talk to, a so-called Infobox to be built, publicity campaigns to be organized and potential sponsors and supporters to be found. Networking had become a fashionable term, as Michael from Mitte's district office explained. It could simply mean sharing a photocopier or distributing flyers for each other. More specifically, Michael knew that it connoted 'the coacting of autonomous parts in clearly defined work relationships', a phrase he had gleaned from a course on modern management techniques. Such notions were self-conscious borrowings from organization studies to characterize his own and his colleagues' actions.

In this context, networking was thought to facilitate an even distribution of knowledge and to avoid wasteful duplication at a time of limited resources. Most youth workers attended countless workshops and regular meetings, imagined as arenas for information and knowledge exchange. In the AG Alex's meetings, for example, the participating youth-work projects would present themselves along with the focus of their work, the facilities at their disposal and the services they provided. A regularly updated timetable listed when and where the respective projects could be found in Alexanderplatz. Important in this context was, in Heiko's words, '*what* kind of work needs to be done *how,* and not *by whom.*'

An additional expectation was the strengthening of the AG Alex's cause. Presenting the AG Alex as a network, it was hoped, would give the participating projects and their demands more weight. In a publicity market for youth-work projects, the AG Alex had a joint stall, and people tending the stall promoted and represented, in the first place, the AG Alex and *not* the institutions employing them. Rather than a mere agglomeration of diverse projects, the AG Alex was presented as a distinct entity. In turn, at a time of diminishing funds for youth work the network was thought to offer protection. All of the network's parts were vital, it was argued, and none could be removed.

Alexanderplatz assumed a defining role within the AG Alex's network. It was to be both literally and metaphorically a platform. It served as a venue for joint events, including demonstrations, graffiti spraying and publicity markets. Youth workers recalled with excitement the summer camps held in Alexanderplatz during the late 1990s, which came with tents, a small swimming pool, a barbecue and a fireplace around which people sat singing songs. By holding these camps, youth workers had sought to call attention to the dire consequences of insufficient funding. They conjured up a worrisome future. Re-enacting a 'real' summer camp seemed particularly effective because it was so incompatible with Alexanderplatz, quite the opposite of what has come to be seen as a wholesome holiday destination for children. Simultaneously, it illustrated inventive and previously unimaginable uses for Alexanderplatz.

It was in these networked events that Alexanderplatz was enacted as the place of young people. There also emerged a different spatiality, where the network is not formed around that particular place but where the networked Alexanderplatz emerges *within* those relations. Alexanderplatz was to be an example of what could be achieved through networking. Shaping Alexanderplatz as a place for young people was regarded as an unusual experiment that required innovative means. Networking seemed innovative because it implied the alignment of what were perceived to be quite disparate actors and institutions around a particular site. Importantly, networking was felt to enable the youth workers to fight for their cause ('the place of young people in Alexanderplatz') in arenas previously beyond their reach. What I described above as hybridity refers to the sense that their network was capable of enjoining some of the distinct institutions and conceptual entities whose reification this book has examined: public and private, planners and citizens and so on. The beach-volleyball field, the Container and the numerous events for young people in Alexanderplatz would have been impossible without enlisting the support of numerous youth-work projects and, importantly, private sponsors and administrators.

People, institutions, telephones and communicative technologies, laws and information, containers and sand, spraying cans and footballs, all were gathered into the networked Alexanderplatz. At issue for AG Alex participants was perhaps less how a seemingly limitless network can be cut, to use Strathern's (1996) memorable phrase, than how it can be created in the first place and what it could be made to do.

Potentialities

For one afternoon in September 2002, Alexanderplatz became the venue for a publicity market for youth-work projects. Such events reflected the ongoing support that the AG Alex received from the local district council which gave permission for such events to be held. Aside from numerous stalls providing information on youth work in Berlin, there was a miniature football field, hip-hop music and break-dancing. Punks, together with streetworkers, manufactured large, wooden benches. Skateboarders showed off their skills on a huge half-pipe and a fence around a building site was given over to graffiti sprayers. This event condensed a broader effort to subvert negative images of young people. Punks were not idle but productive, and graffiti sprayers not destructive but creative. Removed from their usual time and space – the youth club, the skate park, the back streets and the darkness of the night – the doings of young people seemed transformed. These were not simply leisurely pastimes but skilful activities, which could appear spectacular and acceptable to adults too.

Through this event, Alexanderplatz came to demonstrate its perceived potential channelled by the youth workers' challenge to dominant conceptualizations of what social geographers have termed public space as 'adult' space (Holloway and Valentine 2000a; Valentine et al. 1998). Instead of confining young people to schools, kindergartens, playgrounds and youth clubs, the youth workers' ambition was to reposition young people as an unthreatening feature of public space. In an important sense, for youth workers, 'Alexanderplatz – a place for young people' was a confirmation of how young people disrupt common understandings of public space. Streetworkers' practices were claimed to grant legitimacy to young people's presence in public spaces, which they thought was often denied and increasingly jeopardized. As Ulrike, who worked for district Mitte's children and youth office, suggested:

> [Without our efforts] there would be neither a beach-volleyball field nor a meeting point for youth. The streetball field would be there because, through this, Nike can leave its mark on the square. Otherwise, I believe, this would be a 'dangerous place' – however one might imagine it. The police would carry out their duties; and whoever is noisy, stands out, or is complained about would be removed. Nobody would give it a thought. I

don't think that Kaufhof or Forum Hotel would ever think about the youths spending their free time outside their premises – unless they are a disturbance, then they would be removed. Therefore, I'd be very pessimistic.

This was a counterfactual but still ominous future. Spaces where young people can play, socialize, or simply be, I was told, were gradually disappearing in Berlin, as in other cities. Vacant lots had been built on and train stations and shopping malls were highly surveyed and staffed with guards who removed all 'non-consumers' and 'undesirables' from the premises. Streetworkers proffered a dystopian view of Berlin's future development. It partly echoed scholarly commentary regarding the privatization of public space in the neo-liberal city (Caldeira 2000; Davis 1990; Low 2000; 2006; Sorkin 1992), in which the assumed (past) congruence between material and metaphoric public space seems increasingly under threat (cf. Habermas 1989; Holston 1989; Sennett 1994). With the apparent extinction of the public street and square, public life too is soon expected to disappear. The new Alexanderplatz, the one envisioned by Berlin's planners, was imagined to be just another instantiation of an omnipresent progression towards privatization, exclusion and segregation.

In the RKA, the Platzmanagement's ideas found general support. Heiko initiated several meetings and discussions with the planners, in which they commented approvingly on his 'reasonable' outlook, explained to him the administrative ins and outs, and discussed alternative locations for the youth facilities. For his part, Heiko had incorporated planners' and developers' language into his repertoire – a strategy that he thought proved quite successful. Whilst it was Heiko's ambition to translate the youth workers' and young people's interests into those of private sponsors and developers, it remained crucial to be able to tell these interests apart. Social work has always conjoined public and private in different ways (Deleuze 1979: x). What the Platzmanagement sought to highlight was how an apparently public interest could be made to serve private (commercial) ends. For example, by creating Alexanderplatz as a place welcoming to young people one was simultaneously bringing a new generation of customers to the square.

And sometimes, the network had to be cut (Strathern 1996). Youth work, it was explained to me, could not be left to private businesses alone. Private businesses were seen to lack the human resources and expertise for assessing young people's requirements and, significantly, the specific commercial interests could also stand in the way of broader, public objectives. This was a qualified version of neoliberal urban management, where elements of neoliberal urban discourses interact with 'specific substantive or value orders' to create a city of 'actually existing neoliberalism' (Collier and Ong 2005: 14, citing Brenner and Theodore 2002). The state, its servants and those whose profession required them to work in the name of the public good still had to assume overall responsibility, if only by devising and supervising the implementation of youth welfare programs.

In his conversations with planners, Heiko had appropriated their concern with the value of 'urbanity'. For planners, the existing Alexanderplatz lacked a sense of clearly defined public space. To be made urbane, its emptiness needed to be filled (cf. Holston 1989; Stimmann 2001). However, in Heiko's view, urbanity was constituted within social practices rather than a given, tangible quality of place (cf. Corsín Jiménez 2003). Despite partial inroads and acceptance amongst planners, the potential that youth workers saw in Alexanderplatz thus differed sharply from the twin discourse of aesthetics and real estate so prominent in post-unification Berlin. In Heiko's view, Alexanderplatz fostered a public life all of its own. In the new Alexanderplatz, it would be displaced by the cafés, cinemas and similar attractions. The AG Alex's ideas self-consciously contradicted these commercial interests that they believed would determine the square's future shape. They suggested free toilets, multiple seating, sport and play facilities, and sites for streetwork services.

By contrast, for planners such provisions were clearly inimical to public interests. Young people were not part of the development potential that Alexanderplatz promised. As an East German administrator argued: 'In our system, land is too valuable. It has to be marketed.' As a major traffic node and a thoroughfare for hundreds of thousands of people per day, the planners emphasized, Alexanderplatz needed to be 'robust'. Robustness, in this view, was not only a technical category but also an aesthetic and an economic one. It referred to a plain, sturdy and largely undefined space and echoed the image of a well-proportioned 'European' square that had become a urban design ideal in Berlin (Stimmann 2001). What the AG Alex envisaged for Alexanderplatz was 'clutter', unpleasing to the eye and hampering other people's use of the square.

Experts and Citizens Revisited

In their appeals for young people's participation, youth workers invoked two notions in particular: the expert and the citizen. Whilst the expert called to mind ideas of difference and specificity, the citizen evoked sameness and equality. Both conferred legitimacy: the former buttressed the authority of young people's knowledge; the latter confirmed their right to be involved in planning processes. 'Children are their own experts,' some of the youth workers would say. Fathoming the distinct dispositions, tastes and desires of children and youths was considered to be intrinsically difficult for adults.

Instead of consulting self-styled experts on youth matters, one should let young people speak for themselves as individuals with an ability to know themselves and with a right to be consulted conferred on them qua citizens. Ulrike, an East German youth worker in Mitte district's Children and Youth Office, noted that in all the talk about citizen's participation in Berlin it had always been forgotten that children and youth were citizens, too.

Citizens' participation, as argued earlier, has come to be considered an indispensable requirement of German democracy, in general, and planning, in particular. Young people's right to participate was now similarly inscribed in the law. Youth workers regularly referred me to certain paragraphs in the Children and Youth Welfare Law, stating that young people ought to be consulted in all matters pertaining to them and in ways appropriate to their development. The law, it seemed, was felt to substantiate and legitimate their claims, and to make those look less like the 'crazy' ideas of a group of youth workers.

Importantly, both 'expert' and 'citizen' impute agency of a kind. To say that children and youths are agents has become a familiar assertion in the social sciences of late (Amit-Talai and Wulff 1995; Bucholtz 2002; Holloway and Valentine 2000b; James et al. 1998; Skelton and Valentine 1998). What we witness today, as James et al. note, is 'the rise of childhood agency, the transition from "the child" as an instance of a category to the recognition of children as particular persons' (1998: 6). Increasing emphasis is placed on children's rights, including the right to be consulted and the necessity for consent. Alexanderplatz as a place for young people needs to be seen as an inflection of this particular discourse on young people – co-constituted by legal texts, social theory and the practices of youth workers, situated ambivalently, between a desire to let young people speak for themselves and a continued requirement for representation.

Significantly, Alexanderplatz would be crucial in the shaping of young people *as* citizens. Ulrike told me that there had been recent attempts to involve children in the design of playgrounds. In this way, municipalities hoped to avoid splashing out on the latest 'pedagogically approved' equipment that children often found abhorrent. Another expectation was that children would feel less alienated from, and hence treat more respectfully, playgrounds in whose design they had participated. Participation, accordingly, induces a sense of 'property' in children: the playground becomes something to which they have a special relationship (Hann 1998: 5).

The shift from providing playgrounds *for* children to planning playgrounds *together with* children is intriguing not only for the ideas about the child and about property that it implies, but also for what it tells us about how citizens are imagined to be made. Playgrounds, it has been suggested, have been part and parcel of a project of forming proper citizens. Twentieth-century American playgrounds, for example, entailed specific spatial regimes (Gagen 2000). These were to facilitate children's development and to inculcate 'American ways' and expected forms of appropriate, gendered behaviour. Sport and play were considered ways of teaching ideas of fairness and justice constitutive of good citizenship (see also Norman 1991: 24–5). A similar notion, as Simon Schama (1987) notes, also informed a popular seventeenth-century Dutch 'genre of paintings known as *kinderspielen* ('children's games') [which] often showed the children playing in a market square or in front of public buildings, as if to demonstrate the connection between youthful pleasure and the development of a mature civic consciousness' (Worpole 2000: 88).

Significantly, the production of 'proper' citizens in playgrounds was not simply an effect of adult supervision and control, but also of self-reflection and the development of individual conscience (Rose 1999: 88). Playgrounds, in this view, were key to what may be described, à la Foucault, as a project of governing children – conducting their conduct as particular kinds of citizen subjects. The participation of children in the planning of playgrounds may similarly be considered an attempt to bestow on children a particular set of citizenly qualities and skills, albeit slightly different from those desired in the early twentieth century. What participation is assumed to foster is the ability to assess and articulate one's needs, desires and interests, to balance them with those of others and to exercise choice – in short, what it means to be an 'active citizen' (Cruikshank 1999; Rose 1999).

These are the terms in which the participation of young people has been thematized more widely in Germany in recent years. Not only is participation assumed to be *generally* ethical. Regarding young people, participation has come to be seen as a desirable way of equipping them with what are considered democratic skills, such as negotiating interests, accepting other people's opinions, finding compromises and taking responsibility for oneself and others. Teaching democracy became an explicit objective of German youth-work institutions in the aftermath of the Second World War period (Gillis 1981: 199). Now, it seems that young people as agents are encouraged to take matters increasingly into their own hands. Heiko's descriptions of the Platzmanagement's rationale evoked very similar ideas. Enabling youths to participate in democratic processes, teaching them about their rights and obligations, encouraging them to take on responsibility and to respect others in spite of differences were, in his view, essential aspects of a *politische Bildung* ('political education').

Such notions also underpinned the agenda of the Citizens' Foundation that gave support to the Platzmanagement. According to a spokeswoman and the foundation's leaflets, solidarity and self-responsibility were diminishing goods in contemporary society. This well-spoken lady, perhaps in her early sixties and with a background in literary studies, had felt rather alien during the inauguration party for the Container, one of the few times she had personally encountered the young people at Alexanderplatz. Age, class, appearance and language seemed to divide them. But when we discussed the foundation's project at Alexanderplatz, the spokeswoman noted emphatically that '*Führung heißt immer Selbstführung* ('Leading always means self-conduct')', stating a point on which both Weber and Foucault might have agreed with her (Gordon 1987). The aim was not to establish a relationship with, or to act directly upon, young people. Neither the youth workers nor the Foundation understood the welfare they practised as coercive or disabling. Rather, it was welfare that worked by example, reliant on the maximization of one's self-interest and on the capability and willingness of the citizen-subject to govern him- or herself (Cruikshank 1999).

As an exercise in *Selbstverwaltung* ('self-administration'), the Container epitomized this idea. So-called leadership seminars had prepared young people for taking responsibility for the Container. The Container had been the young people's own creation. They were in charge and established the rules. A sign in the entrance to the Container proclaimed that there were to be 'no drugs', 'no sex' and 'no weapons'. Decisions about most activities were made through negotiation; emphasis was placed on solving conflicts through verbal rather than violent means; and sometimes, 'general assemblies' were held to deal with particularly pressing issues. The young people I met appeared to appreciate these objectives. Those involved in realizing the project were very proud of their achievement. Others suggested that the Container, as both a project and a meeting point, had kept them from following a different, and what they felt was a contemptible, path – including drugs and crime. In an important sense, their comments pointed towards the ways in which these young people constructed their identities up against certain images of youth and citizens – images that they were encouraged either to embrace or to reject, but in whose production they themselves also played a part.

Perspectival Disparities

> First of all, there is a different language, and second, there is a different perspective. Do I have a building in the foreground or a human being?... The Platzmanagement was created to act as a catalyst, and ... to translate. Because this [difference] sometimes means that you can talk past each other without understanding what the other side means. (Heiko)

When examined through the lens of a Foucauldian notion of governmentality, social work and urban planning emerge as closely related projects.

Their birth is generally traced back to the same historical period and conceived of as entwined with the invention of 'the social' as a knowable, calculable and governable domain (Rabinow 1989; Rose 1999). Both appear to have sprung from a desire to shape and reform this domain, albeit through different techniques. Significantly, Foucault's studies of governmental rationalities aim not at demonstrating unity – or that all phenomena are reducible to 'government' or 'power' – but contingency and complexity (Rose 1999: 276). When I speak of both planning and youth work in reference to concerns with 'government', this is not to suggest that planners and youth workers make up a team in a tug-of-war pulling on the same end of the rope. More often, they feel themselves to be pulling in quite different directions. The disparities in perspective that members of these professions perceived to exist between each other seemed to make 'translation' necessary.

Youth workers and planners encountered each other and their different perspectives in meetings, workshops and panel discussions, such as the discussion on 'Alexanderplatz: Today, Tomorrow, the Day after Tomorrow' organized by the Platzmanagement in May 2002. For this occasion, youth workers, some administrators, a few journalists and other people interested in the topic gathered in the same public hall in Berlin's town hall where earlier irate residents had discussed the introduction of the tram into Rathausstraße. None of the invited investors and business people from Alexanderplatz turned up. The discussion was chaired by the Berlin Senat's *Ausländerbeauftragte* ('representative for foreigners' affairs') and

Figure 14: 'Alexanderplatz Today, Tomorrow, the Day after Tomorrow'

included a SenStadt administrator, an expert on public space from the German Federal Ministry of Construction, Heiko and a young Kurdish man who frequented the Container. Before and after the event, people stood in the corridor outside talking about their expectations and, later, the actual results of the discussion. Youth workers rehearsed their worries that young people would be forced out of the new Alexanderplatz. The SenStadt administrator's contribution was largely felt to reflect a typical planners' perspective. His lengthy talk about architectural design was illustrated with bird's-eye images of Alexanderplatz, demonstrating its despicable emptiness, and with pictures of exemplary public squares in other cities, including Paris and Rotterdam. He was cut short by the chairwoman's request for him to return to the topic of discussion: Would there be a place for young people in the future Alexanderplatz?

One more example will suffice to illustrate how the different perspectives of planners and youth workers were performed. After many meetings, letters and 'phone calls, Heiko had negotiated a meeting with the highest echelon of Berlin's planning administration, the Building Director Hans Stimmann. Stimmann is known for his stern and controversial views regarding the direction that city planning in Berlin should now take, specifically his proposals for a particular set of architectural principles and for retracing the city's historical structure. As discussed in Chapter II, urban development in post-unification Berlin has been largely guided by a master plan based on a specific politico-aesthetic, the principle of critical reconstruction, which is considered Stimmann's brainchild. The negotiations between youth workers and planners around Alexanderplatz took place against this backdrop of deliberation and struggle over how the historical centre of Berlin could be adequately reinstated.

For his encounter with Stimmann, Heiko arrived dressed in a suit and accompanied by his intern, who sported a shirt rather than his usual T-shirt. Two members of the citizens' foundation, including a countess from a well-known German aristocratic family, provided further support. However, Heiko's attire and aristocratic armour appeared to leave Stimmann unimpressed and his attempt to shift the balance of power remained unsuccessful. Instead, Stimmann focused on demonstrating that Heiko lacked the expertise that would allow him to make authoritative claims regarding urban design. He judged the AG Alex's ideas unsuitable for a central city square and in conflict with official regulations, and questioned Heiko's idea of 'multi-functional' facilities.

Rather condescendingly, Stimmann accused Heiko of disregarding the area's historical meaning and proposed to teach him a lesson in the history of Berlin, which might clarify why young people's facilities were inappropriate. 'This is our gothic old town,' he exclaimed. Young people's facilities would conflict with the church and the town hall nearby. The very idea of a beach-volleyball field in the city centre, he claimed, was unthinkable in any other German city, but here in Berlin people seemed to think that anything goes: 'Our city is so empty, there's so much space, we might as well put up this and that...!'

In planners' commentaries, one thing seemed undisputed: youth workers knew about youth and social problems but not about urban design. Conversely, it was not the task of planners to worry about social or societal matters. Arguably, the planners who deliberated on a new design for Alexanderplatz in the 1990s could claim to have considered the social in the form of a study they had commissioned on the social make-up of Alexanderplatz. In addition, there had been the impressive participative campaign conducted by SenStadt. Indeed, 'society' and 'the social' have long been drawn into planning – through statistics, reports and various forms of popular participation – in Germany as elsewhere. Importantly, however, the youths frequenting Alexanderplatz in the early 2000s had figured neither in the social study nor in the participation procedures. For planners, the young people appeared seemingly out of nowhere.

The meaningful relation that youth workers sensed between young people and Alexanderplatz – and asserted through notions such as *Heimat*, community or public life – apparently eluded planners. For planners, young people were interested less in 'partaking of public life' than in 'staking claims' in Alexanderplatz. From the youth workers' perspective, the robust, plain and undefined Alexanderplatz envisaged by the planners would appear to deny – or at least play down – the presence of certain groups of people that do not fit the image of the ideal user that planners seem to have in mind.

In their exchanges with Heiko, administrators repeatedly noted that instead of promoting sectoral planning or particularistic interests, one needed to plan for the 'common good'. Young people, however, were but one user group amongst many. As Heiko recalled with some bitterness in a conversation with me: 'If I talk about the punks, [the administrators] tell me to remember the youths interested in sport. If I talk about youths interested in sport, they tell me that I mustn't forget the punks.' Such advice undermined the youth workers' claim to a comprehensive outlook. Time and again, youth workers pointed out to me that Alexanderplatz was not for young people alone. Residents, business people, the police, social workers, the municipality, tourists, punks, urban planners and architects were but a few of the diverse groups with vested interests in the square.

Youth workers might have considered rather ironic an administrator's assertion that 'we don't live in neutral space' (where people can do as they please). To them, this was very much how planners saw space. What for planners was a beautiful, unmarked public square, could amount, for youth workers, to a negation of the presence of (young) people.

What I term the perspectival disparities between planners and youth workers were complex indeed. They may be considered to relate quite simply to professional self-interest, but also to ethics, aesthetics and the knowledge practices constitutive of the professional domains. Planners considered theirs to be a trained perspective. One had to learn, as it were, to assume the 'God's eye view'. By contrast, youth workers would seem to have stayed firmly on the ground. They claimed their perspective was that of real people, which was a perspective that allegedly eluded planners. Perspectival disparities acquired peculiar significance when members of the

Figure 15: The Punks' Alexanderplatz

two professions encountered each other. Each contested the ability of the other to see and know in the right way.

The Universal, the Particular and the Robust

In this book I showed how public space continues to be an object of lively debate and social practice in contemporary Berlin. The project 'Alexander-platz – a place for young people' offers a complex counter-example to pre-vailing narratives of the death of urban public space in the contemporary neo-liberal city. Whilst notions of privatization, gentrification and social exclusion are key to the AG Alex's project, participants also achieved a sustained plausible model for what urban development in a contemporary capital city may comprise. Seen as a public space in which diversity resided and could be encountered (as various kinds of people), Alexanderplatz was a place in which one could learn (Basso 1996). It was considered a place where tolerance and pluralism could be practised, and where citizenly ways could be acquired. For the youth workers, the involvement of children in the planning of playgrounds was insufficient. Children's confinement to playgrounds in planning mirrored, in a sense, their confinement to play-grounds in space. Young people needed to be involved in the planning of other spaces too – spaces that were not exclusively for them but that they nevertheless use.

The youth workers registered some surprising successes. In the 2004 competition for the design of the square, the Platzmanagement was so-licited as an expert. It included further workshops and opportunities for public discussion, also used by the young people. The Platzmanagement endorsed the winning design, which includes a vision of Alexanderplatz as a 'stage' for people, with plenty of lighting and seating facilities. A new site nearby has been found for the youth facilities, whilst the building works in Alexanderplatz are slowly taking off, although it has proved difficult to en-list the developers' support. In the light of contemporary pronouncements of the death of 'the social' (Rose 1999), the AG Alex's (partial) success may come as a surprise. I do not wish to deny the extent to which this success is due to the persistence and ingenuity of Heiko, the AG Alex and certain individuals in both the district's administration and SenStadt who sup-ported their aims. The youth workers' project was embroiled in complex local politics, in official planning doctrines and individual power struggles, as well as in concerns about what the capital of the New Germany may look like and, significantly, about the process of its making. It took place in an environment characterized by deliberation and struggle over how an ideal society could be realized in urban space. In this sense, the youth workers' project spoke to concerns both about neo-liberal city development and, more specifically, about the contemporary constitution of public space in Germany and ultimately about notions of Germanness.

In Caldeira and Holston's (2005) discussion, the reconceptualization of 'the social' in planning seems to have failed to produce the purported outcomes. In this chapter, I have examined a persistent and somewhat more successful attempt to build 'the social' into the urban fabric. The material from Alexanderplatz offers important anthropological insight beyond the ethnographic specificities of Berlin, regarding this shift in the thinking about 'the social' in planning. Rather than its redundancy (or resurrection), I argue that we see a *rearticulation* of the social in city planning, an attempt to create a kind of 'social robustness'. Scholars such as Helga Nowotny and her collaborators have recently begun to point to a different imagination of the role of society in the production of scientific knowledge (Nowotny et al. 2001). In this view, social robustness is sought where efforts are made 'to "build into" particular projects not just future demands of the public or customers, society in a weak sense, but an authority that lies beyond the market, in the name of "society" in a strong sense' (Strathern 2005: 466). This is what I mean by a new 'social question'. To paraphrase, where planning was once considered robust if its practices and procedures conformed to those recognized as valid within the professional domain, now planning may be considered robust only if it looks towards 'society'. The seeking of authority beyond the domain of planning makes for what I term 'socially robust' planning.

Robustness is a fitting metaphor to illustrate what was at stake regarding Alexanderplatz and in rethinking planning practices more generally. Arguably, planners and youth workers entertained very different notions of how society could be materialized in the cityscape and of how Alexanderplatz could be made robust. Largely framed by their professional understanding of what makes a good public space, planners spoke of robustness as an aesthetic, economic and technical quality to which public space needed to aspire. This aspiration seemed threatened by the youth workers' demands for what was, at times, derisorily described as sectoral planning. In an important sense, both youth workers and planners accused each other of taking insufficient notice of the social. In the planners' view, youth workers endorsed a technocratic idea of society as consisting of different sectors that could be known empirically and for which distinct spaces could be planned. For the youth workers, planners were preoccupied with the technicalities and economic profit rather than the sociality of the square.

It is not the case, however, that youth workers took the social into account whilst planners did not. Rather, the youth workers' perspective may be understood as a perspective from the *particular*, whilst the planners considered the social as a *totality*. That is to say, the youth workers' concern was with people's particular needs and desires, including those of young people to which their job required them to be especially attuned. Youth, here, was an aggregate entity; but there were also individual youths hanging out in Alexanderplatz today and in the future. This was different from the particularistic perspective which, as I explained in Chapter V, was associated with NIMBYism and individual interests rather than the public good, and of which the youth workers, too, were occasionally accused. Their perspective from the particular could seem in conflict with the position reflected in the planners' reports, namely, a position that revolved around the notion of a larger social totality as a universal form that could be circumscribed and known. In this sense, 'the social' had already been embodied in the social report on Alexanderplatz and in citizens' participation, and thus been considered in the early stages of the planning. Assembled from questionnaires, surveys and statistics, the social had been integrated into Alexanderplatz's new design.

Importantly, however, these forms of conjuring the social were quite different from what the youth workers had in mind. Citizens had influenced the planning process primarily in their role as property owners with certain rights; whilst the social report conjured 'the social' as separate from and even opposed to other domains such as the economy, the environment and the legal. By contrast, in the youth workers' project, Alexanderplatz was a space considered to be inherently social, by virtue of people being there, a quality that could be either imperilled or enhanced. The youth workers' aim was not simply to add a social group that planners seemed to have overlooked. Rather, what the youth workers demanded for Alexanderplatz may be understood as a form of *social* robustness. For them, planning was not just about providing a spatial container for people's activities, but about creating a place that had people's desires, expectations and actual behaviour already built into its design.

Though perhaps rather different from Berlin's contemporary dominant politico-aesthetics of urban form revolving around particular design elements and conventions, the youth workers' Alexanderplatz, too, suggested a particular kind of aesthetics – one highlighting the intrinsic sociality of urban space. I suggest that what we see, here, is a messy coexistence of different discursive registers and practices that people draw on to persuade. The shift towards socially robust planning is by no means linear or absolute. Nor is it a 'top down' reformulation of governmentality. 'Alexanderplatz: a place for young people' is not simply a form of resistance to a prevalent urban governmentality but a rich example of contemporary efforts to reassert the power of the social in the city.

⤙ Chapter VII ⤚

Whose Alexanderplatz?

A muggy, thundery air was hanging over Berlin on the day in May 2002 when SenStadt representatives and the developers signed the amended urban development contracts setting down their mutual rights and obligations in relation to Alexanderplatz. Whilst upstairs in the RKA office the property relations regarding Alexanderplatz had been confirmed once again, down in the square the question of who owned Alexanderplatz and who owned urban space, more generally, was being negotiated quite differently.

When I left the RKA, a little dizzy from the champagne with which we had celebrated the occasion, the atmosphere seemed tense. Numerous police vans and ambulances were assembled particularly around the train station. The stairs leading up to the railway tracks had been closed off. A paramedic I approached explained that some people had jumped onto the tracks, stopping inner-city trains and causing tumult and alarm. In the café where I settled down to observe what was happening, a waitress opined that 'some idiots' had been protesting against the visit of U.S. president George W. Bush scheduled for that week. The following day, newspapers reported that the obstruction of the railway tracks had been part of a 'Reclaim-the-Street' demonstration, attracting about a thousand people. They had managed, with seeming ease and until being removed by police, to bring Alexanderplatz to a standstill.

People disrupting train lines and those smashing the Kaufhof department store's show windows later that evening, were an unwelcome intrusion in Alexanderplatz as envisaged by its planners. They enacted a particular kind of protesting public and, as such, were a fitting anthropological contrast to the citizens summoned in the planning procedures, whose participation gave the plans the stamp of legitimacy.

Contemporary practices of planning, as I pointed out earlier in this book, posit the presence of a public. Without people capable of debate, contest or approval, notions such as participation, transparency and accountability would barely be thinkable. Since the populism of the 1960s and 1970s, which affected governmental rationalities, planning practice and anthropological theory alike, there has been a pervasive desire to include 'real' people in our accounts to bestow the respective professional endeavours with some legitimacy (cf. McDonald 1989). In part, this was a response to the perceived shortcomings of established technocratic and academic knowledge practices. Intriguingly, as Holmes and Marcus (2005) note, even as the statistical mode of analysis and other forms of technocratic knowledge production continue to be powerful, – forms which emerged, in fact, so as to make industrial society knowable – we see the growing importance of 'the para-ethnographic'. This includes an attempt to reference the realities of social life in the context of neo-liberal ideologies that delegate authority to the market (cf. Riles and Myazaki 2005).

In the previous chapter, I discussed an example of what we might see as the growing intrusion of the social back into planning, specifically in the politicized and partly subversive practices of some former technicians of 'the social', namely, the youth workers in Alexanderplatz. Yet the bulk of this book was concerned to show that quite unlike anthropologists who have begun to see themselves as situated people, interacting with the subjects of their research, administrative planners would seem to have largely remained anxiously objective technocrats. In contrast to Holmes and Marcus, my ethnographic interest lay in showing how it is these planners' efforts to embody a view that is distinct, rational and comprehensive – in keen awareness of their own humanity and the relevance of experientially grounded knowledge – which makes them fascinating subjects of anthropological enquiry.

Mediated by specific modes of government, these different knowledge practices frame the struggles over urban place, such as the one charted in this book, and shape the subjectivities of those involved. People express their demands and responsibilities as administrators, planners, experts, citizens or, simply, 'the affected'. These categories are frequently taken as self-evident and unproblematic both in Berlin planning debates and in scholarly analyses. This book, by contrast, has affirmed their enabling qualities and the possibilities they opened up, as well as their limitations. Instead of an abstract normative concept of citizenship, for example, I explored some of the quotidian practices in which the citizen is invoked and embodied: as the constituent of a critical public; a legitimating cipher; a member of society; and an active citizen-in-the-making.

The material discussed in this book presents so many moments in which the citizen is made, remade and unmade – to diverse effects. The new citizen who had arrived in the 1960s did so hand in hand with a different kind of planner, one required to be open to citizens' needs and demands. Planners nonetheless continued to command the final say in what makes the city attractive and what is comprised by the public good. Moreover, whilst having opened up a new type of Latourian *Dingpolitik*, from the 1980s urban planning increasingly became determined by economic imperatives.

Planners now manage space in relation to society, imagined as an aggregate of private interests, and the idea is that consensus can be found through rational debate. Indeed, I would suggest that the mix of numerical, participative and more 'narrative' knowledge practices that planners now deploy have yet to translate into newly conceived kinds of composite and possibly inconclusive results.

This book is itself embedded in a very distinct set of knowledge practices, as it presents a variety of ways in which place is comprehended and known in contemporary Berlin. Starting from Rodman's call to make explicit the 'multivocality' of place, where 'places, like voices, are local and multiple' (1992: 643), this book has suggested – influenced by the post-humanist currents of contemporary social theory – an ontology of place as assemblage. In doing so, I have invoked a variety of sites, at once human and non-human, discursive and material: the planning offices, the living rooms of experts and citizens, the venues for podium discussions and the reality of Alexanderplatz for people who live, work and spend their time there. These sites entail diverse agendas, technological regimes, material practices, people and things; and concerns generated by one site are contested, appropriated and translated by and into another. Together they generate what I earlier termed 'Alexanderplatz multiple'.

The vantage point for this study has been Alexanderplatz's problematization in post-unification Berlin. I began by looking at how Alexanderplatz was problematized in the offices, drawings and pronouncements of the city planners. For them, Alexanderplatz became a complex problem to be solved and a hybrid compound of public and private. It was also a future assembled in meetings, documents, plans and timetables, through the arrangement of tracks and pipes, the selection of street lamps and paving materials – a future eagerly anticipated and continually postponed. Its flip side was Alexanderplatz as an 'object of grievance' of self-conscious citizens and critical experts. In this view, the new Alexanderplatz was an element of what I have called Berlin's emergent topography of immorality. It was generated through concerns about governmental conduct and legitimacy, senses of property and belonging, and through specific practices of consultation and discontent.

The significance accorded to public debate and the participative process in Berlin has been matched only by the contention these practices have spurred. Critical citizens and experts, just like the youth workers, drew on terms and forms of debate similar to those of the planners, but they desired different effects. The pre-established frames of the debate – especially the premise of development – and its process that depoliticized the result and evacuated its conflictual potential, meant that those other 'desirables' must forever recede into the background.

The counterpoint to the planners' Alexanderplatz was, however, not the citizen group's carefully developed square or the youth workers' socially robust square, but rather the square where disorder and disintegration have become manifest. People's commentary on disorder and the solutions they proposed – through street cleaning, policing or social work – suggested that order and disorder are mutually implicated. It also suggests an imagination of Alexanderplatz as the embodiment of a particular temporality of the state, a temporality that is not necessarily reflected in the planners' visions.

My discussion of Alexanderplatz acutely highlights the historicity of the assemblage and its conflictual nature. The RKA engineer, Frau Fürstenau, suggested the following, as we discussed how people saw Alexanderplatz today. She noted that there were dissimilar memories and experiences at work in administrators' perceptions of the square that had become the object of their planning:

> The West [German] administrator finds Alexanderplatz just terrible ....
> The East administrator also finds it terrible, but because it has become like this. Thus, they [East administrators] still have a kind of background: 'Once there was something beautiful.' It was something linked to positive emotions. But the way it is now, it's ugly and it can't go on like this. In this respect, ... the approach of both is the same: 'It is terrible and one has to change something!' – One [the West administrator] has no background and says: 'Alexanderplatz *is* just terrible!' And the other says: 'Alexanderplatz *has become* terrible!'

In the light of images of the New Berlin, the metropolis or the global city, Alexanderplatz could now appear shabby, provincial and altogether inadequate. The disorder and disintegration of Alexanderplatz, as I noted, seemed to parallel the dissolution of the socialist state and, concomitantly, of a former socialist utopia and a specific sociality. Ironically, the plans to revamp Alexanderplatz into a space of planned order, a promise of economic prosperity and a stepping stone towards 'real' unification appeared to transform an unfinished construction of the GDR state into the unfinished construction of another, the FRG. From the clash of temporal orders, destruction and disorder emerged.

How do people make sense of such messiness? The following brief exchange gives an indication. It ensued in a meeting concerning the distribution of water pipes, held in one of the developers' planning office, and involved a male and a female waterworks employee. One of them had produced some drawings of the pipe system in the area around Alexanderplatz, which he had found at home. He had obtained these drawings during

the messy *Wende* period, when most files and documents of GDR administrative institutions had been discarded (along with, as his colleague put
it, years of people's work and lives). 'If the *Wende* hadn't happened,' she
lamented, 'we would have got all the plans we need today.' But her colleague replied, poignantly: 'If the *Wende* hadn't happened, we would not
need these plans today.'

What-ifs, counterfactuals, implicit presences and absences, possible and
actual futures often complicated my research. People wondered how their
lives would have turned out had the *Wende* not happened, and their lives
had turned out despite their expectations. How would Alexanderplatz have
evolved, the GDR planners I interviewed speculated. Their answers, which
suggested that the square was always a work in progress, contradicted readings of Alexanderplatz that posited it as a socialist future made permanent.
Although still existing in materialized form, the Alexanderplatz of GDR
times could appear to be more readily present in archives and in people's
memories. In the words of the visual artist Folke Köbberling, Alexanderplatz was (and is) a contemporary past.[53] Such temporal parallelism seemed
difficult to accommodate in the planning of the future square.

It will have become clear in the preceding pages that the controversy
around Alexanderplatz and similar sites in Berlin (and possibly elsewhere)
has been as much a contestation of space and territory in a unified Germany as a struggle over time. In a sense, Alexanderplatz is a materialization
of what Munn, following Husserl, describes thus: '[A]t a given moment, any
event [read, 'place'] is infused with an ambience of potentialities or "futu-
rity", as well as pasts' (1990: 5). Notions of historicity, memory or transformation only poorly convey this temporal quality. As an urban design object,
Alexanderplatz appeared to have a time in and of itself – the embodiment
of a particular historical moment, now defeated and hopelessly outdated. It
was, in the words of an elderly lady I met in Alexanderplatz, 'a piece of the
East' that Berlin's city builders could not accept.

Urban design formations, similar to the photographs and artefacts discussed by Pinney (2005), are read as 'contextualizing' and 'contemporaneous' of a particular historical era and associated politico-economic and
socio-cultural regimes.[54] Such readings are always evaluative and, therefore, subject to interrogation and challenge. Against official inscriptions of
historicity, East Berliners invoked their own temporal experiences as the
inhabitants of this city that is to be rewritten, and the continuing salience
of the gradually obliterated socialist period in their life trajectories. Such
contestations are as much about the nature and value of urban public space
as they are about how a 'proper' temporality could be materialized in place
– a temporality which would align multiple contradictory pasts, presents
and futures.

Figure 16: Alexanderplatz made of cardboard boxes

The past and history, richly evocative terms in post-unification Berlin, have become key reference points in people's projects and constructions of contemporary futures, including Alexanderplatz. Writing this book was a constant effort to put into words whether the Alexanderplatz that people invoked was a past, present or future – or all of these at once. Alexanderplatz is an (im)possibility that springs out of the gap between the seemingly irreversible concreteness of the existing square and the short-lived provisionality of, for example, temporary events or the cardboard 'Alexanderplatz 2012' that the staff of district Mitte's Children and Youth Office incited passers-by to build during the youth-work publicity market in 2002. 'Ambiguity', 'fluidity' and 'elusiveness' might be the last words that come to mind when one looks at Alexanderplatz, this concrete plane, and the sturdy buildings around it. Yet, they seem to be the words that encapsulate it best.

In conclusion, I wish to turn my notion of 'Alexanderplatz multiple' on its head. I used the notion to convey how each of the different Alexanderplatzes had a reality irreducible to any one of them alone, although none was autonomous either. There was one Alexanderplatz, however, that sometimes appeared to be 'more real' than the others. In people's commentary on Alexanderplatz and on Berlin's planning debates more generally, the following statement was typical: 'There is a lot of talk about "aesthetics" and "history" – but what it is *really* about is economics and money.'

In other words, there seemed to be a distribution of relative realities; and fundamental reality was to be found in the economic realm (cf. Mitchell 2002). For those who attached their hopes and grievances to Alexanderplatz, the question was often less one of a *multiple* than one of a *singular* Alexanderplatz which might, for better or worse, be commodified, owned and transacted, and to which people could lay claim in diverse ways. Framed within this discourse, Alexanderplatz acquired a singular material reality, thus opening up the question of 'whose Alexanderplatz?' For administrative planners, Alexanderplatz was not just a public square but simultaneously an investment project where ownership is distributed between private developers and the public hand, this nebulous entity with planning sovereignty and concomitant rights and obligations to determine Berlin's overall shape. But from a different perspective, Alexanderplatz also belonged to *all* Berliners, an imagined collectivity of citizens distinct from both 'the state' and 'the market'.

This juxtaposition of collective ownership and commodification was thrown into relief by an event in Alexanderplatz in the summer of 2002. It was staged by a couple of artists who called themselves psd°, short for 'public space development',[55] and their friends. They had drawn a chalk circle on the ground between the fountain and the tram tracks, where they felt Alexanderplatz's emptiness to be most apparent. Passers-by stopped to watch the bizarre happening. The following day, a piano, speakers, amplifiers and a table with a huge cake were put up in the centre of the circle. The cake had

Figure 17: Taking one's share in Alexanderplatz

a peculiar design: it was an edible replica of a statistical scheme, representing the percentage of Berliners who had voted for the respective political parties in the last elections and, importantly, also those who had refused or were not eligible to vote. Amplified by a microphone and loudspeakers, the artists announced the distribution of the cake to all passers-by. Taking a share of the cake, they proclaimed, stood for taking one's share in the public space that was Alexanderplatz.

At first people hesitated, but soon curiosity and appetite seemed to win out. An increasingly large crowd gathered to receive their share on paper plates. A lively music programme accompanied the event. One of the passer-by spontaneously sat down at the piano and played some tunes. Alexanderplatz suddenly became a happening place. In addition, the artists began to sell 'shares' in Alexanderplatz – fake certificates embellished with photographs of the square for €27 each. (I am the proud owner of one of these.) Handing out and selling shares was intended to provoke reflection on what stake people held in Alexanderplatz and in public space, more generally. Steeped in self-consciously philosophical ideas (their references spanned from Jürgen Habermas to Peter Sloterdijk), these artists presented public space as 'private space shared'. It was a space created by people with an interest in the fate of their city coming together. The notion of shares was also a pun on the detested sell-out of Berlin, that is, an enacted allegory on real-estate acquisition by private investors. In contrast to the planning procedures for Alexanderplatz, which asked people to evaluate the aesthetics and practicalities of the proposed design, the distribution of shares would require people, quite literally, to re-valuate their relation to Alexanderplatz qua citizen or simply qua Berliner.

As in the claims to autochthony, societal property, or the knowledgeable and experienced engagement with place discussed earlier, the artists' project asked about how people belong to place and how place belongs to people. There were diverse languages of ownership at play – each comprising an array of ideas about people's obligations and entitlements regarding Alexanderplatz. A week later I went along to the screening of a video of the event shown in psd°'s studio space in the Haus des Lehrers, a few floors down from the RKA. There, reflecting on their activities, the artists worried that by explaining the event as 'art', they might have dispelled people's puzzlement all too quickly and kept them from pondering the questions: Who does the *Alex* belong to? Whose place is it?

The question 'whose Alexanderplatz?' forms an endpoint, rather than a starting point, of this book. What I sought to explore were precisely some of the 'whose' – that is, the different positions from which claims to Alexanderplatz were made. The question 'whose Alexanderplatz?' could evoke a variety of replies, pointing to diverse senses of what I called belonging, which did not readily find expression in the legal or economic domains, and which stood in expressed conflict with official definitions. A last anecdote, related to me by the Berliner Zeitungsmann, the man who sold the newspaper *Berliner Zeitung* in Alexanderplatz, brings out the ad hoc and sometimes ironic nature of belonging. Late one evening, in the 1990s, he was busy packing up his stall when the then manager of the Kaufhof department store staggered past. The manager was quite obviously drunk, talking to himself and repeatedly exclaiming: 'Kaufhof belongs to me!' Then, the Berliner Zeitungsmann recalled, chuckling and evidently delighted, he himself exclaimed in response: 'The Alex belongs to me!' – leaving the manager looking dumbfounded.

The primacy of the economic was once again asserted in a public statement regarding the development of the Alexanderplatz project in 2006.[56] The press attaché of Berlin's new Senator for Urban Development, Ingeborg Junge-Reyer, was reported to have stated that the developers in Alexanderplatz could not be forced to build anything they would subsequently be unable to sell or let. Nobody was going to pursue the Alexanderplatz project 'against the market', she said. Nevertheless, the Kollhoff plan would not be scrapped; the contracts with the developers were now extended until 2013.[57] 'So, we still have seven years', the press attaché concluded. In other words, Alexanderplatz has been postponed once more and continues seemingly transfixed in its *Wartestand.*

I do not want to make too much of Alexanderplatz's apparent failure or speculate about its causes. Indeed, the completion of a large new shopping mall just across the street from Alexanderplatz in 2007 is cited as an affirmation of its development potential. Also, as previously noted, I think it would be a mistake *ever* to call Alexanderplatz a failure, not least, because the notion posits a belief in complete objects, projects or places, which would contradict the spirit of my argument in this book. The similarity with Latour's Aramis, the proposed Personal Rapid Transit system in Paris (1996: 281), is palpable. The volatility of economic cycles that seems to jeopardize the project stands in opposition to the construction plan that, to use again the words of the SenStadt administrator, is 'law, persisting into eternity'. As such, it would seem to be unalterable even by the most sceptical voices that can be heard in Berlin's planning debates. Alexanderplatz's feasibility remains intact – at least, in a perfect market and in a world where Berlin will boom as a global city and where greed, mismanagement and corruption have no place (cf. Krätke 2004). Economic and social contingency, however, and incomplete knowledge – although everybody knows they exist – are not assumed in the plan; they acquire visibility only in retrospect (Scott 1998: 343).

It is unlikely that Alexanderplatz will suffer the same surreptitious death as Aramis. Bits of the Kollhoff plan have appeared and will appear, here and there, around the site. Yet Alexanderplatz has shown what I think is a remarkable obduracy in the face of transformation. Two decades after unification it becomes possible to see that the grand obliteration of Berlin's cityscape, initially expected, has been met with a sort of tenacity of urban form. To note this is neither to vindicate nor celebrate GDR planning. Alexanderplatz, as I hope is clear by now, is more than its design.

This book is not against planning. Nor is it specifically a criticism of the planning for Alexanderplatz. The aim of the book has been to demonstrate multiplicity. But it also has suggested the possible reduction of multiplicity to a singularity, for instance, through appeals to planning, law, the public good or economics. I have examined some of the translations and conversions that are going on within that multiple Alexanderplatz. I showed how planners engaged in a work of inscribing the economic, legal, environmental and social aspects into reports, which can subsequently be reincorporated into the design of the square. The citizens, in turn, defined their experienced understanding of Alexanderplatz and then converted it into legal grievances and planning discourse. I suggested how the youth workers sought to make sense of young people's doings in Alexanderplatz, partly in ways that would allow them to find resonance in the planners' and developers' language of urbanity. Finally, I looked at the ways artists incorporated their philosophical, political and technical concerns into an artistic form. Such processes of translating and converting between different domains are, of course, part and parcel of 'modern' life, but we might want to question with Latour (1993) whether we've ever fully managed to be modern in the first place.

The different Alexanderplatzes hang together through 'partial connections', but their contradictions and inconsistencies, spelled out in Berlin's planning debates and in the pages of this book, are all too evident. Creating a sense of wholeness – such as that suggested by planning – is an accomplishment, not a natural given (cf. Mol 2002: 120; Strathern 1991). But so too is complexity, which rests on particular methodological and textual strategies that permit the creation of ever more vantage points and perspectives, and ever more detail. Neither does more or less violence to the reality in question (cf. Mol and Law 2002: 4). My argument is not simply to say that the perspectives of real people are routinely left out of planning; and that merely adding them on – for instance, by participative process or by sending an ethnographer into the field – could remedy the situation. 'Multiplicity' does not mean 'relativity'. I fear that this book would attest to the impossibility of taking 'everything' into account.

This book has had an objective that is categorically different from that of planning. Although mindful that 'solving' the problem of Alexanderplatz has been one of the main concerns of the people who are at the centre of this study, I was not interested in finding a solution myself. Rather, I sought to problematize the very act of problematization – by looking at some of the activities through which it occurs. This, of course, is part of the kind of self-reflexivity we now share with many of our interlocutors. I would like to add to this the question of what it would mean, instead of somehow reconciling perceived conflicts and incongruities, to make do with what is there. I am prepared to detect traces of this kind of approach to place and planning in Alexanderplatz itself. What some might consider the super-imposition of the socialist intervention and current capitalist reversals in Berlin's cityscape, I am tempted to label elasticity. What others describe as patchwork, I should rather call cohabitation (Latour 2005). What may be seen as a market bust, I like to see as obduracy. In the end, it is Alexanderplatz that makes people live things simultaneously.

∽ NOTES ഉ

CHAPTER I

1. Geertz expresses the anthropological rationale thus: 'The locus of study is not the object of study. Anthropologists don't study villages ...; they study *in* villages. You can study different things in different places, and some things ... you can best study in confined localities. But that doesn't make the place what it is you are studying' (1973: 22). Riles's study of the network (Riles 2001) proposes a kind of ethnographic inversion similar to the one I pursue here.
2. 'Großreinemachen auf dem Alex', in *Berliner Zeitung*, 18 September 2008.
3. This book is partly written in the spirit of Latour's *Aramis* (1996) and Mol's *The Body Multiple* (2002). Latour's account of the project of *Aramis* – a French public-transport project that was eventually abandoned – foreshadows important concerns regarding the constitution and failure of techno-social projects, which are invested with enormous financial and political resources. Mol shows how different medical practices relating to atherosclerosis enact the object, the disease, differently. Here, I occasionally adopt her fruitful terminology of the 'enactment' and 'doing' of the object in question.
4. Mol (2002: 66–8) lists various analytic approaches through which social scientists have sought to achieve this kind of de-essentialization. They include the positing of dissimilar 'social worlds', different 'perspectives', distinct explanatory 'frames' invoked by people, or 'modes' of ordering. Contrary to Mol and the Actor Network Theorists she draws on, I keep with Foucault's notions of 'discourse' and 'discursive formation' (Foucault 1972), which I understand to circumscribe an assemblages of words, strategies, practices and technologies, people and objects; whereas the 'network' I treat as an ethnographic term (Chapter VI).
5. In this sense, my account also contributes to the debate on complexity (e.g., Mol and Law 2002).
6. I am grateful to Javier Lezaun for pointing me to Hommels' paper.
7. My discussion focuses primarily on the anthropology of Germany produced in the English-speaking world (see, e.g., Berglund 1998; De Soto 1998; Forsythe 1989; Linke 1999; Norman 1991). There is, of course, a substantial body of work by German anthropologists which will not be reviewed, here.
8. See, e.g., De Soto 1993; 2000a; De Soto and Panzig 1995; Marx Ferree 1997.
9. See, e.g., Carrithers 2006; Ten Dyke 2001.
10. See, e.g., Berdahl 1999b, 2005; Graf et al. 1993; Mandel 1994, 2008; Müller 1992; Veenis 1999; White 1997.

11. See Borneman (1992, 1993, 1994, 1996, 1997, 1998) and Borneman and Senders (2000).
12. See, e.g., De Soto 1997; Richardson 2008; Tumarkin 1997; Wanner 1998; Yampolsky 1995.
13. There are exceptions such as the interest in social change and process and the temporalizing techniques characteristic of ethnographic practice (Boyarin 1994; Fabian 1983).
14. They take inspiration from geographers' non-representational models of space (Massey 1999; Thrift 1996).
15. Anthropological research on the Soviet city and the socialist city, more generally, remained limited due to political and practical constraints (Alexander and Buchli 2007: 12; Sampson 1984).
16. Examples of such ethnographies are, e.g., Ben-Ari 1995; Corsín Jiménez 2003; Finnegan 1998; Lang 1998; Rotenberg and McDonogh 1993; Richardson 2008.
17. Benevolo (1993) and Rykwert (1976) provide two classic historic studies of the city.
18. Abu-Lughod (1994) provides a similarly multiplied account of the struggle around the Lower East Side co-produced by a number of scholars, albeit preserving the distinctiveness domains and corresponding kinds of expertise and knowledges about the place.
19. A precedent of Senat interference with the district's decision-making autonomy was the re-naming of streets after unification (De Soto 1997: 34–5).
20. Thanks to Georgie Born for letting me include parts of our ongoing discussion (Born and Weszkalnys n.d.).

CHAPTER II

21. My discussion of these 'guiding images' is by no means exhaustive. Other future imaginaries for Berlin include the 'City of Talents', invoking notions of an R&D and knowledge industry (Krätke 2004); the 'Multi-cultural City'; and the 'Child and Youth Friendly City', which will be relevant in Chapter VI.
22. Mol's 'politics-of-what' (2002: 172–7) contains a similar proposition.
23. Due to the associated potential for violence and destruction, May Day demonstrations have been a contentious issue in Berlin not least since the 1980s (Lang 1998: 148–53).
24. Lang (1998: 122–9) describes the emergence of this politics in Kreuzberg in the 1970s and '80s.
25. These are questions of political and moral legitimacy and issues of privatization, which are now reported more widely from the post-socialist world (e.g., Alexander and Buchli 2007: 20–7; Bodnár 2001).
26. The notion of self-fulfilling prophecy was first coined in 1949 by Robert K. Merton to describe a certain set of economic behaviour. For example, if Bank X is predicted or rumoured to go bankrupt, customers will rush in and withdraw their money and, in effect, cause the bankruptcy of the bank.
27. These texts are on par with Jacobs' *Death and Life of Great American Cities* (1962) in the Anglo-American world.

28. Both globalization and post-socialism are understood to manifest themselves in cities in similarly problematic ways, including social segregation, gentrification, sub-urbanization and the privatization of property. In the post-socialist city, these processes tend to be depicted as the immediate result of capitalism *per se*. There is, however, an interesting tension regarding understandings of the 'post-socialist city', spelled out in the collection *Cities after Socialism* (Andrusz et al. 1996; see also Bodnár 2001: ch.2; French 1995: 5). The contributions suggest two broad views: one claims that 'state socialist urbanization was merely a special variant of a more general 'stages' model of global urban development' (Harloe 1996: 13); the other 'insists on the qualitatively different nature of socialist and capitalist cities' (Harloe 1996: 26). In the latter view, changes in the urban make-up emerge not as symptoms of a particular stage of urban evolution in the global era, but through the juxtaposition of radically different politico-economic systems, socialism and capitalism. In Germany, this contrast may be expressed in terms of East and West, e.g., when West German enterprises seize the opportunity of new eastern markets; or wealthy *Wessis* reclaim their property in the East (cf. Häußermann 1996a).

29. Anthropologists have long pointed to the varied construction of history (e.g., Comaroff and Comaroff 1992; Hastrup 1992; Kaneff 2004; Tonkin et al. 1989).

30. The so-called *Volkspalast* initiative brought together a number of Berlin arts institutions (Staiger n.d.). Intriguingly, it was partly sponsored by the European Commission's Urban Catalyst funding programme, which has aimed to investigate interim usages of public spaces. Such activities thus become increasingly inscribed and defined as *usages* of a particular kind. The non-productivness of space, instead of being considered aberrant, is transformed into cherished instances of urban creativity, as also evinced by a recent SenStadt publication (Senatsverwaltung 2007).

31. The institution in charge of managing and selling former GDR state-owned property after unification.

CHAPTER III

32. 'Schwarzer Tag für schwarzen Markt: heißes Pflaster Alex', *Neue Berliner Illustrierte*, 5/1990

33. 'Sittenspiegel um die Welt-Zeit: der Berliner Alexanderplatz, gründlich gewendet, Anlaß für Ekel oder Wohlgefühl', *Der Morgen*, 23.06.1990; 'Spekulanten ade – wer kommt jetzt? Alex wurde ein Zentrum der Straßenkriminalität', *BZ am Abend*, 02.07.2005

34. 'Das malträtierte Herz der Stadt. Berlin Alexanderplatz: Ortsbeschreibung eines deutschen Zustands', *Süddeutsche Zeitung*, Nr. 68, 20./21.03.1993

35. Attempts to create built environments that have specific effects on people's sense of being are not new. Such environments are imagined to entail what Nancy Munn (2003) has termed 'transposable qualities'. An example is the 1850s design for New York's Central Park, especially the creation of 'scenes' or 'views'. They were assumed to have a 'poetic' influence and 'qualities [which]

had the power to act on people's inner states of being or mind, and so make life 'healthier and happier' in the city' (Munn 2003: 102).

36. *Ostalgie* is frequently diagnosed in the domain of consumption, for example, in the revival of former GDR brands; but as I have shown in my research it is important to take seriously the other, 'rationalized' frameworks that people invoke for their choices (Weszkalnys 2000; cf. Berdahl 1999b; Boyer 2006). On the phenomenon of nostalgia more generally, see Chase and Shaw (1989), Lowenthal (1989), Wilson (1997).

37. A West German policeman I met opined that such fears were characteristic of East Germans unfamiliar with risks of ordinary cities. Perceptions of crime and danger may vary in relation to gender, age, ethnicity, individual feelings of vulnerability, and so on. Ewald (2000) relates fear of crime among East Germans to the experience of disappointment attendant on unification, especially among economically marginal workers.

38. In the Anglo-Saxon world, they would perhaps be referred to as 'crusties' or 'New Age travellers'.

Chapter IV

39. St. Nicholas day is celebrated in Germany on December 6.

40. There also emerged a new understanding that – rather than determining a single best path – planning implied a choice among alternatives or even among alternative futures (Albers 1980; 1997; Holston 1999: 158).

41. This kind of account is readily provided by political scientists (Lenhart 2001; Strom 2001).

42. I thank Rosemary Butcher for first suggesting the notion when I told her about Alexanderplatz.

43. Part of this analysis has benefited from much fruitful discussion with Simone Abram, and we will examine the work of the plan in much detail elsewhere (Abram and Weszkalnys, forthcoming).

Chapter V

44. None of my interlocutors pointed to a previous involvement in a GDR citizen group (Krämer-Badoni and Wiegand 1996; Neubert 1997).

45. On the development of citizenship in Brazil, see the fascinating study by Holston (2008).

46. Bebauungsplan I-B 4a "'Alexanderplatz': Auswertung der Beteiligung der Bürger gemäß §3 Abs. 2 BauGB, 7. April 1999", pp. 8–9 (unpublished document).

47. Arguably, my own identity as a West German ethnographer would seem to pose some methodological problems. It could be understood as one reason for the citizen group members' relative lack of emphasis on the issue of East and West.

48. No official opinion poll was ever conducted. However, some numbers were published in newspapers. Opinions collected during the exhibition of the com-

petition results showed that 56 per cent were against high-rise constructions, compared to 33 per cent in favour (Tagesspiegel 11.6.1993, cit. in an 'Open Letter' by the Bürgervertretung in March 1994). According to an evaluation of the survey conducted during the Alex-Info-Bus event, 65 per cent objected to high-rise buildings; only 10 per cent agreed that certain buildings should be destroyed (Lenhart 2001: 223 ftn.288).

49. For a marvellous account of residents attempting to forge new kinds of futures in the face of apparently ceaseless change in the built environment, in the very different context of urban Malaysia, see Baxstrom (2008).

CHAPTER VI

50. Andrew Barry and I developed the notion in the context of a research project conducted jointly with Georgina Born and Marilyn Strathern on contemporary modes of interdisciplinarity (Barry and Weszkalnys 2006). Arendt (2003) provides a classic discussion of the 'social question'.

51. Senatsverwaltung für Schule, Jugend und Sport (1999) 'Leitlinien für eine Kinder- und Jugendfreundliche Stadt'. Berlin.

52. Unlike the networks conjured by actor-network theory (ANT), the networked Alexanderplatz that emerged from the activities of the youth workers was not recognized to enjoin humans and objects in agentive relationships (Law and Hassard 1999); but some of the ideas that prompted ANT thinkers to conceive of the network in such ways seemed to have resonance.

CHAPTER VII

53. Köbberling conducted a project in the late 1990s eliciting people's descriptions of Alexanderplatz See http://www.folkekoebberling.de

54. What Pinney (2005) does not acknowledge is that the authors of the 'contextualizing objects' that give evidence of contemporaneity and whose origin he locates in the late eighteenth century (e.g., the German romanticists including Goethe, Herder, etc.) were actually producing objects that, like Pinney's Indian photograph, were largely un-contemporaneous. These objects propelled, rather than mirrored or inscribed, the idea of a German nation-state.

55. The artists were Dietrich Toellner and Peter Sandhaus. See http://www.ps-d.de

56. 'Hochhaus-Pläne für den Alex liegen weiter auf Eis', in *Berliner Morgenpost*, 12.03.2006

57. The existing plans are unlikely, if not impossible, to revise due to the developers' potential claims for compensation.

⊰ BIBLIOGRAPHY ⊱

Abram, S. 1998. 'Introduction: Anthropological Perspectives on Local Development.' In S. Abram and J. Waldren (eds), *Anthropological Perspectives on Local Development.* London and New York, Routledge: 1–17.

———. 2000. 'Planning the Public: Some Comments on Empirical Problems for Planning Theory.' *Journal of Planning Education and Research* 19(4): 351–357.

Abram, S. and G. Weszkalnys (eds) forthcoming *Elusive Promises – planning in the contemporary world.* Oxford, Berghahn.

Abu-Lughod, J. (ed). 1994. *From Urban Village to East Village.* Cambridge, MA, and Oxford, Blackwell.

Abu-Lughod, L. 1990. 'The Romance of Resistance: Tracing Transformations of Power through Bedouin Women.' *American Ethnologist* 17(1): 41–55.

———. 1991. 'Writing Against Culture.' In R. G. Fox (ed). *Recapturing Anthropology: Working in the Present.* Santa Fe, New Mexico, School of American Research Press: 137–162.

Adams, W. M. 1995. 'Green Development Theory? Environmentalism and Sustainable Development.' In J. Crush (ed). *Power of Development.* London and New York, Routledge: 87–99.

Albers, G. 1980. 'Town Planning in Germany: Change and Continuity under Conditions of Political Turbulence.' In G. E. Cherry (ed). *Shaping an Urban World.* London, Mansell: 145–160.

———. 1997. *Zur Entwicklung der Stadtplanung in Europa.* Braunschweig and Wiesbaden, Vieweg.

———. 1998. 'Wer plant die Planer?' In U. Altrock, D. Frick and T. Kuder (eds), *Zwischenbilanz: Standortbestimmung und Perspektiven der Stadt- und Regionalplanung.* Berlin, Institut für Stadt-und Regionalplanung, Technische Universität Berlin.

Alexander, C. 2007. 'Soviet and Post-Soviet Planning in Almaty, Kazakhstan.' *Critique of Anthropology* 27(2): 165–181.

Alexander, C. and V. Buchli 2007. 'Introduction.' In C. Alexander, V. Buchli and C. Humphrey (eds), *Urban Life in Post-Soviet Asia.* London, UCL Press: 1–39.

Alexander, C., V. Buchli and C. Humphrey (eds) 2007. *Urban Life in Post-Soviet Asia.* London, UCL Press.

Amit-Talai, V. and H. Wulff (eds) 1995. *Youth Cultures: A Cross-Cultural Perspective.* London and New York, Routledge.

Andrusz, G., M. Harloe and I. Szelenyi (eds) 1996. *Cities after Socialism: Urban and Regional Change and Conflict in Post-Socialist Societies.* Cambridge, MA, Blackwell.

Appadurai, A. 1988. 'Putting Hierarchy in Its Place.' *Cultural Anthropology* 3(1): 36–49.

———. 2000. 'Deep Democracy: Urban Governmentality and the Horizon of Politics.' *Public Culture* 14(1): 21–47.

Arendt, H. 2003. 'The Social Question.' In P. Baehr (ed). *The Portable Hannah Arendt*. New York, Penguin.

Augé, M. 1998. *A Sense for the Other*. Stanford, California, Stanford University Press.

Bahro, R. 1990 (1977). *Die Alternative: Zur Kritik des real existierenden Sozialismus*. Frankfurt am Main, Bund Verlag.

Barry, A. 1999. 'Demonstrations: Sites and Sights of Direct Action.' *Economy and Society* 28(1): 75–94.

———. 2001. *Political Machines: Governing a Technological Society*. London and New York, Athlone.

Barry, A., G. Born and G. Weszkalnys 2008. 'Logics of Interdisciplinarity.' *Economy and Society* 37(1): 20–49.

Barry, A. and G. Weszkalnys 2006. 'The New Social Question.' *Department of Geography, UCL*. London.

Barta, P. I. 1996. *Bely, Joyce, and Döblin: Peripatetics in the City Novel*. Gainesville, University Press of Florida.

Basso, K. H. 1996. 'Wisdom Sits in Places: Notes on a Western Apache Landscape.' In S. Feld and K. H. Basso (eds), *Senses of Place*. Santa Fe, New Mexico, School of American Research Press: 53–90.

Bätzner, N. 2000. 'Der Siedlungsbau der 20er Jahre – Laboratorium sozialer und formaler Experimente.' In T. Scheer, J. P. Kleihues and P. Kahlfeldt (eds), *Stadt der Architektur – Architektur der Stadt: Berlin 1900–2000*. Berlin, Nicolai: 148–159.

Bauausstellung Berlin, G. (ed). 1984. *Modelle für eine Stadt – Internationale Bauausstellung Berlin: Die Neubaugebiete, Dokumente-Projekte I*. Berlin, Siedler.

Baumann, G. 1986. *Contesting Culture: Discourses of Identity in Multi-Ethnic London*. Cambridge, Cambridge University Press.

Baxstrom, R. 2008. *Houses in Motion: The Experience of Place and the Problem of Belief in Urban Malaysia*. Stanford, CA, Stanford University Press.

Ben-Ari, E. 1995. 'Contested Identities and Models of Action in Japanese Discourses of Place-Making.' *Anthropological Quarterly* 68(4): 203–218.

Bender, B. (ed). 1993. *Landscape: Politics and Perspectives*. Oxford, Berg.

Benevolo, L. 1993. *The European City*. Oxford and Cambridge, MA, Blackwell.

Benninghaus, C. 1999. 'Die Jugendlichen.' In U. Frevert and H.-G. Haupt (eds), *Der Mensch des 20. Jahrhunderts*. Frankfurt/Main and New York, Campus Verlag: 230–253.

Berdahl, D. 1999a. *Where the World Ended: Re-unification and Identity in the German Borderland*. Berkeley, CA, and London, University of California Press.

———. 1999b. '"(N)Ostalgie" for the Present: Memory, Longing, and East German Things.' *Ethnos* 64(2): 192–211.

———. 2005. 'The Spirit of Capitalism and the Boundaries of Citizenship in Post-Wall Germany.' *Comparative Studies in Society and History* 47(2): 235–251.

Berglund, E. K. 1998. *Knowing Nature, Knowing Science: An Ethnography of Local Environmental Activism.* Cambridge, White Horse Press.

Beuermann, C. and B. Burdick 1998. 'The German Response to the Sustainability Transition.' In T. O'Riordan and H. Voisey (eds), *The Transition to Sustainability: The Politics of Agenda 21 in Europe.* London, Earthscan Publications: 174–188.

Binder, B. 2000a. 'Inszenierung von Erinnerung: Geschichtspolitik und der symbolische Umbau Berlins zur Hauptstadt. Ein Werkstattbericht.' *Vokus* 10(2): 4–27.

———. 2000b. 'Political Stage-Setting. The Symbolic Transformation of Berlin.' In B. Stråth (ed), *Myth and Memory in the Construction of Community: Historical Patterns in Europe and Beyond.* Bruxelles, PIE Lang: 137–155.

———. 2001a. 'Capital under Construction: History and the Production of Locality in Contemporary Berlin.' *Ethnologia Europaea* 31(2): 19–40.

———. 2001b. 'Eine Hauptstadt wird gebaut: Zur Produktion neuer Wahrnehmungsweisen in Berlin.' In E. Fischer-Lichte, C. Horn, S. Umathum and M. Warstat (eds), *Wahrnehmung und Medialität.* Tübingen and Basel, A. Francke Verlag: 177–196.

Blaut, J. 1993. *The Colonizer's Model of the World. Geographical Diffusionism and Eurocentric History.* New York, Guilford Press.

Bobbio, N. 1989. 'The Great Dichotomy: Public/Private.' *Democracy and Dictatorship.* Minneapolis, University of Minnesota Press.

Bodenschatz, H. 1987. *Platz frei für das neue Berlin: Geschichte der Stadterneuerung seit 1871.* Berlin, Transit.

———. 1995. *Berlin: Auf der Suche nach dem verlorenen Zentrum.* Hamburg, Junius.

Bodnár, J. 1998. 'Assembling the Square: Social Transformation in Public Space and the Broken Mirage of the Second Economy in Postsocialist Budapest.' *Slavic Review* 57(3): 489–515.

———. 2001. *Fin de Millénaire Budapest: Metamorphoses of Urban Life.* Minneapolis and London, University of Minnesota Press.

Born, G. 1995. *Rationalizing Culture: IRCAM, Boulez, and the Institutionalization of the Musical Avant-Garde.* Berkeley and London, University of California Press.

———. 2006. 'The Social and the Aesthetic: Methodological principles in the study of cultural production.' Paper presented at Yale University.

———. 2009. 'The social and the aesthetic: Methodological principles in the study of cultural production.' In I. Reed and J. Alexander (eds.), *Meaning and Method: the Cultural Approach to Sociology.* Boulder, Co., Paradigm: 123–74.

Born, G. and G. Weszkalnys n.d. 'From Multi-site to Problematization: Anthropology's Changing Objects'. (manuscript)

Borneman, J. 1992 *Belonging in the Two Berlins: Kin, State, Nation.* Cambridge, Cambridge University Press.

———. 1993. 'Uniting the German Nation: Law, Narrative, and Historicity.' *American Ethnologist* 20(2): 288–311.

————. 1994. 'Time-Space Compression and the Continental Divide in German Subjectivity.' *New Formations* 21(1): 102–118.

————. 1996. 'Narrative, Genealogy, and the Historical Consciousness: Selfhood in a Disintegrating State.' In E. V. Daniel and J. M. Peck (eds), *Culture/Contexture: Explorations in Anthropology and Literary Studies*. Berkeley, CA, and London, University of California Press: 214–234.

————. 1997. 'State, Territory, and National Identity Formation in the Two Berlins 1945–1995.' In A. Gupta and J. Ferguson (eds), *Culture, Power, Place: Ethnography at the End of an Era*. Durham, Duke University Press: 93–117.

————. 1998. '*Grenzregime* (Border Regime): The Wall and its Aftermath.' In T. M. Wilson and H. Donnan (eds), *Border Identities: Nation and State at International Frontiers*. Cambridge, Cambridge University Press: 162–190.

Borneman, J. and S. Senders 2000. 'Politics without a Head: Is the 'Love Parade' a New Form of Political Identification?' *Cultural Anthropology* 15(2): 294–317.

Bourdieu, P. 1977. *Outline of a Theory of Practice*. Cambridge, Cambridge University Press.

————. 1990. *The Logic of Practice*. Stanford, CA, Stanford University Press.

Bourgois, P. 1995. *In Search of Respect: Selling Crack in El Barrio*. Cambridge, Cambridge University Press.

Boyarin, J. 1994. 'Space, Time, and the Politics of Memory.' In J. Boyarin (ed), *Remapping Memory – The Politics of Timespace*. Minneapolis and London, University of Minnesota Press: 1–37.

Boyer, D. 2006. 'Ostalgie and the Politics of the Future in Eastern Germany' *Public Culture* 18(2): 361–381.

Brandstädter, S. 2007. 'Transitional Spaces: Postsocialism as a Cultural Process.' *Critique of Anthropology* 27(2): 131–145.

Brenneis, D. 1994. 'Discourse and Discipline at the National Research Council: A Bureaucratic *Bildungsroman*.' *Cultural Anthropology* 9: 23–36.

Brenner, N. and N. Theodore 2002. 'Cities and the Geographies of "Actually Existing Neoliberalism"'. In N. Brenner and N. Theodore (eds), *Spaces of Neoliberalization: Urban Restructuring in North America and Western Europe*. Oxford, Blackwell: 2–32.

Bridger, S. and F. Pine 1998. 'Introduction.' In S. Bridger and F. Pine (eds), *Surviving Post-Socialism: Local Strategies and Regional Responses in Eastern Europe and the Former Soviet Union*. London and New York, Routledge: 1–15.

Brubaker, R. 1992. *Citizenship and Nationhood in France and Germany*. Cambridge, MA, and London, Harvard University Press.

Buchli, V. 1999. *An Archaeology of Socialism*. Oxford and New York, Berg.

Bucholtz, M. 2002. 'Youth and Cultural Practice.' *Annual Review of Anthropology* 31: 525–552.

Buck-Morss, S. 2000. *Dreamworld and Catastrophe: The Passing of Mass Utopia in East and West*. Cambridge, MA, and London, MIT Press.

Burawoy, M. and K. Verdery 1999. 'Introduction.' In M. Burawoy and K. Verdery (eds), *Uncertain Transitions: Ethnographies of Change in the Postsocialist World*. Lanham, Maryland, and Oxford, Rowman & Littlefield: 1–18.

Burchell, D. 1995. 'The Attributes of Citizens: Virtue, Manners and the Activity of Citizenship.' *Economy and Society* 24(4): 540–558.

Caldeira, T. and J. Holston 2005. 'State and Urban Space in Brazil: From modernist planning to democratic interventions.' In A. Ong and S. J. Collier (eds), *Global Assemblages: Technology, Politics, and Ethics as Anthropological Problems.* Malden, MA, and Oxford, Blackwell: 393–416.

Caldeira, T. P. R. 2000. *City of Walls: Crime, Segregation and Citizenship in Sao Paulo.* Berkeley and London, University of California Press.

Calhoun, C. 1992. 'Introduction: Habermas and the Public Sphere.' In C. Calhoun (ed), *Habermas and the Public Sphere.* Cambridge, MA, and London, MIT Press: 1–50.

Candea, M. 2007. 'Arbitrary Locations: In Defence of the Bounded Fieldsite.' *Journal of the Royal Aanthropological Institute* 13: 167–184.

Carrier, J. G. 1997. 'Introduction.' In J. G. Carrier (ed), *Meanings of the Market: The Free Market in Western Culture.* Oxford and New York, Berg: 1–68.

Carrier, J. G. and D. Miller 1999. 'From Private Virtue to Public Vice.' In H. L. Moore (ed), *Anthropological Theory Today.* Cambridge, Polity Press: 24–47.

Carrithers, M. B. 2006. '"Witnessing a shipwreck" German figurations in facing the past to face the future.' *Revista de Antropología Social* 15: 193–230.

Casey, E. S. 1996. 'How to Get from Space to Place in a Fairly Short Stretch of Time: Phenomenological Prolegomena.' In S. Feld and K. H. Basso (eds), *Senses of Place.* Santa Fe, New Mexico, School of American Research Press: 13–52.

Chapman, M. 1978. *The Gaelic Vision in Scottish Culture.* London, Croom Helm.

Chase, M. and S. Shaw 1989. 'The Dimensions of Nostalgia.' In C. Shaw and M. Chase (eds), *The Imagined Past: History and Nostalgia.* Manchester, Manchester University Press: 1–17.

Cochrane, A. and A. Jonas 1999. 'Reimagining Berlin: World City, National Capital or Ordinary Place?' *European Urban and Regional Studies* 6(2): 145–164.

Collier, J. F., B. Maurer and L. Suárez-Navaz 1995. 'Sanctioned Identities: Legal Constructions of Modern Personhood.' *Identities* 2(1–2): 1–27.

Collier, S. J. and A. Ong 2005. 'Global Assemblages, Anthropological Problems.' In A. Ong and S. J. Collier (eds), *Global Assemblages: Technology, Politics, and Ethics as Anthropological Problems.* Malden, MA, and Oxford, Blackwell: 3–21.

Comaroff, J. L. and J. Comaroff (eds) 1992. *Ethnography and the Historical Imagination.* Studies in the ethnographic imagination. Boulder and Oxford, Westview Press.

Cooper, M. 1999. 'Spatial Discourses and Social Boundaries: Re-imagining the Toronto Waterfront.' In S. M. Low (ed), *Theorizing the City: The New Urban Anthropology Reader.* New Brunswick, N.J., and London, Rutgers University Press: 377–99.

Corbin, A. 1986. *The Foul and the Fragrant: Odor and the French Social Imagination.* Cambridge, MA, Harvard University Press.

Corsín Jiménez, A. 2003. 'On Space as Capacity.' *Journal of the Royal Anthropological Institute* 9(1): 137–153.

Creed, G. W. and B. Ching 1997. 'Recognizing Rusticity: Identity and the Power of Place.' In B. Ching and G. W. Creed (eds), *Knowing Your Place: Rural Identity and Cultural Heritage.* New York and London, Routledge: 1–38.

Cruikshank, B. 1999. *The Will to Empower: Democratic Citizens and Other Subjects.* Ithaca and London, Cornell University Press.

Crush, J. S. 1995. 'Introduction: Imagining Development.' In J. S. Crush (ed), *Power of Development.* London, Routledge: 1–24.

Dahn, D. 1994. *Wir bleiben hier oder Wem gehört der Osten: Vom Kampf um Häuser und Wohnungen in den neuen Bundesländern.* Reinbek bei Hamburg, Rowohlt.

Das, V. 1995. *Critical Events: An Anthropological Perspective on Contemporary India.* Oxford and Delhi, Oxford University Press.

Davis, M. 1990. *City of Quartz: Excavating the Future in Los Angeles.* London, Verso.

de Certeau, M. 1984. *The Practice of Everyday Life.* Berkeley, Los Angeles, and London, University of California Press.

De Soto, H. G. 1993. 'Equality/Inequality: Contesting Female Personhood in the Process of Making Civil Society in Eastern Germany.' In H. G. De Soto and D. Anderson (eds), *The Curtain Rises: Rethinking Culture, Ideology, and the State in Eastern Europe.* Atlantic Highlands, N.J., Humanities Press International: 289–304.

———. 1997. '(Re)Inventing Berlin: Dialectics of Power, Symbols and Pasts, 1990–1995.' *City and Society* 8(1): 29–49.

———. 1998. 'Reading the Fools' Mirror: Reconstituting Identity Against National and Transnational Political Practices.' *American Ethnologist* 25(3): 471–488.

———. 2000a. 'Contested Landscapes: Reconstructing Environment and Memory in Postsocialist Saxony-Anhalt.' In D. Berdahl, M. Bunzl and M. Lampland (eds), *Altering States: Ethnographies of Transition in Eastern Europe and the Former Soviet Union.* Ann Arbor, University of Michigan Press: 96–113.

———. 2000b. 'Crossing Western Boundaries: How East Berlin Women Observed Women Researchers from the West after Socialism, 1991–1992.' In H. G. De Soto and N. Dudwick (eds), *Fieldwork Dilemmas: Anthropologists in Postsocialist States.* Madison, Wisconsin, University of Wisconsin Press: 73–99.

De Soto, H. G. and C. Panzig 1995. 'From Decollectivization to Poverty and Beyond: Women in Rural East Germany before and after Unification.' In D. A. Kideckel (ed), *East-Central European Communities: The Struggle for Balance in Turbulent Times.* Boulder, Westview Press: 179–196.

Deleuze, G. 1979. 'Foreword: The Rise of the Social.' In J. Donzelot (ed), *The Policing of Families: Welfare Versus the State.* London, Hutchinson: ix–xxvii.

Deleuze, G. and F. Guattari 1987. *A Thousand Plateaus: Capitalism and Schizophrenia.* Minneapolis, University of Minnesota Press.

Dieser, H. 1996. 'Restitution: Wie funktioniert sie und was bewirkt sie?' In H. Häußermann and R. Neef (eds), *Stadtentwicklung in Ostdeutschland: Soziale und räumliche Tendenzen.* Opladen, Westdeutscher Verlag: 129–138.

Dilley, R. 1992. 'Contesting Markets: A General Introduction to Market Ideology, Imagery and Discourse'. In R. Dilley (ed), *Contesting Markets: Analyses of Ideology, Discourse and Practice*. Edinburgh, Edinburgh University Press: 1–34.

———. 1999. 'Introduction: The Problem of Context'. In R. Dilley (ed), *The Problem of Context*. New York and Oxford, Berghahn: 1–46.

Döblin, A. 1990 (1929). *Berlin Alexanderplatz: The Story of Franz Biberkopf*. New York, Continuum.

Donald, J. 1999. *Imagining the Modern City*. London, Athlone.

Dörries, C. 2000. 'Pulsierender Stadtkörper'. In Senatsverwaltung für Stadtentwicklung Berlin (ed), *z.B. Berlin - Zehn Jahre Transformation und Modernisierung*. Berlin, Edition Foyer.

Douglas, M. 1966. *Purity and Danger*. London, Routledge & Kegan Paul.

Driskell, D. 2002. *Creating Better Cities with Children and Youth: A Manual for Participation*. London and Sterling, VA, Earthscan Publications.

du Gay, P. 2000. *In Praise of Bureaucracy: Weber – Organization – Ethics*. London, Thousand Oaks, and New Delhi, Sage Publications.

Düwel, J. and N. Gutschow 2001. *Städtebau in Deutschland im 20. Jahrhundert: Ideen – Projekte – Akteure*. Stuttgart, Leipzig, Wiesbaden, Teubner.

Elias, N. 1994 (1939). *The Civilizing Process*. Oxford, Blackwell, 1994.

Engler, W. 1999. *Die Ostdeutschen: Kunde von einem verlorenen Land*. Berlin, Aufbau-Verlag.

Englund, H. and J. Leach 2000. 'Ethnography and the Meta-Narratives of Modernity'. *Current Anthropology* 41(2): 225–248.

Epstein, D. 1998. 'Afraid/Not: Psychoanalytic Directions for an Insurgent Planning Historiography'. In L. Sandercock (ed), *Making the Invisible Visible: A Multicultural Planning History*. Berkeley and Los Angeles, CA, University of California Press: 209–226.

Ewald, U. 2000. 'Criminal Victimisation and Social Adaptation in Modernity: Fear of Crime and Risk Perception in the New Germany'. In T. Hope and R. Sparks (eds), *Crime, Risk, and Insecurity: Law and Order in Everyday Life and Political Discourse*. London and New York, Routledge: 166–199.

Fabian, J. 1983. *Time and the Other: How Anthropology Makes its Object*. New York, Columbia University Press.

Fainstein, S. S. 1994. *The City Builders: Property, Politics, and Planning in London and New York*. Oxford and Cambridge, MA, Blackwell.

Fainstein, S. S., I. Gordon and M. Harloe. 1992. *Divided Cities: New York and London in the Contemporary World*. Oxford and Cambridge, MA, Blackwell.

Färber, A. 2005. 'Vom Kommen, Bleiben und Gehen: Anforderungen und Möglichkeiten urbaner Praxis im Unternehmen Stadt. Eine Einleitung'. *Berliner Blätter* 37: 7–20.

Fardon, R. 1995. 'Introduction: Counterworks'. In R. Fardon (ed), *Counterworks: Managing the Diversity of Knowledge*. London and New York, Routledge: 1–22.

Feld, S. and K. H. Basso (eds) 1996. *Senses of Place*. Santa Fe, New Mexico, School of American Research Press.

Ferguson, J. 1990. *The Anti-Politics Machine : "Development," Depoliticization, and Bureaucratic Power in Lesotho.* Cambridge, Cambridge University Press.

———. 1997. 'The Country and the City on the Copperbelt.' In A. Gupta and J. Ferguson (eds), *Culture, Power, Place: Explorations in Critical Anthropology.* Durham and London, Duke University Press: 137–154.

Ferguson, J. and A. Gupta 2002. 'Spatializing States: Toward an Ethnography of Neoliberal Governmentality.' *American Ethnologist* 29(4): 981–1002.

Finnegan, R. 1998. *Tales of the City: A Study of Narrative and Urban Life.* Cambridge, Cambridge University Press.

Fischler, R. 1995. 'Strategy and History in Professional Practice: Planning as World Making.' In H. Liggett and D. C. Perry (eds), *Spatial Practices: Critical Explorations in Social/Spatial Theory.* Thousand Oaks, California, and London, Sage: 13–58.

Flierl, B. 1992. 'Hochhäuser für Berlin – wozu und wo?' In H. G. Helms (ed), *Die Stadt als Gabentisch: Beobachtungen der aktuellen Städtebauentwicklung.* Leipzig, Reclam-Verlag: 445–470.

———. 1996. 'Der Zentrale Ort Berlin – Zur räumlichen Inszenierung sozialistischer Zentralität.' In G. Feist, E. Gillen and B. Vierneisel (eds), *Kunstdokumentation 1945–1990, SBZ/DDR: Aufsätze, Berichte, Materialien.* Köln, Dumont.

———. 2001. 'Zwischen DDR-Moderne und Planwerk-Inszenierungen in Berlin-Mitte.' In H. Stimmann (ed). *Von der Architektur- zur Stadtdebatte: Die Diskussion um das Planwerk Innenstadt.* Berlin, Braun: 75–81.

Forsythe, D. 1989. 'German Identity and the Problem of History.' In E. Tonkin, M. McDonald and M. Chapman (eds), *History and Ethnicity.* London and New York, Routledge: 137–156.

Forty, A. 2000. *Words and Buildings: A Vocabulary of Modern Architecture.* London, Thames & Hudson.

Foster, J. 1999. *Docklands: Cultures in Conflict, Worlds in Collision.* London, UCL Press.

Foucault, M. 1980 (1976). 'Questions on Geography.' In C. Gordon (ed), *Power/ Knowledge – Selected Interviews and Other Writings 1972–1977 by Michel Foucault.* Harlow, Longman: 63–77.

———. 1991 (1978). 'Governmentality.' In G. Burchell, C. Gordon and P. Miller (eds), *The Foucault Effect: Studies in Governmentality.* London, Harvester Wheatsheaf: 87–104.

———. 1999 (1969). *The Archaeology of Knowledge.* London, Routledge.

———. 2000 (1982). 'Technologies of the Self.' P. Rabinow (ed), *Michel Foucault – Ethics.* London, Penguin Books: 223–251.

———. 2002 (1982). 'Space, Knowledge, and Power.' In J.D. Faubion (ed), *Michel Foucault – Power.* London, Penguin Books: 349–364.

———. 2003 (1963). *The Birth of the Clinic.* London, Routledge.

French, R. A. 1995. *Plans, Pragmatism and People: The Legacy of Soviet Planning for Today's Cities.* London, UCL Press.

Frisby, D. 2001. *Cityscapes of Modernity: Critical Explorations.* Cambridge, Polity.

Gagen, E. A. 2000. 'Playing the Part: Performing Gender in America's Playgrounds.' In S. L. Holloway and G. Valentine (eds), *Children's Geographies: Playing, Living, Learning*. London and New York, Routledge: 213–229.

Gal, S. 1991. 'Between Speech and Silence.' In M. di Leonardo (ed), *Gender at the Crossroads of Knowledge: Feminist Anthropology in the Postmodern Era*. Berkeley, University of California Press: 175–203.

Gal, S. and K. A. Woolard 2001. 'Constructing Languages and Publics: Authority and Representation.' In S. Gal and K. A. Woolard (eds), *Languages and Publics: The Making of Authority*. Manchester and Northampton, MA, St. Jerome Publishing: 1–12.

Gell, A. 1992. *The Anthropology of Time: Cultural Constructions of Temporal Maps and Images. Explorations in anthropology*. Oxford and Providence, Berg.

Gillis, J. R. 1981. *Youth and History: Tradition and Change in European Age Relations, 1770–Present (Expanded Student Edition)*. New York and London, Academic Press.

Glaeser, A. 1998. 'Placed Selves: The Spatial Hermeneutics of Self and Other in the Postunification Berlin Police.' *Social Identities* 4(1): 7–38.

———. 2000. *Divided in Unity: Identity, Germany, and the Berlin Police*. Chicago and London, University of Chicago Press.

Gordon, C. 1987. 'The Soul of the Citizen: Max Weber and Michel Foucault on Rationality and Government.' In S. Lash and S. Whimster (eds), *Max Weber, Rationality and Modernity*. London, Allen & Unwin: 293–316.

———. 1991. 'Governmental Rationality: An Introduction.' In G. Burchell, C. Gordon and P. Miller (eds), *The Foucault Effect: Studies in Governmentality*. London, Harvester Wheatsheaf: 1–52.

Graf, W., W. Hansen and B. Schulz 1993. 'From *The* People to *One* People: The Social Bases of the East German "Revolution" and its Preemption by the West German State.' In H. G. De Soto and D. G. Anderson (eds), *The Curtain Rises: Rethinking Culture, Ideology, and the State in Eastern Europe*. Atlantic Highlands, N.J., Humanities Press International: 207–230.

Graffunder, H. 1973. 'Neue Bebauung der Rathausstraße.' *Deutsche Architektur* (June): 340–345.

Green, S. 1997. *Urban Amazons: Lesbian Feminism and Beyond in the Gender, Sexuality and Identity Battles of London*. London, Macmillan.

Greenhouse, C. J. 1996. *A Moment's Notice: Time Politics Across Cultures*. Ithaca, NY, and London, Cornell University Press.

Gregory, S. 1998. *Black Corona: Race and the Politics of Place in an Urban Community*. Princeton, N.J., Princeton University Press.

Grillo, R. D. 1985. *Ideologies and Institutions in Urban France: The Representation of Immigrants*. Cambridge, Cambridge University Press.

———. 1997. 'Discourses of Development: The View from Anthropology.' In R. D. Grillo and R. L. Stirrat (eds), *Discourses of Development: Anthropological Perspectives*. Oxford and New York, Berg: 1–33.

Grundmann, S. 1984. *Die Stadt*. Berlin, Dietz Verlag.

Gupta, A. 1995. 'Blurred Boundaries: The Discourse of Corruption, the Culture of Politics, and the Imagined State.' *American Ethnologist* 22(3): 375–402.

Gupta, A. and J. Ferguson 1997a. 'Beyond 'Culture': Space, Identity, and the Politics of Difference.' In A. Gupta and J. Ferguson (eds), *Culture, Power, Place: Explorations in Critical Anthropology*. Durham and London, Duke University Press: 33–51.

———. 1997b. 'Culture, Power, Place: Ethnography at the End of and Era.' In A. Gupta and J. Ferguson (eds), *Culture, Power, Place: Explorations in Critical Anthropology*. Durham and London, Duke University Press: 1–32.

———. 1997c. 'Discipline and Practice: 'The Field' as Site, Method, and Location in Anthropology.' In A. Gupta and J. Ferguson (eds), *Anthropological Locations: Boundaries and Grounds of a Field Science*. Berkeley and Los Angeles, CA, University of California Press: 1–46.

Haag, A. 1992. *'Deine Sehnsucht kann keiner stillen': Rainer Werner Fassbinders BERLIN ALEXANDERPLATZ – Selbstbildreflexion und Ich-Auflösung*. München, Trickster.

Habermas, J. 1989 (1962). *The Structural Transformation of the Public Sphere: An Inquiry into a Category of Bourgeois Society*. Cambridge, Polity.

Hain, S. 1992. 'Berlin Ost: 'Im Westen wird man sich wundern'.' In K. von Beyme, W. Duth, N. Gutschow, W. Nerdinger and T. Topfstedt (eds), *Neue Städte aus Ruinen: Deutscher Städtebau der Nachkriegszeit*. München, Prestel Verlag.

———. 1996. 'Vom Kollektivplan zum Hauptstadtwettbewerb. Ein Jahrzehnt Stadtplanung.' In Institut für Regionalentwicklung und Strukturplanung (ed), *Archäologie und Aneignung. Ideen, Pläne und Stadtfigurationen. Aufsätze zur Ostberliner Stadtentwicklung nach 1945*. Erkner (bei Berlin): 73–96.

———. 2000a. 'Urbanistik und Architektur beim neoliberalen Ausbau der Zitadelle Berlin. Ein Fall revanchistischer Stadtentwicklungspolitik.' In A. Scharenberg (ed), *Berlin: Global City oder Konkursmasse? Eine Zwischenbilanz zehn Jahre nach dem Mauerfall*. Berlin, Karl Dietz Verlag: 111–128.

———. 200b. 'Zwischen Arkonaplatz und Nikolaiviertel. Stadt als soziale Form versus Inszenierung. Konflikte bei der Rückkehr in die Stadt.' In T. Scheer, J. P. Kleihues and P. Kahlfeldt (eds), *Stadt der Architektur, Architektur der Stadt: Berlin 1900–2000*. Berlin, Nicolai.

———. 2001. 'Struggle for the Inner City – A Plan Becomes a Declaration of War.' In W. J. V. Neill and H.-U. Schwedler (eds), *Urban Planning and Cultural Inclusion: Lessons from Belfast and Berlin*. Basingstoke, Palgrave: 69–84.

Hall, P. 1996. *Cities of Tomorrow: An Intellectual History of Urban Planning and Design in the Twentieth Century (Updated Edition)*. Oxford and Malden, MA, Blackwell.

Hann, C. 1998. 'Introduction: The Embeddedness of Property.' In C. Hann (ed), *Property Relations: Renewing the Anthropological Tradition*. Cambridge, Cambridge University Press: 1–47.

Hannerz, U. 1980. *Exploring the City: Inquiries Toward an Urban Anthropology*. New York, Columbia University Press.

————. 1992. *Cultural Complexity: Studies in the Social Organization of Meaning.* New York, Columbia University Press.

Hansen, T. B. and F. Stepputat 2002. 'Introduction: States of Imagination.' In T. B. Hansen and F. Stepputat (eds), *States of Imagination: Ethnographic Explorations of the Postcolonial State.* Durham and London, Duke University Press.

———— (eds). 2002. *States of Imagination: Ethnographic Explorations of the Postcolonial State.* Durham and London, Duke University Press.

Haraway, D. 1991. *Simians, Cyborgs, and Women: The Reinvention of Nature.* London, Free Association Books.

Harley, J. B. 1988. 'Maps, Knowledge, and Power.' In D. Cosgrove and S. Daniels (eds), *The Iconography of Landscape: Essays on the Symbolic Representation, Design, and Use of Past Environments.* Cambridge, Cambridge University Press: 277–312.

Harloe, M. 1996. 'Cities in Transition.' In G. Andrusz, M. Harloe and I. Szelenyi (eds), *Cities after Socialism: Urban and Regional Change and Conflict in Post-Socialist Societies.* Cambridge, MA, Blackwell: 1–29.

Hartung, K. 1999. 'Doppelgesicht. Über die Paradoxien Berlins.' In M. Michel, I. Karsunke and T. Spengler (eds), *Berlin Metropole, Kursbuch 137.* K. Berlin, Rowohlt: 7–36.

Harvey, D. 1989. *The Condition of Postmodernity: An Enquiry into the Origins of Cultural Change.* Oxford, Basil Blackwell.

Hastrup, K. (ed). 1992. *Other Histories.* London and New York, Routledge.

Häußermann, H. 1996a. 'From the Socialist to the Capitalist City: Experiences from Germany.' In G. Andrusz, M. Harloe and I. Szelenyi (eds), *Cities after Socialism: Urban and Regional Change and Conflict in Post-Socialist Societies.* Oxford and Cambridge, MA, Blackwell: 214–231.

————. 1996b. 'Von der Stadt im Sozialismus zur Stadt im Kapitalismus.' In H. Häußermann and R. Neef (eds), *Stadtentwicklung in Ostdeutschland.* Opladen, Westdeutscher Verlag: 5–48.

Häußermann, H. and A. Haila 2005. 'Cities of Europe: changing contexts, local arrangements, and the challenge to urban cohesion.' In Y. Kazepov (ed), *Cities of Europe: changing contexts, local arrangements, and the challenge to urban cohesion.* Oxford, Blackwell: 43–63.

Häußermann, H. and A. Kapphan 2000. *Berlin: von der geteilten Stadt zur gespaltenen Stadt. Sozialräumlicher Wandel seit* Opladen, Leske und Budrich.

Häußermann, H. and E. Strom 1994. 'Berlin: the Once and Future Capital.' *International Journal of Urban and Regional Research* 18(2): 335–346.

Hebdige, D. 1979. *Subculture: The Meaning of Style.* London, Methuen.

Hecht, T. 1998. *At Home in the Street: Street Children of Northeastern Brazil.* Cambridge, Cambridge University Press.

Herzfeld, M. 1991. *A Place in History: Social and Monumental Time in a Cretan Town.* Princeton, N.J., Princeton University Press.

————. 1992. *The Social Production of Indifference: Exploring the Symbolic Roots of Western Bureaucracy.* New York, Berg.

Hindess, B. 1986. '"Interests" in Political Analysis.' In J. Law (ed), *Power, Action and Belief: A New Sociology of Knowledge?* London, Routledge & Kegan Paul: 112–131.

Hirsch, E. 1995. 'Landscape: Between Place and Space.' In E. Hirsch and M. O'Hanlon (eds), *The Anthropology of Landscape: Perspectives on Place and Space.* Oxford, Clarendon Press.

Hirsch, E. and M. O'Hanlon (eds) 1995. *The Anthropology of Landscape: Perspectives on Place and Space.* Oxford, Clarendon Press.

Holloway, S. L. and G. Valentine 2000. 'Children's Geographies and the New Social Studies of Childhood.' In S. L. Holloway and G. Valentine (eds), *Children's Geographies – Playing, Living, Learning.* London and New York, Routledge: 1–26.

—— (eds) 2000. *Children's Geographies – Playing, Living, Learning.* London and New York, Routledge.

Holmes, D. R. and G. E. Marcus 2005. 'Cultures of Expertise and the Management of Globalization: Toward the Re-Functioning of Ethnography.' In A. Ong and S. J. Collier (eds), *Global Assemblages: Technology, Politics, and Ethics as Anthropological Problems.* Malden, MA, and Oxford, Blackwell: 393–416.

Holston, J. 1989. *The Modernist City: An Anthropological Critique of Brasília.* Chicago and London, University of Chicago Press.

——. 2008. *Insurgent Citizenship: Disjunctions of Democracy and Modernity in Brazil.* Princeton, N.J., Princeton University Press.

Holston, J. and A. Appadurai 1999. 'Introduction: Cities and Citizenship.' In J. Holston (ed), *Cities and Citizenship.* Durham and London, Duke University Press: 1–18.

Hommels, A. 2005. 'Studying Obduracy in the City: Toward a Productive Fusion between Technology Studies and Urban Studies.' *Science, Technology & Human Values* 30(3): 323–351.

Howe, L. 1990a. *Being Unemployed in Northern Ireland.* Cambridge, Cambridge University Press.

——. 1990b. 'Urban Anthropology: Trends in its Development since 1920.' *Cambridge Anthropology* 14(1): 37–66.

Howell, P. 1993. 'Public Space and the Public Sphere: Political Theory and the Historical Geography of Modernity.' *Society and Space* 11: 303–322.

Humphrey, C. 1999. 'Traders, 'Disorder', and Citizenship Regimes in Provincial Russia.' In M. Burawoy and K. Verdery (eds), *Uncertain Transitions: Ethnographies of Change in the Postsocialist World.* Lanham, Maryland, and Oxford, Rowman & Littlefield: 19–52.

Humphrey, C. 2002. 'Rituals of death as a context for understanding personal property in socialist Mongolia.' *Journal of the Royal Anthropological Institute* 8(1): 65–87.

Huyssen, A. 1997. 'The Voids of Berlin.' *Critical Inquiry* 24(1): 57–81.

Ingold, T. 1996. 'The concept of society is theoretically obsolete.' In T. Ingold (ed), *Key Debates In Anthropology.* London, Routledge: 41–82.

Isin, E. F., 2000. 'Introduction: Democracy, Citizenship and the City.' In E. F. Isin (ed), *Democracy, Citizenship and the Global City.* London and New York, Routledge: 1–22.

Jacobs, J. 1962. *The Death and Life of Great American Cities.* London, Jonathan Cape.

Jaffe, R. and M. Onneweer. 2006. 'Futurities: On the Temporal Mediation of Landscapes.' *EASA Biennal Conference.* Bristol, UK.

Jahn, O. and S. Opalka 2004. *Tod im Milliardenspiel. Der Bankenskandal und das Ende eines Kronzeugen.* Berlin, Transit Buchverlag.

James, A. 1986. 'Learning to Belong: the Boundaries of Adolescence.' In A. P. Cohen (ed), *Symbolising Boundaries: Identity and Diversity in British Cultures.* Manchester, Manchester University Press: 155–170.

James, A., C. Jenks and A. Prout 1998. *Theorizing Childhood.* Cambridge, Polity Press.

James, I. 2003. *Re-making Urban Space: Writing Social Realities in the British City.* University of St. Andrews. (PhD dissertation)

James, W. and D. Mills (eds). 2005. *The Qualities of Time: Anthropological Approaches.* Oxford and New York, Berg.

James-Chakraborty, K. 2000. *German Architecture for a Mass Audience.* London and New York, Routledge.

Johnston, L. 1992. *The Rebirth of Private Policing.* London and New York, Routledge.

Kaneff, D. 2003. *Who Owns the Past? The Politics of Time in a 'Model' Bulgarian Village.* New York and Oxford, Berghahn.

Kapferer, B. 2005. 'Introduction.' In B. Kapferer (ed), *The Retreat of the Social: The Rise and Rise of Reductionism.* New York and Oxford, Berghahn: 1–18.

Kern, S. 1983. *The Culture of Time and Space 1880–1918.* London, Weidenfeld and Nicolson.

Kieren, M. 1994. 'Which way to 'Alex' please?' In K. Feireiss (ed), *Alexanderplatz: Städtebaulicher Ideenwettbewerb Alexanderplatz = Urban Planning Ideas Competition.* Berlin, Ernst & Sohn.

Kil, W. 1992. 'Prenzlauer Berg – Aufstieg und Fall einer Nische.' In H. G. Helms (ed), *Die Stadt als Gabentisch: Beobachtungen der aktuellen Städtebauentwicklung.* Leipzig, Reclam-Verlag: 508–520.

———. 2000. *Gründerparadiese: Vom Bauen in den Zeiten des Übergangs.* Berlin, Verlag Bauwesen.

Kil, W. and B. Kündiger 1998. 'Alexanderplatz – drei Wettbewerbe, drei Weltstadtvisionen.' In H.-J. Pysall (ed), *Das Alexanderhaus, der Alexanderplatz.* Berlin, Jovis.

King, A. D. 1996. 'Introduction: Cities, Texts and Paradigms.' In A. D. King (ed), *Re-presenting the City: Ethnicity, Capital and Culture in the 21st Century Metropolis.* Basingstoke, Macmillan: 1–19.

Knecht, M., 1999. 'Einleitung: Die andere Seite der Stadt.' In M. Knecht (ed), *Die andere Seite der Stadt: Armut und Ausgrenzung in Berlin.* Köln, Weimar, and Wien, Böhlau Verlag: 8–28.

Kracauer, S. 1996. *Berliner Nebeneinander – Ausgewählte Feuilletons 1930–33.* Zürich, Edition Epoca.

Krämer-Badoni, T. and E. Wiegand. 1996. 'Bürgerinitiativen nach der Wende. Zur Entstehung von Stadtteil- und Bürgerinitiativen in der Stadt Leipzig seit 1989.' In H. Häußermann and R. Neef (eds), *Stadtentwicklung in Ostdeutschland.* Opladen, Westdeutscher Verlag: 205–218.

Krätke, S. 1999. 'Berlin's Regional Economy in the 1990s: Structural Adjustment or 'Open-Ended' Structural Break?' *European Urban and Regional Studies* 6(4): 323–338.

———. 2004. 'City of talents? Berlin's regional economy, socio-spatial fabric and "worst practice" urban governance' *International Journal of Urban and Regional Research* 28(3): 511–29.

Krätke, S. and R. Borst 2000 *Berlin – Metropole zwischen Boom und Krise.* Opladen, Leske + Budrich.

Kuhle, H. 1995. 'Auferstanden aus Ruinen: Der Alexanderplatz.' In B. Wilczek (ed), *Berlin – Hauptstadt der DDR 1949 – Utopie und Realität.* Baden Baden, Elster Verlag.

Kulick, D. 1995. 'Introduction. The Sexual Life of Anthropologists: Erotic Subjectivity and Ethnographic Work.' In D. Kulick and M. Wilson (eds), *Taboo – Sex, Identity and Erotic Subjectivity in Anthropological Fieldwork.* London and New York, Routledge: 1–28.

Ladd, B. 1990. *Urban Planning and Civic Order in Germany, 1860–1914.* Cambridge, MA, and London, Harvard University Press.

———. 1997. *The Ghosts of Berlin: Confronting German History in the Urban Landscape.* Chicago and London, University of Chicago Press.

———. 1999. 'Altstadterneuerung und Bürgerbewegung in den 1980er Jahren in der DDR.' In H. Barth (ed), *Planen für das Kollektiv.* Erkner (bei Berlin), Institut für Regionalentwicklung und Strukturplanung: 89–93.

Lang, B. 1998. *Mythos Kreuzberg: Ethnographie eines Stadtteils (1961–1995).* Frankfurt and New York, Campus.

Lass, A. 1994. 'From Memory to History: The Events of November 17 Dis/membered.' In R. Watson (ed), *Memory, History, and Opposition under State Socialism.* Santa Fe, New Mexico, School of American Research Press: 87–104.

Latham, A. 2006a. 'Anglophone Urban Studies and the European City: Some Comments on Interpreting Berlin.' *European Urban and Regional Studies* 13(1): 88–92.

———. 2006b. 'Berlin and Everywhere Else: A Reply to Allan Cochrane.' *European Urban and Regional Studies* 13(4): 377–379.

Latour, B. 1993. *We Have Never Been Modern.* London, Harvester Wheatsheaf.

———. 1996. *Aramis: or the Love of Technology.* Cambridge, MA, and London, Harvard University Press.

———. 2005. 'From Realpolitik to Dingpolitik: or How to Make Things Public.' In B. Latour and P. Weibel (eds), *Making Things Public: Atmospheres of Democracy.* Cambridge, MA, and London, The MIT Press: 14–41.

Law, J. and J. Hassard (eds). 1999. *Actor Network Theory and After.* Oxford and Malden, MA, Blackwell.

Lawrence, D. L. and S. M. Low 1990. 'The Built Environment and Spatial Form.' *Annual Review of Anthropology* 19: 453–505.

Lees, A. 1985. *Cities Perceived: Urban Society in European and American Thought 1820–1940.* Manchester, Manchester University Press.

Lefebvre, H. 1991. *The Production of Space.* Oxford, Basil Blackwell.

Lemon, A. 2000. 'Talking Transit and Spectating Transition: The Moscow Metro.' In D. Berdahl, M. Bunzl and M. Lampland (eds), *Altering States: Ethnographies of Transition in Eastern Europe and the Former Soviet Union.* Ann Arbor, University of Michigan Press: 14–39.

Lenhart, K. 2001. *Berliner Metropoly: Stadtentwicklungspolitik im Berliner Bezirk Mitte nach der Wende.* Opladen, Leske + Budrich.

Levine, M. A. 2004. 'Government Policy, The Local State, and Gentrification: The Case of Prenzlauer Berg (Berlin), Germany ' *Journal of Urban Affairs* 26(1): 89–108.

Li, T. M. 2005. 'Beyond 'the State' and Failed Schemes.' *American Anthropologist* 107(3): 383–394.

Lindenberger, T. 2008. 'Asociality' and Modernity: The GDR as a Welfare Dictatorship.' In K. Pence and P. Betts (eds), *Socialist Modern: East German Everyday Culture and Politics.* Ann Arbor, University of Michigan Press: 211–233.

Lindstrom, L. 1990. *Knowledge and Power in a South Pacific Society.* Washington, DC, Smithsonian Institute Press.

Linke, U. 1999. *German Bodies: Race and Representation after Hitler.* New York and London, Routledge.

Lompscher, K. 2000. 'Stadtidee Dienstleistungen. Zum Zusammenhang von Stadtentwicklungsdiskurs und Dienstleistungsentwicklung in Berlin seit 1990.' In A. Scharenberg (ed), *Berlin: Global City oder Konkursmasse? Eine Zwischenbilanz zehn Jahre nach dem Mauerfall.* Berlin, Karl Dietz Verlag: 82–95.

Low, S. M. 1996. 'The Anthropology of Cities: Imagining and Theorizing the City.' *Annual Review of Anthropology* 25: 383–409.

———. 1997. 'Theorizing the City: Ethnicity, Gender and Globalization.' *Critique of Anthropology* 17(4): 403–409.

———. 1999. 'Introduction: Theorizing the City.' In S. M. Low (ed), *Theorizing the City: The New Urban Anthropology Reader.* New Brunswick, N.J., and London, Rutgers University Press: 1–33.

———. 2000. *On the Plaza: The Politics of Public Space and Culture.* Austin, Texas, University of Texas Press.

———. 2003. 'The Edge and the Center: Gated Communities and the Discourse of Urban Fear.' In S. M. Low and D. Lawrence-Zúñiga (eds), *The Anthropology of Place and Space: Locating Culture.* Malden, MA, and Oxford, Blackwell: 387–407.

Low, S. M. and D. Lawrence-Zúñiga (eds) 2003. *The Anthropology of Space and Place: Locating Culture.* Malden, MA, and Oxford, Blackwell.

Lowenthal, D. 1989. 'Nostalgia tells it like it wasn't.' In C. S. M.Chase (ed), *The Imagined Past: History and Nostalgia.* Manchester, Manchester University Press: 18–32.

Lücke, D. 1998. 'Die Weltzeituhr.' In H.-J. Pysall (ed), *Das Alexanderhaus, der Alexanderplatz.* Berlin, Jovis.

Macdonald, S. 2001. 'Behind the Scenes at the Science Museum: Knowing, Making, Using.' M. In Bouquet (ed), *Academic Anthropology and the Museum.* Oxford, Berghahn: 117–140.

Malkki, L. H. 1997. 'National Geographic: The Rooting of Peoples and the Territorialization of National Identity among Scholars and Refugees.' In A. Gupta and J. Ferguson (eds), *Culture, Power, Place: Explorations in Critical Anthropology.* Durham and London, Duke University Press: 52–74.

Mandel, R. 1994. "Fortress Europe' and the Foreigners within: Germany's Turks.' In V. A. Goddard, J. R. Llobera and C. Shore (eds), *The Anthropology of Europe: Identities and Boundaries in Conflict.* Oxford and Providence, Berg: 113–124.

———. 2008. *Cosmopolitan Anxieties: Turkish Challenges to Citizenship and Belonging in Germany.* Durham and London, Duke University Press.

Marcus, G. E. 1998. *Ethnography Through Thick & Thin.* Princeton, N.J., Princeton University Press.

Marcuse, P. 1998. 'Reflections on Berlin: The Meaning of Construction and the Construction of Meaning.' *International Journal of Urban and Regional Research* 22(2): 331–338.

Marx Ferree, M. 1997. 'German Unification and Feminist Identity.' In J. W. Scott, C. Kaplan and D. Keates (eds), *Transitions, Environments, Translations: Feminism in International Politics.* London and New York, Routledge: 46–55.

Massey, D. 1999. 'Space-time, 'Science' and the Relationship Between Physical Geography and Human Geography.' *Transactions of the Institute of British Geographers (N.S.)* 24: 261–276.

Matthews, H., M. Limb and M. Taylor 2000. 'The "Street as Thirdspace".' In S. L. Holloway and G. Valentine (eds), *Children's Geographies: Playing, Living, Learning.* London and New York, Routledge: 63–79.

Mayer, M. 1999. 'Urban Movements and Urban Theory in the Late-20th-Century City.' In R. A. Beauregard and S. Body-Gendrot (eds), *The Urban Moment: Cosmopolitan Essays on the Late-20th-Century City.* Thousand Oaks, London, New Delhi, Sage: 209–238.

———. 2000. 'Social Movements in European Cities: Transitions from the 1970s to the 1990s.' In A. Bagnasco and P. les Galès (eds), *Cities in Contemporary Europe.* Cambridge, Cambridge University Press: 131–152.

McDonald, M. 1989. *'We are not French!': Language, Culture and Identity in Brittany.* London, Routledge.

———. 1993. 'The Construction of Difference: An Anthropological Approach to Stereotypes.' In S. Macdonald (ed), *Inside European Identities.* Oxford, Berg: 219–236.

McDonogh, G. W. 1993. 'The Geography of Emptiness.' In R. Rotenberg and G. W. McDonogh (eds), *The Cultural Meaning of Urban Space.* Westport, CN, and London, Bergin & Garvey: 3–15.

———. 1999. 'Discourses of the City: Policy and Response in Post-Transitional Barcelona.' In S. M. Low (eds.), *Theorizing the City: The New Urban Anthro-*

pology Reader. New Brunswick, N.J., and London, Rutgers University Press: 342–376.

———. 2003. 'Myth, Space, and Virtue: Bars, Gender, and Change in Barcelona's Barrio Chino.' In S. M. Low and D. Lawrence-Zúñiga (eds), *The Anthropology of Space and Place: Locating Culture.* Malden, MA, and Oxford, Blackwell: 264–283.

Merton, R. K. 1949. *Social Theory and Social Structure.* New York, Free Press.

Midgley, J. 1986. 'Community Participation: History, Concepts and Controversies.' In J. Midgley (ed), *Community Participation, Social Development and the State.* London and New York, Methuen & Co.

Miller, D. 2005. 'Materiality: An Introduction.' In D. Miller (ed), *Materiality.* Durham and London, Duke University Press: 1–50.

Mitchell, T. 1988. *Colonising Egypt.* Cambridge, Cambridge University Press.

Mitchell, T. 1991. 'The Limits of the State: Beyond Statist Approaches and their Critics.' *American Political Science Review* 85(1): 77–96.

———. 2002. *Rule of Experts: Egypt, Technopolitics, Modernity.* Berkeley, University of California Press.

Mitscherlich, A. 1996 (1965). *Die Unwirtlichkeit unserer Städte: Anstiftung zum Unfrieden.* Frankfurt/Main, Suhrkamp Verlag.

Miyazaki, H. and A. Riles. 2005. 'Failure as Endpoint.' In A. Ong and S. J. Collier (eds), *Global Assemblages: Technology, Politics, and Ethics as Anthropological Problems.* Malden, MA, and Oxford, Blackwell: 320–331.

Mol, A. 2002. *The Body Multiple: Ontology in Medical Practice.* Durham and London, Duke University Press.

Mol, A. and J. Law 2002. 'Complexities: An Introduction.' In J. Law and A. Mol (eds), *Complexities: Social Studies of Knowledge Practices.* Durham and London, Duke University Press: 1–22.

Mommsen, W. 1989. *The Political and Social Theory of Max Weber – Collected Essays.* Cambridge, Polity Press.

Mönninger, M. 2001. 'Die Stadt als Zivilisationsmodell der Zukunft?' In H. Stimmann (ed), *Von der Architektur- zur Stadtdebatte: Die Diskussion um das Planwerk Innenstadt.* Berlin, Braun: 37–43.

Moore, H. L. 1986. *Space, Text and Gender: An Anthropological Study of the Marakwet of Kenya.* Cambridge, Cambridge University Press.

Moughtin, C. 1999. *Urban Design: Street and Square (Second Edition).* Oxford, Auckland, Boston, Johannesburg, Melbourne, and New Delhi, Architectural Press.

Müller, B. 1992. With the Boundary in Mind: East-West German Stereotypes and the Problems of Transition in Three Enterprises in East Berlin. *2nd EASA Conference.* Prague.

Munn, N. D. 1990. 'Constructing Regional Worlds in Experience: Kula Exchange, Witchcraft and Gawan Local Events.' *Man* 25(1): 1-17.

———. 2003 (1996). 'Excluded Spaces: The Figure in the Australian Aboriginal Landscape.' In S. M. Low and D. Lawrence-Zúñiga (eds), *The Anthropology of Space and Place: Locating Culture.* Malden, MA, and Oxford, Blackwell: 92–109.

Navaro-Yashin, Y. 2002. *Faces of the State: Secularism and Public Life in Turkey.* Princeton, N.J., and Oxford, Princeton University Press.

Nelson, N. and S. Wright 1995. 'Participation and Power.' In N. Nelson and S. Wright (eds), *Power and Participatory Development: Theory and Practice.* London, Intermediate Technology: 1–18.

—— (eds). 1995. *Power and Participatory Development: Theory and Practice.* London, Intermediate Technology.

Neubert, E. 1997. *Geschichte der Opposition in der DDR 1949.* Berlin, Links.

Neumann, D. 1995. *'Die Wolkenkratzer kommen!' Deutsche Hochhäuser der zwanziger Jahre.* Braunschweig and Wiesbaden, Vieweg.

Neumeyer, F. 2001. 'Dem Verschwinden der Stadt entgegengedacht.' In H. Stimmann (ed), *Von der Architektur- zur Stadtdebatte: Die Diskussion um das Planwerk Innenstadt.* Berlin, Braun: 29–35.

Nora, P. and L. D. Kritzman 1998. *Realms of Memory: The Construction of the French Past.* New York and Chichester, Columbia University Press.

Norman, K. 1991. *A Sound Family Makes a Sound State: Ideology and Upbringing in a German Village.* Stockholm, University of Stockholm.

Nowotny, H., P. Scott and M. Gibbons 2001. *Re-thinking Science: Knowledge and the Public in an Age of Uncertainty.* Cambridge, Polity Press.

Okely, J. 1992. 'Anthropology and Autobiography: Participatory Experience and Embodied Knowledge.' In J. Okely and H. Callaway (eds), *Anthropology and Autobiography.* London and New York, Routledge: 1–28.

Ortner, S. B. 1995. 'Resistance and the Problem of Ethnographic Refusal.' *Comparative Studies in Society and History* 37(1): 173–193.

Osborne, T. and N. Rose 1999. 'Do the Social Sciences Create Phenomena? The Example of Public Opinion Research.' *British Journal of Sociology* 50(3): 367–396.

Ouroussoff, A. and C. Toren 2005. 'Discussion: Anthropology and Citizenship.' *Social Anthropology* 13(2): 207–209.

Overing, J. 1985. 'Introduction.' *Reason and Morality.* J. Overing Ed. London and New York, Tavistock Publications: 1–28.

Paley, J. 2001. *Marketing Democracy: Power and Social Movements in Post-Dictatorship Chile.* Berkeley, Los Angeles, London, University of California Press.

Pardo, I. 2000. 'Introduction – Morals of Legitimacy: Interplay between Responsibility, Authority and Trust.' In I. Pardo (ed), *Morals of Legitimacy: Between Agency and System.* New York and Oxford, Berghahn.

Parkin, D. 1982. 'Introduction.' In D. Parkin (ed), *Semantic Anthropology.* London and New York, Academic Press: xi–li.

Parman, S. 1998a. 'Introduction: Europe in the Anthropological Imagination.' In S. Parman (ed), *Europe in the Anthropological Imagination.* Upper Saddle River, N.J., Prentice Hall: 1–16.

——. 1998b. 'The Meaning of 'Europe' in the American Anthropologist (Part I).' In S. Parman (ed), *Europe in the Anthropological Imagination.* Upper Saddle River, N.J., Prentice Hall.

Passaro, J. 1997. "You Can't Take the Subway to the Field!': 'Village' Epistemologies in the Global Village.' In A. Gupta and J. Ferguson (eds), *Anthropological Loca-*

tions: Boundaries and Grounds of a Field Science. Berkeley and Los Angeles, CA, University of California Press: 147–162.

Pierre, J. (ed). 1998. *Partnership in Urban Governance: European and American Experience.* Basingstoke, Macmillan.

Pinney, C. 2005. 'Things Happen: Or, From Which Moment Does That Object Come?' In D. Miller (ed), *Materiality.* Durham and London, Duke University Press: 256–272.

Pratt, M. L. 1986. 'Fieldwork in Common Places.' In J. Clifford and G. E. Marcus (eds), *Writing Culture: The Poetics and Politics of Ethnography.* Berkeley, CA, and London, University of California Press: 27–50.

Preuss, U. K. 2003. 'Citizenship and the German Nation.' *Citizenship Studies* 7(1): 37–55.

Rabinow, P. 1989. *French Modern: Norms and Forms of the Social Environment.* Chicago and London, University of Chicago Press.

———. 2003 (1982). 'Ordonnance, Discipline, Regulation: Some Reflections on Urbanism.' In S. M. Low and D. Lawrence-Zúñiga (eds), *The Anthropology of Space and Place: Locating Culture.* Malden, MA, and Oxford, Blackwell: 353–362.

Rada, U. 1997. *Hauptstadt der Verdrängung: Berliner Zukunft zwischen Kiez und Metropole.* Berlin, Schwarze Risse / Rote Straße.

Reed, A. 2002. 'City of Details: terpreting the Personality of London.' *JRAI* 8(1): 127–141.

Ribbe, W. 1998. 'Politik und Gesellschaft am Alexanderplatz.' In H.-J. Pysall (ed), *Das Alexanderhaus, der Alexanderplatz.* Berlin, Jovis.

Richardson, M. 2003 (1982). 'Being-in-the-Market Versus Being-in-the-Plaza: Material Culture and the Construction of Social Reality in Spanish America.' In S. M. Low and D. Lawrence-Zúñiga (eds), *The Anthropology of Space and Place: Locating Culture.* Malden, MA, and Oxford, Blackwell: 74–91.

Richardson, T. 2008. *Kaleidoscopic Odessa: History and Place in Contemporary Ukraine.* Toronto, University of Toronto Press.

Richie, A. 1998. *Faust's Metropolis: A History of Berlin.* London, HarperCollins.

Riedel, M. 1972. 'Bürger, Staatsbürger, Bürgertum.' In O. Brunner, W. Conze and R. Koselleck (eds), *Geschichtliche Grundbegriffe: Ein Historisches Lexikon zur politisch-sozialen Sprache in Deutschland (Vol.1).* Köln, Weimar, Wien, Böhlau Verlag.

Riles, A. 1998. 'Infinity Within the Brackets.' *American Ethnologist* 25(3): 378–398.

———. 2000. *The Network Inside Out.* Ann Arbor, University of Michigan Press.

———. 2006. 'Introduction: In Response.' In A. Riles (ed), *Documents: Artifacts of Modern Knowledge.* Ann Arbor, University of Michigan Press: 1–38.

Robe, C. 1999. "...und raus bist du!' Wie soziale Probleme in der Berliner Innenstadt ausgeblendet werden.' In M. Knecht (ed), *Die andere Seite der Stadt: Armut und Ausgrenzung in Berlin.* Köln, Weimar, and Wien, Böhlau Verlag: 30–41.

Rodman, M. 1992. 'Empowering Place: Multilocality and Multivocality.' *American Ethnologist* 94(3): 640–656.

Rogers, S. C. 1998. 'Strangers in a Crowded Field: American Anthropology in France.' In S. Parman (ed), *Europe in the Anthropological Imagination.* Upper Saddle River, N.J., Prentice Hall: 17–33.

Ronneberger, K., S. Lanz and W. Jahn (eds) 1999. *Die Stadt als Beute.* Bonn, Dietz.

Rose, C. M. 1994. *Property and Persuasion: Essays on the History, Theory, and Rhetoric of Ownership.* Boulder, San Francisco and Oxford, Westview Press.

Rose, N. 1999. *Powers of Freedom: Reframing Political Thought.* Cambridge, Cambridge University Press.

Rose, N. and P. Miller 1992. 'Political Power Beyond the State: Problematics of Government.' *BJS* 43(2): 173–205.

Rotenberg, R. 1993a. 'Introduction.' In R. Rotenberg and G. McDonogh (eds), *The Cultural Meaning of Urban Space.* Westport, CT, and London, Bergin & Garvey: xi–xix.

———. 1993b. 'On the Salubrity of Sites.' In R. Rotenberg and G. McDonogh (eds), *The Cultural Meaning of Urban Space.* Westport, CT, and London, Bergin & Garvey: 17–29.

Rotenberg, R. and G. McDonogh (eds) 1993. *The Cultural Meaning of Urban Space.* Westport, CT, and London, Bergin & Garvey.

Ruddick, S. M. 1996. *Young and Homeless in Hollywood: Mapping Social Identities.* New York and London, Routledge.

Rutheiser, C. 1996. *Imagineering Atlanta: The Politics of Place in the City of Dreams.* London, Verso.

Rutheiser, C. 1999. 'Making Place in the Nonplace Urban Realm: Notes on the Revitalization of Downtown Atlanta.' In S. M. Low (ed), *Theorizing the City: The New Urban Anthropology Reader.* New Brunswick, N.J., and London, Rutgers University Press: 317–341.

Rykwert, J. 1976. *The idea of a Town: The Anthropology of Urban Form in Rome, Italy and the Ancient World.* London, Faber.

Sampson, S. L. 1984. *National Integration through Socialist Planning: An Anthropological Study of a New Romanian Town.* Boulder, East European Monographs.

Sanders, T. and H. G. West 2003. 'Power Revealed and Concealed in the New World Order.' In H. G. West and T. Sanders (eds), *Transparency and Conspiracy: Ethnographies of Suspicion in the New World Order.* Durham and London, Duke University Press: 1–37.

Sassen, S. 1991. *The Global City: New York, London, Tokyo.* Princeton, N.J., Princeton University Press.

———. 2000. 'Ausgrabungen in der "Global City".' In A. Scharenberg (ed), *Berlin: Global City oder Konkursmasse? Eine Zwischenbilanz zehn Jahre nach dem Mauerfall.* Berlin, Karl Dietz Verlag: 13–26.

Schama, S. 1987. *The Embarrassment of Riches: An Interpretation of Dutch Culture in the Golden Age.* London, Collins.

Scheffler, K. 1989 (1910). *Berlin – Ein Stadtschicksal.* Berlin, Fannei & Walz.

Schlör, J. 1998. *Nights in the Big City: Paris, Berlin, London 1840–1930.* London, Reaktion Books.

Schwartzman, H. B. 1989. *The Meeting: Gatherings in Organizations and Communities.* New York and London, Plenum Press.

Schwedler, H.-U. 2001. 'The Urban Planning Context in Berlin: a City Twice Unique.' In W. J. V. Neill and H.-U. Schwedler (eds), *Urban Planning and Cultural Inclusion: Lessons from Belfast and Berlin.* Basingstoke, Palgrave: 24–41.

Scott, J. C. 1998. *Seeing like a State.* New Haven and London, Yale University Press.

Scott, J. W. 1994. 'The Evidence of Experience.' In J. Chandler, A. Davidson and H. Harootunian (eds), *Questions of Evidence: Proof, Practice, and Persuasion across the Disciplines.* Chicago and London, University of Chicago Press: 363–387.

Selle, K. n.d. Stadtentwicklung als Verständigungsarbeit - Entwicklungslinien, Stärken – Schwächen und Folgerungen, http://www.pt.rwth-aachen.de/publikationen/manuskripte/selle/Verstaendigung.html. (no longer available)

Senatsverwaltung für Stadtentwicklung Berlin. 2003. *Alexanderplatz, Berlin-Mitte. Begrenzt-offener freiraumplanerischer Ideen- und Realisierungswettbewerb.* Berlin.

—— (ed) 2000. *z.B. Berlin – Zehn Jahre Transformation und Modernisierung.* Berlin, Edition Foyer.

—— (ed) 2001. *Alexanderplatz Berlin: Geschichte, Planung, Projekte – History, Planning, Projects.* Berlin, Senatsverwaltung für Stadtentwicklung, Planen, Bauen, Wohnen, Umwelt, Verkehr.

—— (ed) 2007. *Urban Pioneers.* Berlin, Jovis Verlag.

Sennett, R. 1994. *Flesh and Stone: The Body and the City in Western Civilization.* London and Boston, Faber and Faber.

——. 2003. *Respect: The Formation of Character in an Age of Inequality.* London, Penguin Books.

Shields, R. 1996. 'A Guide to Urban Representation and What to Do About It: Alternative Traditions of Urban Theory.' In A. D. King (ed), *Re-presenting the City: Ethnicity, Capital, and Culture in the 21st Century Metropolis.* Basingstoke, Macmillan: 227–252.

Shore, C. 1993. 'Inventing the 'People's Europe': Critical Approaches to European Community 'Cultural Policy.' *Man* 28: 779–800.

Shore, C. and S. Wright 1997. 'Policy: A New Field of Anthropology.' In C. Shore and S. Wright (eds), *Anthropology of Policy: Critical Perspectives on Governance and Power.* London and New York, Routledge: 3–42.

Sibley, D. 1995. *Geographies of Exclusion: Society and Difference in the West.* London and New York, Routledge.

Sieber, R. T. 1993. 'Public Access on the Urban Waterfront: A Question of Vision.' In R. Rotenberg and G. McDonogh (eds), *The Cultural Meaning of Urban Space.* Westport, CT, and London, Bergin & Garvey: 173–193.

Siedler, W. J. 1993 (1961). *Die gemordete Stadt: Abgesang auf Putte und Straße, Platz und Baum.* Berlin, Siedler.

Siemann, W. 1995. 'Die deutsche Hauptstadtproblematik im 19. Jahrhundert.' In H.-M. Körner and K. Weigand (eds), *Hauptstadt: Historische Perspektiven eines deutschen Themas.* München, Deutscher Taschenbuch Verlag: 249–260.

Simmel, G. 1980 (1903). 'The Metropolis and Mental Life.' In I. Press and M. E. Smith (eds), *Urban Place and Process: Readings in the Anthropology of Cities.* New York and London, Macmillan: 19–30.

Skelton, T. and G. Valentine (eds) 1998. *Cool Places: Geographies of Youth Cultures.* London and New York, Routledge.

Smail, D. and C. Ross. 2000. 'New Berlins and New Germanies: History, Myth and the German Capital in the 1920s and 1990s.' In M. Fulbrook and M. Swales (eds), *Representing the German Nation: History and Identity in Twentieth-Century Germany.* Manchester, Manchester University Press: 63–76.

Soja, E. W. 1996. *Thirdspace : Journeys to Los Angeles and Other Real-and-imagined Places.* Cambridge, MA, and Oxford, Blackwell.

Sorkin, M. (ed). 1992. *Variations on a Theme Park: The New American City and the End of Public Space.* New York, Hill and Wang.

Spülbeck, S. 1996. 'Anti-Semitism and Fear of the Public Sphere in a Post-Totalitarian Society (East Germany).' In C. M. Hann and E. Dunn (eds), *Civil Society: Challenging Western Models.* London, Routledge: 64–78.

Ssorin-Chaikov, N. 2003. *The Social Life of the State in Subarctic Siberia.* Stanford, CA, Stanford University Press.

———. 2006. 'Heterochrony: On Birthday Gifts to Stalin, 1949.' *JRAI* 12(2): 355–376.

Staiger, U. n.d. 'Cities, Citizens, Contested Cultures: Berlin's Palace of the Republic and the politics of public space.' (manuscript)

Stallybrass, P. and A. White. 1986. *The Politics and Poetics of Transgression.* Ithaca, NY, Cornell University Press.

Stimmann, H. 1994. 'Kritische Rekonstruktion und steinerne Architektur für die Friedrichstadt.' In A. Burg (ed), *Neue Berlinische Architektur: Eine Debatte.* Berlin, Birkhäuser Verlag.

———. 1995a. 'Neue Berliner Büro- und Geschäftshäuser.' In A. Burg (ed), *Berlin Mitte - die Entstehung einer urbanen Architektur = Downtown Berlin - Building the Metropolitan Mix.* Berlin, Birkhäuser Verlag.

———. 1995b. 'Städtebau und Architektur für die Hauptstadt.' In W. Süß (ed), *Hauptstadt Berlin: Berlin im wiedervereinigten Deutschland (Vol.2).* Berlin, Berlin Verlag.

———. 1998. 'Wettbewerb 1992 – und wie weiter?' In H.-J. Pysall (ed), *Das Alexanderhaus, der Alexanderplatz.* Berlin, Jovis.

———. 2001. 'Das Gedächtnis der europäischen Stadt.' In H. Stimmann (ed), *Von der Architektur- zur Stadtdebatte: Die Diskussion um das Planwerk Innenstadt.* Berlin, Braun: 11–27.

Stock, M. 1994. 'Youth Culture in East Germany: From Symbolic Dropout to Politicization.' *Communist and Post-Communist Studies* 27(2): 135–143.

Stolcke, V. 1995. 'Talking Culture: New Boundaries, New Rhetorics of Exclusion in Europe.' *Current Anthropology* 36(1): 1–24.

Stoller, P. 1996. 'Spaces, Places, and Fields: The Politics of West African Trading in New York City's Informal Economy.' *American Anthropologist* 98(4): 776–788.

———. 2002. 'Crossroads: Tracing African Paths on New York City Streets.' *Ethnography* 3(1): 35–62.

Stratford, E. 2002. 'On the Edge: A Tale of Skaters and Urban Governance.' *Social and Cultural Geography* 3(2): 193–206.

Strathern, M. 1987. 'The Limits of Auto-Anthropology.' In A. Jackson (ed), *Anthropology at Home*. London and New York, Tavistock Publications: 16–37.

———. 1991. *Partial Connections*. Savage, MD, Rowman and Littlefield.

———. 1992. *After Nature: English Kinship in the Late Twentieth Century*. Cambridge, Cambridge University Press.

———. 1996. 'Cutting the Network.' *JRAI* 2(n.s.): 517–535.

———. 2000b. 'New Accountabilities; Anthropological Studies in Audit, Ethics and the Academy.' In M. Strathern (ed), *Audit Cultures: Anthropological Studies in Accountability, Ethics and the Academy*. London and New York, Routledge: 1–18.

———. 2002. 'Externalities in Comparative Guise.' *Economy and Society* 31(2): 250–267.

———. 2004. *Commons and Borderlands: Working paper on interdisciplinarity, accountability and the flow of knowledge*. Cambridge, Sean Kingston.

———. 2005. 'Robust Knowledge and Fragile Futures.' In A. Ong and S. J. Collier (eds), *Global Assemblages: technology, politics, and ethics as anthropological problems*. Malden, MA, and Oxford, Blackwell: 464–481.

——— (ed). 2000a. *Audit Cultures: Anthropological Studies in Accountability, Ethics and the Academy*. London and New York, Routledge.

Strieder, P. 2000. 'Prinzip Großstadt.' In Senatsverwaltung für Stadtentwicklung (ed), *z.B. Berlin – Zehn Jahre Transformation und Modernisierung*. Berlin, Edition Foyer.

———. 2001. 'Alexanderplatz Berlin.' In Senatsverwaltung für Stadtentwicklung (ed), *Alexanderplatz Berlin: Geschichte, Planung, Projekte - History, Planning, Projects*. Berlin, Senatsverwaltung für Stadtentwicklung, Planen, Bauen, Wohnen, Umwelt, Verkehr: 3.

Strom, E. A. 2001. *Building the New Berlin: The Politics of Urban Development in Germany's Capital City*. Lanham, MD, and Oxford, Lexington Books.

Süchting, W. and P. Weiss 2001. 'A New Plan for Berlin's Inner City: Planwerk Innenstadt.' In W. J. V. Neill and H.-U. Schwedler (eds), *Urban Planning and Cultural Inclusion: Lessons from Belfast and Berlin*. Basingstoke, Palgrave: 57–68.

Süß, W. and R. Rytlewski (eds) 1999. *Berlin, die Hauptstadt: Vergangenheit und Zukunft einer europäischen Metropole*. Bonn, Bundeszentrale für Politische Bildung.

Ten Dyke, E. A. 2001. *Dresden: Paradoxes of Memory in History*. London, Routledge.

Thiele, G. and C. S. Taylor 1998. *Jugendkulturen und Gangs: Eine Betrachtung zur Raumaneignung und Raumverdrängung in den neuen Bundesländern und den USA*. Berlin, VWB Verlag für Wissenschaft und Bildung.

Thompson, E. P. 1967. 'Time, Work-Discipline, and Industrial Capitalism.' *Past and Present* 38: 56–97.

Thrift, N. 1996. *Spatial Formations.* London, Sage Publications.

Till, K. E. 2005. *The New Berlin: Memory, Politics, Place.* Minneapolis, University of Minnesota Press.

Tonkin, E., M. McDonald and M. Chapman (eds) 1989. *History and Ethnicity.* London, Routledge.

Topfstedt, T. 1988. *Städtebau in der DDR 1955–1971.* Leipzig, VEB E.A. Seemann Verlag.

Tscheschner, D. 1998. 'Der Alexanderplatz unter der Hypothek des Verkehrs.' In H.-J. Pysall (ed), *Das Alexanderhaus, der Alexanderplatz.* Berlin, Jovis.

Tsing, A. 2000. 'The Global Situation.' *Cultural Anthropology* 15(3): 327–360.

Tumarkin, N. 1997. *Lenin lives!: The Lenin Cult in Soviet Russia.* Cambridge, MA, and London, Harvard University Press.

Vale, L. J. 1992. *Architecture, Power and National Identity.* New Haven and London, Yale University Press.

Valentine, G., T. Skelton and D. Chambers. 1998. 'Cool Places: An Introduction to Youth and Youth Cultures.' In T. Skelton and G. Valentine (eds), *Cool Places: Geographies of Youth Cultures.* London and New York, Routledge: 1–32.

van Vree, W. 1999. *Meetings, Manners and Civilization: The Development of Modern Meeting Behaviour.* London and New York, Leicester University Press.

Veenis, M. 1999. 'Consumption in East Germany: The Seduction and Betrayal of Things.' *Journal of Material Culture* 4(1): 79–112.

Verdery, K. 1996. *What Was Socialism and What Comes Next?* Princeton, N.J., Princeton University Press.

Wanner, C. 1998. *Burden of Dreams: History and Identity in Post-Soviet Ukraine.* University Park, Pennsylvania, Pennsylvania State University Press.

Warner, M. 2002. 'Publics and Counterpublics.' *Public Culture* 14(1): 49–90.

Watson, S. and W. K. 2005. 'Spaces of Nostalgia: The Hollowing Out of a London Market.' *Social & Cultural Geography* 6(1): 17–30.

Weber, M. 1991 (1922) 'Bureaucracy.' In H. H. Gerth and C. W. Mills (eds), *From Max Weber: Essays in Sociology.* London, Routledge: 196–244.

———. 1992 (1919). *Politik als Beruf.* Stuttgart, Reclam.

Weck, M. 1992. 'Der ironische Westen und der tragische Osten.' *Kursbuch* (190): 76–89.

Weintraub, J. 1997. 'The Theory and Politics of the Public/Private Distinction.' In J. Weintraub and K. Kumar (eds), *Public and Private in Thought and Practice: Perspectives on a Grand Dichotomy.* Chicago and London, University of Chicago Press: 1–42.

Welch Guerra, M. 1999. *Hauptstadt Einig Vaterland: Planung und Politik zwischen Bonn und Berlin.* Berlin, Verlag Bauwesen.

Weszkalnys, G. 2000. Inventing the East: Some Perceptions of *Ostprodukte* in Contemporary Berlin. *Department of Social Anthropology,* University of Cambridge. (BA dissertation)

———. 2007. 'The Disintegration of a Socialist Exemplar: Discourses on Urban Disorder in Alexanderplatz, Berlin.' *Space and Culture* 10(2): 207–230.

————. 2008. 'A Robust Square: youth work, planning and the making of public space in contemporary Berlin.' *City and Society* 20(2): 251–274.

White, J. B. 1997. 'Turks in the New Germany.' *American Anthropologist* 99(4): 754–769.

Williams, R. 1973. *The Country and the City.* London, Chatto and Windus.

Wilson, E. 1997. ' Looking Backward, Nostalgia and the City ' In S. Westwood and J. Williams (eds), *Imagining Cities: Scripts, Signs, Memories.* London and New York, Routledge: 127–139.

Winkler, H. A. 2003. 'Wofür Berlin steht. Die widerspruchsvolle Geschichte der Stadt.' In K. Biedenkopf, D. Reimers and A. Rolfink (eds), *Berlin – was ist uns die Hauptstadt wert?* Opladen, Leske + Budrich: 15–24.

Wise, M. Z. 1998. *Capital Dilemma: Germany's Search for a New Architecture of Democracy.* New York, Princeton Architectural Press.

Wolle, S. 1999 *Die heile Welt der Diktatur: Alltag und Herrschaft in der DDR 1971.* Bonn, Bundeszentrale für politische Bildung.

Wood, D. 1985. 'Doing Nothing.' *Outlook* 57: 3–20.

Worpole, K. 2000. *Here Comes the Sun: Architecture and Public Space in Twentieth-Century European Culture.* London, Reaktion Books.

Wulff, H. 1995. 'Introduction: Introducing Youth Culture in its Own Right – The State of the Art and New Possibilities.' In V. Amit-Talai and H. Wulff (eds), *Youth Cultures: A Cross-Cultural Perspective.* London and New York, Routledge: 1–18.

Yampolsky, M. 1995. 'In the Shadow of Monuments: Notes on Iconoclasm and Time.' In N. Condee (ed), *Soviet Hieroglyphics: Visual Culture in Late Twentieth-Century Russia.* Bloomington and Indianapolis, Indiana University Press: 93–112.

Zohlen, G. 2000. 'Die IBA est divisa in partes tres.' In T. Scheer, J. P. Kleihues and P. Kahlfeldt (eds), *Stadt der Architektur, Architektur der Stadt: 1900.* Berlin, Nicolai.

Zucker, P. 1959. *Town and Square: From the Agora to the Village Green.* New York, Columbia University Press.

Zukin, S. 1991. *Landscapes of Power: from Detroit to Disney World.* Berkeley and Oxford, University of California Press.

⊰ INDEX ⊱